Praise for *On*

'Heale's style is to weave sociological analysis with the first-hand testimonies of gang members in their own words. Thus the book's triumph is the authenticity that runs through every page, the sense that we are up close with the reality of gang life beyond the headlines – its casual violence, petty dramas and often mind-numbing banality' *The Times*

'The question is, is this a good book? No. It's a brilliant book. If you, as the reader, want to gain knowledge of some of the darker places in our nation, *One Blood* provides the window . . . Above all, Heale displays a real understanding of the complex make-up of gangs and those involved. There is so much quality information in this book that it is impossible to highlight it all here. I recommend you read it' Shaun Bailey, *Evening Standard*

'A thoughtful book. Heale's investigation couldn't be more timely or more urgent' *Daily Telegraph*

'One of the strengths of Heale's book is that it is carefully calculated not to be shocking. He talks to many gang members and former members, but is never voyeuristic . . . It is a welcome relief from the majority of journalistic coverage, which seems only interested in angelic victims and evil perpetrators' *Independent*

'Heale never sensationalises, judges or empathises. Rather, he coolly and authoritatively exposes a social underclass which, having given up dreaming of something better, no longer much cares whether it lives or dies' *Metro*

'In this timely, vividly written and absorbing book, investigative journalist Heale talks to gang members across the country, as well as police, psychologists and youth workers, about their backgrounds, motives and lives, analysing the effects of inner-city warfare on society. Scary, depressing, important' *thelondonpaper*

'The author manages to draw their personal stories and tragedies involving individuals in the sub-culture without sensationalism or moral judgement, while at the same time painting pictures in the reader's mind of the deprivation and hopelessness of inner-city youth that spawns this phenomenon. This is a must-read book for anyone wanting to understand the growing problem of youths drifting into a life of crime, drugs, gangs and murder' *Newcastle Sunday Sun*

ONE BLOOD

Inside Britain's New
Gang Culture

JOHN HEALE

POCKET
BOOKS

LONDON · SYDNEY · NEW YORK · TORONTO

First published in Great Britain by Simon & Schuster UK Ltd, 2008
This edition first published by Pocket Books, 2009
An imprint of Simon & Schuster UK Ltd
A CBS COMPANY

3 5 7 9 10 8 6 4 2

Simon & Schuster UK Ltd
1st Floor
222 Gray's Inn Road
London WC1X 8HB

www.simonandschuster.co.uk

Simon & Schuster Australia
Sydney

A CIP catalogue record for this book
is available from the British Library.

ISBN: 978-1-84739-281-7

Printed by CPI Cox & Wyman, Reading, Berkshire RG1 8EX

To Mum, Dad and FB

CONTENTS

ACKNOWLEDGEMENTS

Thanks to Professor John Pitts for permission to reproduce his work, to Methuen Publishing for permission to use extracts from Beatrix Campbell's *Goliath*, to my agent Andrew Lownie and editor Kerri Sharp for their hard work, help and support, and the scores of brave and dedicated people who agreed to help me with my research: above all to Kevin, Rob, Mark, Paula, Nat, AK, DJ, JS, Mike, Pat, Tony and Jason.

We pray for better days.

PREFACE

'We be of one blood, thou and I,' Mowgli answered . . . 'my
kill shall be thy kill if ever thou art hungry.'

Rudyard Kipling, *The Jungle Book*

I met my first gang member several years ago, while working as a
researcher for a television documentary about gangs in south
London. A youth worker had arranged an introduction, and so one
afternoon I waited for him, a little scared, in a small room at the
youth club. He came in, a stocky black man covered in expensive
jewellery and wearing gold in his teeth. It had taken me weeks of
phone calls in order to get access to him, weeks of telling the youth
worker that the documentary would not sensationalize the gang
member's life, that there had to be room to write about the positive,
and other assurances regarding protection of his anonymity.

As our interview progressed, a number of things struck me. The
first was how witty and intelligent this man was. He had me laughing my head off a number of times, coming out with pithy
statements about where he lived. He would have made an excellent
guest on any TV chat show.

The second thing was the nature of the horrors he described.
Lives in his area were cheap. He would become angry when talking

about the police or the authorities, but most of the killings were described in a blunt, matter-of-fact tone. He told of a shocking litany of violence in the area, and a huge number of incidents that had never been reported, including brutal attacks in which young girls were either victims or protagonists. He told me about the large amount of money he had made from dealing drugs, and the early age at which children were involved in the trade – some as young as nine or ten. At one point he said: 'It's like the Nazis – you switch off your emotions in order to survive. You ever see that documentary about Hitler, *Seven Steps to Tyranny*? It's like we done that to ourselves.'

The third thing was a set of photographs on the wall behind him. The pictures showed a group of children in a rustic idyll: walking up moors, kayaking, visiting a farm. And I was surprised to notice that he was there, among them.

'Where were those photos taken?' I asked.

'Lake District. We went there last summer. I help out here.'

'You help out here? But you're a gang member. You're involved in all the stuff you've told me about?'

'For life.'

It's due to such contradictions that the media has struggled to give a representation of the 'gang situation'. 2007 was the year that the notion of violent youth street gangs really entered the public consciousness in the UK. In terms of the overall number of homicides it was not an exceptionally violent year, but what caught the public's attention was a series of high-profile killings of teenagers which in their brutality and callousness seemed to mark a worsening of the problem.

The picture that has been put forward is muddled. Take, for example, the coverage of Alex Kamondo's murder in June 2006. He was heading home from celebrating his GCSE results with two friends. They got off a bus in Kennington, south London, whereupon they were confronted by a large gang of youths who pushed them into a side street. The gang wielded an array of weapons, including hockey sticks and baseball bats. Kamondo was stabbed through the chest with a Samurai sword. As the media reported, another tragic killing of an innocent.

But later that month the *Daily Mail* published an exclusive: 'The Life and Death of a Gangsta.'[1] It said: 'A *Daily Mail* investigation has found that, far from being innocent, he was another victim of the destructive gang culture in Britain's inner cities.' If this statement seems contradictory, other lines in the piece were even more confusing: '[Alex's father] told reporters: "Alex loved music and was doing his exams at school. He wanted to go to college and do electrical engineering. He was a lovely boy with lots of friends." Yet the photographs of Alex calling himself "Tiny Alien" and posturing with his fellow gang members on the Man Dem Crew website are there for everyone to see.'

The possibility that both lives might co-exist was not even on the radar. And this is indicative of the troubled relationship between the media and gang-involved youths. They are at once villains and victims. On the one hand, sensational headlines about violence sell – but at the same time, there is an awareness that the problem is about more than the actions of immoral individuals. The problem for the media has been how this can be explored in any depth, while making an extremely complex issue accessible and interesting to the public.

This book will attempt to show how and why these contradictions exist in gang life. It aims to provide some suggestions as to how the problem (as loosely defined within media reports) can be solved.

A word on the methodology. All names in the book have been changed, and certain details have been altered in order to protect sources, be they gang members, current or ex-police officers or community workers, all of whom have kindly given their time to talk to me and explain the situation in their area. This is obviously frustrating for both writer and reader, both of whom strive for authenticity. I can only ask for the reader's trust that their words are a fair representation of reality.

This is a book about gangs more than about gangsters: I do not delve into their private or family lives in intricate detail, though I know some of them well. The gang problem is so large, and encompasses so many different people, that while this would be an interesting method, it would only reveal the most general of truths about the problem. But just as that first interviewee was much more than a gang member, so I have met dozens of muggers, drug dealers – even, on occasion, murderers – who are fathers, community figures, skilled footballers, musicians and more. To imagine their words can encapsulate all of their experiences, or indeed the experiences of the community in which they live, is to project one's own assumptions about the 'ghetto' onto them; an easy thing to do. However, I hope my interviewees' words provide a contrast to what I consider the most common public perceptions of gang members to be.

Finally, this book is not an attempt to make excuses for any crimes that gang members have committed: ultimately, these are individuals with free will who have made the wrong choices in life. I wish to show the background against which those choices have been made. This is a book about a social problem; a problem which will never be solved until it is understood.

John Heale, London, 2008

ONE

From Leyton to Chingford: Welcome to Gangland

Here is melodrama . . . Here are unvarnished emotions. Here
also is a primitive democracy . . . The gang, in short, is *life*,
often rough and untamed . . .

Frederic Thrasher, *The Gang* (1927)

Alex is looking at his feet and fiddling with his gold ring. He does-
n't want to talk about this; doesn't want to dredge up old ground.
But my perception of the events is so wrong that, laughing, he is
drawn into a response:

'Ha, ha, ha! You fucking kidding me? It wasn't about the lyrics.
Maybe at first, but in the end it was about people not respecting
their positions. It was an internal beef. All Chingford. OK, so Shaks
is an MC: he's a very talented boy. And Goodz is talented too: he's
just signed to Polydor. Now the thing is he's got to keep that cor-
porate image up.

'He's distanced himself from the gang. So the young guys don't see
no love coming from Goodz. Now you see, I think he was gonna
give back – that's what you got to do when you make it, you give
back. It's just that he was consolidating his position. Anyway, Shaks

1

writes this rhyme, says Goodz is dissing us. Nothing heavy: it's like . . . he's said that – now you've got to go on the mike. Take me on.

'But it don't work like that. You see, Shaks is a Younger. If you're a Younger, you don't do that. So Goodz locks him in his car, and tells him to take back what he said. It's like . . . this is music, I understand that, but just show some respect. But Shaks isn't backing down. And suddenly we're on to a whole new level. This isn't about music any more.

'This is where Richie turns up. He says leave the boy alone; he's only young. He's got the crew with him – a load of guys from Piff. And the crew are like . . . OK, this is outside the music, we're saying you leave the boy alone, you're not listening – we're going to have to pay you a visit.

'So these threats are escalating. Now these are serious players: maybe he was angry, maybe he was scared. I don't know. Probably both. But Goodz decides to make a call. He phones Titch and tells him to come down. Titch knows what he's going up against, and he knows he's going to need an arsenal.

'Later they walk around a corner with their guns drawn and they see Richie and some of Piff. He sees them, and just says, "Now you've drawn it, you're going to have to use that." Worst thing he could have said . . .

'Later that day the boys ran up and smashed up Goodz's house and his car. The family had evacuated earlier. They still want to kill him. Weird shit. They all grew up together.'

From the *Guardian*, 3 November 2006:

A rapper outraged because his half-brother was 'disrespected' in a song lyric was jailed with a confederate for 30 years yesterday after a revenge attack ended in murder. Carl Dobson, 23 – also known as the grime rap star Crazy Titch – killed music producer Richard

Holmes last November as a row over the lyrics escalated disastrously, the Old Bailey heard . . . A handgun was held to the victim's head before he was shot in the back as he tried to escape. The attackers also shot him in the leg with a Mach 10 machine gun.

The murder of Richard Holmes is a model killing in today's Gangland. It happened for the same reasons most gang murders take place: it was about respect. To lose respect is to put yourself at risk. As the informant says, once the disrespect moved outside the abstract, impersonal world of lyrics, it moved closer to the final situation – the only way it could be resolved was through violence.

The killing was about the disrespect shown by a teenager – Shaks or Shabah Shah – aged sixteen at the time of the murder. Young men have become the prevalent force in Gangland in the last decade. Perversely, they don't always have the power, but they are the ones who do many of the killings, and the ones who are killed. They are the ones most likely to show disrespect, because they stand to gain the most by enforcing their reputation.

To understand why these changes have occurred – why young people are dying on our streets every month – we need to understand Gangland, and what has happened to it. Gangland is ultimately a state of mind: thousands of people live within it, go to work, raise their children, and live otherwise unremarkable lives. At the same time, for some it exists as a very clearly defined physical area.

At the junction of Hall Road and Langthorne Road in Leytonstone, east London, the two roads' street signs sit next to each other. One says 'Langthorne Road, E11'. The other should say 'Hall Road, E15', but the number five has been sprayed over with black spray paint. It reads 'E11' as well.

On Hall Road, opposite the street signs, lie the gigantic white concrete slabs that comprise the flats of Blackthorne Court. They are connected by rickety blue metal walkways. The central block of flats is called Gean Court. Its façade gives away little: one sees few windows at the front of the building. At the back of the block is a small car park. The rear is festooned with satellite dishes. At the foot of the wall, in tiny black marker pen, are the words 'RIP Paule' (sic).

In April 2007 Paul Erahon, aged fourteen, and his friend, aged fifteen, were assaulted by a group of youths. A teenager demanded Paul 'come here', and then threatened: 'This could get physical. You don't want me to have to come over there.' Paul was attacked by the group as the teenager shouted: 'Go on, Youngers.' A second group of youths then rushed to the scene and joined in the attack. In total, there were seventeen people attacking Paul and his friend.

The youths were armed with bats and a samurai sword. As the blows rained down upon him, Paul screamed at them not to shank him. They did: they stabbed him through the heart with a seven-inch samurai sword, and stabbed his friend five times. The wounded boys staggered out into Hall Road. One neighbour saw them and thought they were drunk. They made it further down the street, and Paul collapsed, dying a few yards from his home. He murmured, 'I'm dying, I'm dying' as his parents raced to his side. He was pronounced dead half an hour later.

Three boys were convicted of murder and two of manslaughter following a three-month trial. It was alleged that they committed the murder to earn their spurs within the Cathall gang.

Paul lived in a small cul-de-sac next to Blackthorne Court. It sits uneasily next to the flats: the close, with its neat two-bedroom houses and smart cars out the front, looks like it has been picked up and transposed from a provincial town. Attached to the railings next to it are lanterns, a teddy bear, roses and cards: 'RIP forever'; 'We will miss you'.

A few hundred yards west of Blackthorne Court, Leyton High Road runs through the middle of the borough of Waltham Forest. A little further to the west, you find the area where the old high-rise Oliver Close Estate was. A labyrinthine hotchpotch of newly built red-brick houses and small 1980s blocks of flats, this doesn't look like gang territory, but it is.

Continue for a mile north up Leyton High Road, past the shops owned by Turks, Albanians and Asians, selling a random selection of cheap goods, past the fried chicken shops, the garages, the tube station, over a bridge which has cars shooting along the A12 below, past more shops, cafes, garages, past an incongruous cricket ground, the remaining tower block on the Beaumont Estate suddenly looms large on the right. It dominates the road; a soaring, rotting column too large to take in at once. The closer you get, the more the decay is defined – rotting windows, peeling paintwork. Around are smaller blocks of neater, newer flats, another hotchpotch, and between the flats are building sites. The shells of torn-down buildings are visible above the wooden boards, the concrete crumbled like meringue, the steel wires that supported them jutting out like the ribs of a decaying carcass. Soon they will all be gone – the Beaumont Estate, like the Oliver Close Estate a few years ago, is undergoing redevelopment.

Continuing up Leyton High Road, past bookmakers, more cheap stores, a scruffy pub, a Cash Converters, you reach the junction with Lea Bridge Road. It's like coming up for air. The hustle and bustle die down for another half-mile as the road becomes a leafy strip of terraced houses running all the way to Walthamstow station. Continue further, past the station and the common on the right, and the road reverts to how it was – claustrophobic, noisy, cluttered. It runs like this for another mile, before you see the grandiose Town Hall, with vast lawns stretched out in front of it. Half a mile to the west lies Priory Court, its buildings, like most of Gangland, a mix of small red-brick houses and large pastel blocks of flats. A mile north of that is the North Circular, the Chingford Hall Estate, like the others, hunched behind it.

This is Gangland. For the most part, it looks modern and safe. It exists in several incongruous pockets, all of them tucked away off the beaten track, most of them newly built. Life goes on around Gangland; ordinary people with regular day jobs living cheek by jowl with the most disadvantaged and potentially violent members of society.

The modern gang evolved in places like these due to the overwhelming changes in the structure of British crime that have taken place in the last 25 years. Andy's story may help to explain this transition.

He is immensely stocky: his powerful frame belies his fifty years. His jowls and unimpressed glare give him the appearance of a grouchy bulldog. He addresses his audience, a dozen or so teenage boys, with a gruff, East End accent: 'Oo d'you fink I am?' Some mutter 'cop'; others suggest he's a careers advisor. Silence. He looks at each of them in turn. He nods. 'Oh, right. Do you now?'

Andy was an enforcer and robber for a white crime syndicate for thirty years, until the police caught him holding up a bank in south London. While on day release, he was approached by a charity to work with youths in deprived areas. He's been at this for months now; heading into youth centres and schools to talk to them about gangs and the damage they do. The kids will listen to him – this is a bona fide criminal. But he finds it a struggle. It's a hard world for him to understand: Andy's east London is not the same east London inhabited by his audience.

'Yeah, I was in a gang. We used to play football in the park. Once I was a big boy, I suppose you could say I was in a gang, but all this –' he mimes pulling a hood up over his head, '– nah . . . it's something new.'

Andy's gang made most of their money from hold-ups. 'I'd get a call, every other month or so. We'd meet and talk through what the job was: post office, bank, lorries – we'd do the lot. Someone above me would have done most of the planning; he'd have done the reconnaissance and all the rest of it. We'd just get told what we were doing, what our cut was, and off we'd go – job done, sit around, wait for the next call. It was a successful freelance role I had, if you will. It was a very happy and prosperous few years for me. Until I got nicked. The bank had tiny CCTV cameras which our man hadn't spotted. They had footage of me, and I got fifteen years.'

By the early 1990s, improved technology was making it harder and harder for criminals like Andy to ply their trade. At the same time, heroin, cocaine and, most importantly, crack began to flood into London. There was more money to be made, more regularly, in drugs, and provided it was done well dealing posed few of the risks associated with the kind of blags carried out by Andy's crew.

'I was working for a small team that had its links, but we were a little group of mates who'd known each other since we were young,' says Andy, shaking his head. 'But the kids I'm dealing with . . . however much they make, there's always someone above them. It's a corporation – a criminal corporation.'

His assessment is accurate. Before a user gets hold of any drugs, they have travelled down an elaborate supply chain. Crack is a product in a competitive market: it needs to be marketed, packaged and distributed. The people who sell it need to be protected, and the people who threaten them have to be negated. Until demand is saturated, which it won't be until everyone is using it, there will be a demand for people to work in the corporation that provides it.

A common misconception is that only those at the very top of a gang stand to make any money: in fact, this is not always the case.

At the top end of the drugs chain, a dealer will usually sell the drugs he has bought at double the price. The dealer to whom he has sold it will add an extra 50 per cent to that price when he sells it to a user. Professor John Pitts of the University of Bedfordshire produced a report in 2007 which analysed the gangs of Waltham Forest.[1] In the Oliver Close area he estimated there are around 150 people spending on average £50 per week on drugs. The weekly drug-spend is therefore £7500. This means that someone at the top of the chain will stand to make £130,000 per year, and if he has five dealers working for him, each of those will hypothetically stand to make £26,000: a healthy annual salary. It should be stressed that these numbers are speculative, and that the risks run by those at the bottom of the market usually outweigh the benefits. But the Oliver Close gang is a subsidiary of Piff City, the leaders of which have been at the top of their game for years. They have made more money than Andy's gang could ever have hoped for.

Some of the crack that reaches the borough is smuggled in from South America by established London criminals and distributed through their networks of dealers. The other source is Jamaica – the crack is processed there and carried by drugs mules, usually women.

Few things are simple in Gangland. Your day-to-day activities, your role, your future, the people with whom you work, the people with whom you fight – all are uncertain, transient. But, paradoxically, most gang members have a clearly defined perception of how the drug market is structured. The best way to understand the way that market works is to imagine the process by which fruit is sold in a supermarket. In this case the producers operate in Jamaica and South America. The international criminals who sell the drug are wholesalers. The top gang members to whom they sell, the Elders and Faces, are the supermarket's head office. Below them are the Youngers: the branch managers. And working the supermarket's tills and on the shop floor are the Shotters.

In terms of the drug trade, what we see in the estates around Walthamstow and Leyton is the same structure we see across the nation. Most of the gangs in this book started at roughly the same time, the 1980s, doing the same things: theirs has been a natural evolution into their current state. Eerie though this may seem, the fact they mirror each other shouldn't surprise us.

It started when Dan was thirteen years old, with his friend Joe. He and Joe walked from their estate to school every day. Joe's brother, Mike, was sixteen. He'd been excluded from their school a year previously for threatening someone with a knife. Dan knew about Mike, and Joe would always tell him that he was fine; happier than ever. He hung around with the other kids on the estate, apparently, and he was never bored.

Dan rarely hung around with Joe or his brother after school. He knew Joe's brother was in a crew, but at that point it had not been something they had spoken about at any length. Dan would stay at home, keep to himself. He liked his Playstation; he liked listening to his records. He wanted to be a hip-hop producer. He hadn't played in the park near the estate since some boys had asked him what he thought he was doing there. He couldn't stay there: he wasn't in C Crew. Dan said C Crew didn't own the park, and one of them had punched him in the face. He'd run home and washed the blood off his nose, scampering past his mother so as not to alert her.

One day, Mike was waiting outside the school for Dan and Joe. He said to Dan: 'Is that him?' and pointed to a boy who had been bullying both of them. Dan was surprised that Joe had told Mike about it, but said it was. Mike nodded, and they walked home together. The next day, Joe ran up to Dan at the end of school. Breathless with excitement, he told him to come to the boys' toilet. Inside were Mike, and two of his friends. They were in a cubicle, shoving the boy's head in a toilet, and holding a knife to his throat.

'Do you want to die? Are you fucking stupid? Then don't ever fuck with my bro again!'

The boy was crying and crying. They all started laughing at him. 'I think he's shit himself.' And with that Mike slammed the toilet lid on his head, and walked out. The boy never so much as looked at Dan again. But Mike kept showing up outside school to walk home with Dan and Joe. They'd talk about music, football and girls. One day Mike asked Dan if he wanted to see his arsenal. Joe told him he should go – it was amazing. They went to a flat belonging to one of Mike's friends. Dan was nervous, but Joe told him not to worry. Inside were a group of young men playing Playstation in the front room, the air thick with bong smoke. Mike took him to the kitchen at the back, and there on the table was a small pistol. Did Dan want to hold the gun? He did. It felt heavier than he expected. He pointed it around the kitchen, his arm aching under the weight. He put it down. Mike seized Dan by the arm, and told him if he breathed a word of this to his mother, he was dead. He owed Mike.

A little later, Dan ran into Mike in the estate. He told Dan he needed a favour. He needed Dan to take a package to a friend's for him. Dan didn't think twice. He wanted respect, protection, the money (£30 for delivering it). Over the months, the money kept coming Dan's way, and the jobs kept coming too. Most of the time it was simple – take this package to a guy at Walthamstow Central, keep an eye out for the cops when the boys are doing something – and all the while he saw his mother less and less every evening, all the while his school work got worse and worse. Even if Dan had wanted to stop doing this, he couldn't. Mike knew where he lived, knew his routes home from school. But for now he didn't want to – he loved having respect from Mike. And anyway, the money was stacking up in a shoebox under his bed. He bought himself brand new trainers and CDs.

Soon Dan began to take a more active role, seeking Mike out for jobs. Every job he did, bigger and bigger, gave him a little bit more to talk about with the guys with the Playstation, the weed, the fancy clothes, the nice car out front. He liked them. There was still aggression from C Crew if he walked across the park – soon the guys told him if he ever needed a piece in order to shoo them off, it was his. One day they saw him on his way home from school, and started shouting and running after him. He got to Mike's. Mike gave him a gun, unloaded, and told him to see if they wanted to fuck with him. He walked back there, and the minute they saw him, he pulled it out. They sprinted away. It wasn't their area any more.

The most common errands Dan did involved taking drugs to Shotters, or dealers. He managed the 'shop floor', a place that takes many forms in this trade. The Shotter might work just on the street; he will have the protection of the gangsters he has bought the drugs from – or will be a member of that gang – and will sell in that area. The threat posed to Shotters by rival gangs and the police can mean a closed market comes into play: they will take orders by mobile phone or will operate from crack houses. When the police tried to close these down in early 2006, the Shotters switched to moped deliveries. Then the police gave up, and the crack houses reappeared.[2]

Some of the kids from C Crew were at Dan's school, and they hated Mike's crew. There were always fights between the two. Dan and Joe were well and truly in with the kids who called themselves members of Mike's crew, by now; C Crew feared them. One day a mass fight broke out in the playground: one kid pulled a knife on Dan. They wrestled and both were left with slash marks. The teachers broke the fight up, but all those involved in the incident were expelled. Dan was fifteen. His mother was aghast at the expulsion, but not shocked. This had been coming for months; she'd seen it happen to others.

With no school, Dan did everything Mike expected of him. He carried drugs to the dealers. He hung around near Mike's flat, and if there was anyone there who had beef with Mike's boys, he'd make threats. Once he told a bunch of guys to fuck off, and they drew guns and walked towards him. He was terrified, and he ran back to Mike's flat. Mike and his friends grabbed their arsenal and started firing out of the windows at them. The guys ran away. Dan got a lot of respect after that. In fact, it was at that very time that he became a fully fledged Younger.

Dan's looks betray his young years: he is now seventeen. His brown skin is smooth, his eyes bright and intense. At the same time, there is something terribly old and hard about him. His language is infused with violence, informed by the acts he's seen or heard about on a daily basis. He talks about the ineffectiveness of the police, and says he wants to take an axe to all their heads. It doesn't sound like an empty threat. Politicians are worse – he'd shoot them, bang bang, all of them, the useless fucks. The speed of his speech is infectious – a nonstop babble of film and television quotes, the only education he's ever had.

'You ever watched the last *Star Wars* film?' he asks, before sipping his Coke in a fast-food joint near Walthamstow Central Station. 'You know how Anakin has that choice, between the light and the dark side? That's all the road is – it's an illusion. Every time you think you're making progress, you're digging yourself in deeper and deeper. You think you're becoming the big man, and then before you know it you're in jail. Suddenly there's no Man Dem behind you – it's just you and a guy who doesn't give a shit, because he's got nothing to lose. The way I've told it looks like the road chose me: it didn't. I chose the road. Ain't got no one to blame but myself.'

*

Most youths join gangs between the ages of twelve and fourteen – the age where it becomes apparent that if you're not affiliated you're susceptible to harassment, theft, violent assault and rape. Professor Pitts' report highlighted the fact that 40 per cent of these members were either occasional or reluctant affiliates.[3] They were coming to the Youth Offending Team because they were present at the scene of a crime, but were not necessarily the individual who committed the offence. Sometimes they join because they know of the risks to them and their family if they don't. All the rude boys in Waltham Forest know about the fifteen-year-old boy who was asked to join Beaumont. They told him to do a robbery – he refused. They beat him up and raped his fifteen-year-old sister. To be neutral is to be at the bottom of the pile, and this risk is amplified if someone has left a gang.

In terms of the drug trade, Dan was the Younger to Mike's Elder. Beyond Mike lay the Faces. The Faces are all adults, and their ages can range from 21 to 50. Gang members use the term to describe all sorts of individuals. The Faces in Waltham Forest have generally lived here since the drugs came, and are either affiliated to or are members of the criminal families that took control of the trade in the 1990s. They control operations on the estates, but rarely live on them. Some have made good money, and own several properties here and abroad, often moving around to avoid detection. Their detachment from the area only serves to emphasize the awe in which they are held when they do appear in it. But it is not enough to single out the Faces as the villains of the piece. The more people you talk to, the more surprising is the picture that emerges.

Richard sips his tea in a cafe in Walthamstow Market. A middle-aged black man, his shades perched on top of his cropped hair, he looks around the cafe. There's no one in there but us, but still he keeps his voice low. He has lived in Leyton all his life. He watched the Faces rise to the top of the pile, knows some of them on first-name terms and, had he stuck at the gang life, he would have been one himself.

'When we started, it was all about business. If you want business, you need stability. If you went into another person's area, you were provoking them into retaliating in some way. And that was bad business. There were no crews. You had people working for you, and you had an agreement with the people who worked in other areas, but that was it. There'd be the odd fight between a bunch of people from here and a bunch of people from Forest Gate, but most of the fights we had were with the National Front.'

It is only when Richard talks about the ancient kingdom of Babylon that he gets excited. He left the gang life and took a job working in church administration, where he became interested in ecclesiastical scripture. He wants to write books about it. 'I stopped when the fighting began. But you must understand that most Faces are like me. They know what's good and bad business. There's no money in fighting.'

Richard tells me about one well-known Face in the area. 'Many people here see him as a modern-day Robin Hood. He's like a community worker. He has one aim and one aim only: to sing and rap his boys out of the ghetto. The money that comes from the gang is invested in music – studios, promotion, club nights. If someone makes it to a major label, they give back. That's the rule. If I had the money to stop the gang problem, he'd be one of the first people who'd get it. Yeah, they still make their money through drugs. That's how it is here.'

Not all the Faces are philanthropists, but in some cases success, money and respect for the area in which they grew up has made them less threatening as individuals to those who live in Gangland. Elsie is sitting in a church hall. A small, frail woman, she breaks into a broad smile, throws her head back and laughs when I mention the name of a well-known Face in her area. 'You mean Joel. Let me tell you some-thing – a few months ago I saw Joel on the estate. First time in ages – I don't know what he was doing there. And I walked right up to him, and I told him I knew my friend's son was hanging around with some of his gang. I told him I didn't want him to be a part of it, and I would tell the police everything I knew about him. He says to me: do you know who I am? And I tell him, of course I know who you are, I've lived here longer than you have; I knew your mother. I say, you've made your money, you've got everyone scared of you, but I'm asking this of you as a mother. And he muttered something, and I knew it would be OK. Everyone here thinks I'm crazy.

'Let me tell you about another one of these so-called Faces. I knew his mother too. One time he came in with his new trainers, his lip, and he starts back-chatting her. Well, she walks up to him and bang! She butts him right between the eyes. He's out cold. He comes round, and says, "Momma, how can you do that to me?" And she says, "Don't think, just because you're the big man here, I'm not your mother no more. And that I don't know how to check you when you play up."'

Don't be fooled: these are high-powered criminals who have com-mitted all manner of serious crimes. But in terms of the violence on the street, their current input is often negligible. It happens on their behalf – under the umbrella of a body they may have envisaged and named – but not always at their behest. Richard sees some of the Faces as Don Corleone figures, struggling to maintain control of empires that have lost the rules and respect they once had. 'No Face I know would ever have recruited a child when they were on the street. They wouldn't have shot at someone's house with their family inside. But there's been an escalation. Everyone's a gangster now. And if one gang decides it's acceptable, so it has to be for them too. Usually the precedent isn't set by a Face – it's an Elder, trying to make a name for himself.'

*

JOHN HEALE

While the British media often mentions gangs by names, it rarely gets the essence of their make-up. What, if anything, is a gang? It has developed into a catch-all term to describe all sorts of urban groups, but criminologists and community safety professionals have struggled with the term for a long time. Perhaps the best and most simple definition has been offered by Simon Hallsworth and Tara Young of London Metropolitan University: 'A relatively durable, predominantly street-based group of young people who see themselves (and are seen by others) as a discernable group for whom crime and violence is integral to the group's identity.'[4]

They place the gang between two extremes: below it the peer group ('a small, unorganized, transient grouping occupying the same space with a common history. Crime is not integral to their self-definition'), and above it the organized criminal group ('Members are professionally involved in crime for personal gain operating almost exclusively in the "grey" or illegal marketplace'). For Hallsworth and Young, each tier feeds upward – peer-group members become street gang members, who one day become members of organized criminal groups. However, they would also admit that in practice the distinctions between all three groups are blurred. There are members of peer groups who interact with the organized gangs and every other permutation.

I have drawn my own simple definition of what constitutes a gang for the purposes of this book. All of the gangs covered are groups that have a name and a territory, and are involved in serious drug dealing or violent crime. Even this definition, though broad, must be qualified. The first major point to bear in mind is that not all gang-involved young people are gang members. It is common for a young person to be associated with a crew, yet not regard themselves as a member of that gang. They may identify with the culture, but more often than not it is where they live or who their friends are that leads others to perceive them as gangsters. This is

16

important; as I have mentioned media coverage often draws a line between 'gang' and 'non-gang', when in fact the line is far more blurred.

This may also appear to contradict the clear drug-dealing structure that we have seen so far. It is a complex issue, which will be dealt with in the first four chapters. The second chapter will mention some of the causes behind today's gangs. The third chapter will, in the light of this knowledge, explain how they can be both organized and disorganized, and the fourth chapter will show how they have changed in recent years. With this theory in place the book will then look around the country to see how the pattern is mirrored.

For now we shall look at the gangs as individual bodies. In the light of how well ordered the drug trade is, the gangs themselves appear chaotic. There are two large gangs in Waltham Forest: Piff City and Beaumont. Piff City is based around the Chingford Hall Estate and parts of Leyton, while Beaumont is found around the estate of the same name. Both gangs are large and, as such, have elements of the criminal organization at the top, but the less-involved members could be seen as street gangsters, or peer-group members. If asked, they would all say they were members of the gangs, but the level of crime they commit varies a great deal. Some are killers or high-level drug dealers with connections across the country: they might be dotted around the borough, a long way from the estates where the gangs originated, while others are young people who are local to the estate and whose principal criminal activity consists of anti-social behaviour.

This disorganization is also true of the gangs' relationships. Professor Pitts' report attempts to detail the endless cycle of alliances and altercations ('beefs') within the borough.[5] At the time of the report's publication in 2007, a simple overview would read thus: the main battle is between the Beaumont Gang and Piff City. Then come the smaller gangs. Drive is based around the centre of the borough: Wood Street, Marlow, Atlee Terrace and Coppermill. It contains around 30 to 40 members. It is aligned with Priory Court, a small gang of about 30 which is allied through family ties to Beaumont, and it is also aligned with Oliver Close, which is part of Piff, thus at war with Beaumont. Priory Court, for its part, also has family links with Cathall, which happens to be part of Piff City. If this is hard for a reader to follow, it gives a good indication of how chaotic the lives of those involved with gangs are. Later chapters will show that, contrary to popular belief, many of these rivalries and alliances have nothing to do with competition for drugs markets. As we shall see, to truly understand the gangs, it helps to dispense with their names altogether.

Bill, a local pastor, and his outreach team (six youths, aged between fifteen and sixteen) are striding through Gangland. They are looking for the Youngers. Once his team finds them, they talk about what's happening on the street. Sometimes they talk about God. It might not sound hopeful, but Bill and his team receive a good response. Bill's team all hail from the area, and the fact they talk the language of the street makes them more respected than any social worker. The chatter in the car is of rap music: 'DMX's new stuff is the *bomb*.' 'Yeah, but can he do it live? That's the test.' It is of football, of another worker who says he's ill: 'He's way too scared to come down these ends.' As we enter the estate, the chatter dies down. We get out.

The estate, given its reputation, doesn't seem intimidating. Everything is modern – the buildings are a mixture of new houses and a central courtyard which is flanked by new blocks of flats, freshly painted in bright colours. In another part of the city, it would be positively luxurious. But this is what you notice about Gangland the more time you spend there. These days, the estates are rarely dilapidated. Money has been invested in regeneration: with a few exceptions it is brand new, or in the process of being built. It's the same all over London – ambitious schemes to rebuild the homes of the poor, in the hope that doing so will rebuild their lives. On the one hand, it has undoubtedly improved living standards. But on the other, the movement of established residents has damaged the sense of community, while in the midst of all this newness, the same problems remain. The brand new buildings do not stop the tenants suffering from low incomes or unemployment. The relocation of residents to low-rise accommodation can make life harder for any families who are involved in the gangs – a flat in a tower block is far harder to shoot at.

The things that threaten you are the things you least suspect. A twenty-something man cycles past on a tiny BMX bicycle. He cuts a preposterous figure, but the outreach workers shrink from his glare as he cycles past. He's a gang member who's on a perfect mode of transport from which to 'gun and run'.

Everything happens so quickly on the street. We take a walk around a block of flats, and when we return to the entrance a heavily muscled man is being held down by several police officers. A crowd of teenagers are shouting at them. When did they get there – the man, the police, the Youngers? The place seemed deserted when we arrived.

In terms of crime, Britain is two very distinct nations. One nation, Gangland, is regularly afflicted by crime of all kinds – the other, rarely. The first nation is so fraught that only the most serious crime makes the headlines; the other so rarely afflicted that any serious crime that happens there is reported in minute detail. Tim Hope, a Professor of Criminology at Keele University, has demonstrated this with his use of the British Crime Survey.[6]

The survey divides neighbourhoods into ten categories on the basis of the intensity of the criminal victimization of their residents.

By 1992, the chances of a resident in the lowest crime neighbour-hood being assaulted had fallen to a point where it was barely measurable. Residents in the highest crime neighbourhoods, by contrast, risked being assaulted twice a year. They also experienced twice the rate of property crime and four times the rate of personal crime than those in the next worst category. Indeed, by 2003 Hope was arguing that 'half the country suffers four fifths of the total amount of household property crime.' The other half suffers the remainder. These findings point to a significant redistribution of victimization towards the poorest and most vulnerable over the intervening ten years. An estate like this lies at the heart of Gangland.

Back with the pastor, we find a bunch of Youngers hanging out on a corner near the main road. 'Two weeks ago,' says one of them, 'they stabbed Billy. He was right here, innit. Three of them, and one of them put a blade in his leg. We found him and fucked him right up, bruv. He's never going to talk. We've done him before as well. He'll never talk.'

Professor Pitts' report made the point that crime in an area like this bears several hallmarks: it is committed by and against the young local residents (all of whom are of a similar age, ethnicity and class); and the same people are victimized again and again. Crime in these areas is also embedded – these adolescents will not grow out of it. More importantly, it is under-reported; in an estate like this, no one talks. Crimes become infamous: for instance, the man who threatened to inform on the Beaumont Boys. They kidnapped him, stabbed him seventeen times and sent the video to his mother. Did it happen? There are no official reports of it, but that means little – the 2000 British Crime Survey estimated that the true extent of crime is four and a half times larger than reported: 77 per cent of crime is in what criminologists call 'the dark figure'.[7] Besides, the point is that everyone thinks it did.

Being in a gang usually means being part of the drug business, and being part of the drug business means involvement in gun-related violence. I look at the Younger who has just finished talking. He's wearing a T-shirt that says 'If you see the police – Warn a Brother', with the Warner Brothers' 'WB' symbol behind it. You see that symbol around – on cars, on the Youngers' bikes. Some things mark him out as a teenager – he is tall, but gangling rather than imposing. He has a teenager's downy moustache and acne, yet he talks like a killer. 'We got heat. You need one with our rep. We all share. Ain't gonna talk about it no more.'

The gun is intrinsic to the business. Everyone wants one and they are easily accessible: a group of teenagers will club together to buy one, or they can be hired. There were twelve fatal shootings in Waltham Forest between 2005 and 2006, but 493 incidents of gun-enabled crime, which comprises everything from threats with a replica to murder. Fifty-three per cent of perpetrators were aged between eleven and twenty years old, and 19 per cent of the victims were aged between one and ten years old.[8]

'We need it. There's beef around here,' continues another Younger. 'It's gonna be like at the King's Head.' The reasons for tension can be unexpected. Last year there had been a killing in the borough, and the police were after the wrong man. Word spread they were looking for him and it was assumed a rival gang had grassed him up. It culminated in a shoot out at a local pub involving youths in bullet-proof vests. Like most shooting incidents, it went unreported.

Life in Gangland is geared around violence. All of the Youngers are wearing gloves. It's a part of gang wear; a reference to the fact that combat leaves forensic evidence on one's hands.[9] Violence is a young man's trade. Their offences will be posted on websites, which shows their fearlessness – they are untouchable. Being mugged is often the prelude to a life of street crime: earn respect, or you're fair game.

The Younger continues, looking down at his shoes. 'It's always over the rocks.' He stabs an angry finger up the road, towards the Beaumont Estate. 'Too many of that lot are using what they sell. Bad for business, blood. They're strung out, and then they come down, then it kicks off over nothing.'

Clive, a pensioner, is tired of the Youngers in his road. He's seen a bunch of them smashing up every car in the street. He's seen a gang of fifty attack another gang, leaving one man injured with knife wounds to his head. 'It scares me so much. They never make a sound, then suddenly all hell breaks loose. I don't want to open the door. I keep the lights off in the front room. I don't want anyone to know I'm in – but then I wonder, if they think the house is empty will they try to come in anyway?' His road shouldn't have seen all this. It's a quiet, respectable cul-de-sac in the Chingford area. For some reason a gang decided the young people in it have a relationship with one of their rivals. They don't. But neutral territory can become gang territory by default.

Next door, his neighbours, a young couple, are scared to let their children play on the lawn outside the house. What if a bullet were to hit them? The weight of terror that young gang members create among their community is almost impossible to quantify. They are simply a constant stress, a threat which can never be confronted for fear of recriminations.

Everything about James screams gang: the thin designer wind-cheater, the black gloves, the spotless trainers, the way his eyes dart around the coffee shop where I meet him. He's not happy out of his turf. He smokes a cigarette nervously. He doesn't trust me. He hardly trusts anyone. Like Dan, his language is infused with violence and films. He is a gang Elder.

'I don't plan more than six months ahead, bruv. I don't know what'll happen to me by then.'

No one thinks about the end point when they join a gang. Those who are most involved are highly likely to end up doing a long prison sentence, descend into drug addiction, or be killed. These people are, whatever the Government says, economically and socially excluded. To be thus, to see no hope for their future, leaves them angry and frustrated. The daily brutalities of their lives mean they occupy a different world to most of us – a world in which they have switched off their emotions.

'You know what I think? I reckon the reason we don't get help in the ghetto is because the system needs us.'

You all a bunch of fuckin' assholes. You know why? You don't have the guts to be what you wanna be? You need people like me. You need people like me so you can point your fuckin' fingers and say, 'That's the bad guy.' So . . . what that make you? Good? You're not good. You just know how to hide, how to lie. Me, I don't have that problem. Me, I always tell the truth. Even when I lie. So say good night to the bad guy! Come on. The last time you gonna see a bad guy like this again, let me tell you. Come on. Make way for the bad guy. There's a bad guy comin' through! Better get outta his way!

I lose count of the number of times I hear a gang member deliver a variation of this speech. It's from Brian De Palma's 1983 film *Scarface*. It's delivered by Tony Montana (played by Al Pacino), the gangster who has worked his way up from nothing, who addresses the patrons of the expensive restaurant he's in. It's easy to see why this speech appeals. It emphasizes that the gang's crimes are not theirs, but a fault of the system. There is a distance from reality here. The option to live off welfare, to train in something – they aren't considered acceptable in Gangland. You'll become a victim. 'I'm trying to get out. The last few months is the first time I've been able to feel. I can't describe it. Ever since I can remember, I've wanted to be a hit man.'

Another film homage, this time to *Goodfellas*. James tells me about a gunfight that took place on the Lea Bridge Road, interspersed with language reminiscent from popular gangster movies. Some boys from Hackney had been hassling the Shotters. So he and his crew turned up there, and saw them. They had their vests on, and the other crew didn't. They shot out of the car window, and hit one of them in the leg. His friends tried to drag him to their car, firing back at James and his crew. He felt the passenger window smash, and a bullet flew past his nose. Both cars whirled away from each other, back to their estates.

I have a friend who lives on that road. She's a doctor. Didn't they care who they hit?

'That's just the rules of the road. It's like the Serengeti. If you see something move, you clip it.'

Gang members are emotionally unavailable. The only passion many of them feel is for their area; not for people. In a lifestyle where death is so common, friendship is simply too much of a risk.

The role of the police will be a constant theme, but comments made to me by one former gang member provide an idea of how even they can have a negative impact. He told me about the problems that have occurred since a Face called Razor was sent down for money laundering. It's the best way for the police to catch people at the top level: the wall of silence on the street means that financial investigations, Al Capone-style, are the best way to catch them. But the effects can be unexpected: 'Ever since they sent Razor down, it's been hell. Razor controlled the street. No one fucked with Razor, because if they did they thought he'd hit them twice as hard. But Razor was clever. He knew his Sun Tzu. Very rare that he'd take any action at all. He knew how to instil fear without doing anything. He made sure the Elders didn't step out of line – didn't send the Youngers off to fight unless they knew it was necessary, made sure that no one from his crew was stepping out of line. It'd be bad business.

'But now he's gone everyone wants to be the new Razor. And these new guys think that power comes from the gun. They don't get what made him so powerful. You've got Youngers throwing their weight around, hoping to scare everyone, you've got Elders making them do crazy shit hoping the Faces will let them take his place – it's fucked up. If they could shoot straight, we'd already have had one bloodbath. And fuck knows how much more shit is going to go down once Razor gets out of jail . . .'

It is by such issues that everyone's lives are affected here. There are dozens of Elders in this borough, perhaps 200 Youngers; and hundreds more young people who are affiliated to a gang if not part of the core. When you include the parents and siblings affected by them, the number runs into the thousands. When you include the number of residents in the area affected by the violence and crime that's a part of gang life, that number of people skyrockets further, to a point where it cannot be quantified. They are not distressed on an irregular basis: if they live in Gangland, it dominates their lives.

Further Education colleges are perceived by the area's youth as 'belonging' to the gangs, subsumed as they are by the wider territorialism. This issue can influence the youths' decisions on which college they choose to attend, depending on where they live. I met one youth in the area who had changed college due to the fact that he lived in Chingford but was attending an institution primarily seen as Beaumont. This notional affiliation hasn't led to many serious incidents so far, but there have been two stabbings outside one of them. Youth workers find what they do is shaped by gang territories: they can't get the youths from an area together to play sport or games, or dance, or do drama – because another gang's Youngers will intimidate them en route. The most successful projects involve bussing the youths to a destination outside the city. Once there, they usually get on, even if they are from opposing gangs. How much difference does that make when they get back home? It is hard to say, but one youth worker told me in no uncertain terms that she felt the lure of gangsterism was too strong, no matter how often the children were brought together in neutral territory.

When the Hackney crew invaded James's territory, it was something of an oddity. Previously, the only connection the Waltham Forest boys had with their neighbouring borough was one of business; it was rare for them to head over the Lea to engage with them. One of the good things about Waltham Forest's Gangland is that it is mostly self-contained. Everyone knows who their aggressors and allies are. But Hackney's gangs were changing. There were new players on the scene, and they were unafraid to spread their wings.

TWO

Hackney

Mr and Mrs Veneering were bran-new people in a bran-new house in a bran-new quarter of London.
Charles Dickens, Our Mutual Friend

Karl is walking through Mare Street on a summer day when the grey clouds are looming overhead and the air is thick with heat and moisture. He walks past the austere Town Hall, now a bookmaker's, and past the run-down pound stores that line the borough's main road, a road which in architecture and scale has something of the village high street about it, but which in half the people's faces carries the marks of success, and in the other half failure.

Karl is with a thirteen-year-old boy, a friend of his younger brother's, and is escorting him to a flat near the boundary where, were the boy to slip it, he would be in danger. Karl sees the man as they walk under the railway bridge. At first, there is the recognition; a moment of unfamiliarity, like seeing an old friend. Then there is confusion; as both men pause, staring at each other, the question rattles instantaneously into Karl's brain – surely he won't do anything in this crowded street? The pause is deadly: Karl has shown his hand, and he has nothing. With horrible slowness, the man pulls the pistol out of his jacket and begins to attach a silencer to it; here, in the midst of everything, Karl grabs the boy and turns to run. Most of the shoppers lining the street do not notice.

Veep.

From slow motion to fast forward, they reach the entrance to the estate in what seems like seconds.

Veep.

All thought has been supplanted by fear – everything is happening as if on autopilot. Karl doesn't know where the bullets are going – all he knows, as he hears the deadly, high-pitched squeaks, is that they need to keep moving, and quickly.

Veep.

A cry: the boy has been hit in the leg, and the danger is coming. He drags him to a shop across the road and bangs on the door, begging those inside to let him in. They have locked the door.

And suddenly the awful danger is gone, as quickly as it appeared. Perhaps the gunman thought the police were coming. Perhaps he lost his nerve. Karl doesn't know. Later that day some of Karl's gang beat up the owner of the shop for failing to help them. The beating received a couple of inches' coverage in the *Hackney Gazette*. The shooting was never reported.

Across the borough, further south, I meet Nathan. Something of an extreme case, aspects of his background are nonetheless depressingly familiar. He remembers his father by the beatings he dished out before he left. His mother worked two jobs in order to keep him and his two brothers in food and clothes. She'd be up at six in the morning, and not get home until ten every night. He remembers how, little by little, she began to work less and less, and drink more and more, until eventually she'd just given up and was trying to survive on benefits. School never appealed to him. He remembers, aged twelve, going out into the night to deal for the first time, remembers earning £100 for the first time, remembers his first gun (a shotgun), his first shoot-out (on Murder Mile), and his first sentence (possession of a loaded firearm).

'If I'm going to tell you about this, I want you to put this in the book,' he says, quietly. 'You talk about Waltham Forest; you talk about Southwark, Lewisham, all the rest. And yeah, there're some players there. But Hackney – it's different. You understand? The boys here are more serious than everyone else. Everyone is banging. I mean *everyone*. So don't even try to compare what I'm telling you with all that shit. This place is more serious. You get me?' He says this with an odd mixture of shame and pride.

There were more fatal and non-fatal shootings recorded by Operation Trident (the Metropolitan Police's initiative to deal with gun crime in London's black community) in Hackney than anywhere else in 2005/6 – 37, ahead of Southwark (34) and Lambeth (32).

Nathan's clothes cost a lot more than mine. He's wearing brand new trainers, a bright blue puffa jacket and a heavy gold chain. He's a 21-year-old mix of Thai and Caribbean. His skin is pock-marked; burned out and depleted. His eyes dart around the coffee shop as he toys with his mobile. Every five minutes or so it goes off. He pauses and smiles. His gold tooth glints at me: 'OK, now we can continue.'

Nathan takes a sip of his coffee, and nods. It's good. He thinks for a minute about his area: 'The big difference between Hackney and everywhere else is that at the top level we're individual agents. So when you hear the media talk about, "Ooh, the Riders have a beef with the fucking whatevers," well, what they're describing is the fact a guy's got a click together to smoke someone, and that someone's got their people together because they know it's kicking off. You understand? When a new crew gets formed, it's just because a leader like Cummings, or whoever, has left, so he's got to get some new blood under his wing for a job. And having a name for your crew just makes it easier to get kids on board.' This particular leader has been sent down for life: in 2002 Daniel Cummings got out of his car, walked up to Adrian Crawford, a Tottenham gang member, and calmly shot him in the face. He thought that the fear he inspired in others would protect him; for once it didn't.

It's very hard to establish eye contact with Nathan when he's talking business. Engage him on any other subject – women, music, cars – and he's a bundle of energy and passion, riffing at breakneck speed. Like many heavily involved gang members, he has a studied charm. When it comes to business, he thinks and talks robotically.

'Because we're independent, we don't have time to fuck around. The Trident stats imply we're better shots than other boroughs. I'd say that's wrong. It's not that we aim better, it's that we've got it in us to walk up to the target, look him in the eyes and pull the trigger. The other thing about Hackney boys is that we're very well connected. I've spent years inside. We know everyone. Burger Bar Boys from Birmingham, Aggis from Bristol – people would tie their laces in a way to show what gang they were a member of. And if we can roll, we'll roll. It makes life hard for the police. You need to smoke someone . . . they know he's going to be dropped. They're watching you, but all of a sudden these niggers appear from nowhere and the police are like, "Who the fuck are they?"'

I met Nathan the day he'd been released from Rochester Prison. It was a very important day for him. He left with a £53 warrant and a licence with a list of conditions: not to carry firearms, not to leave the country without express permission, and more. He'd been given a series of appointments – he had to see his housing officer for accommodation, he'd had to make his appointment to claim benefits; and missing any of those, for whatever reason, would mean that it would have to be rescheduled for weeks in advance. He'd have £53 on which to survive, and no home. Once the appointments were done, that was it. He could look for a job, but he has a criminal record, no vocational skills – it's a lottery as to which courses your prison will provide; usually only basic literacy and numeracy. There is no job incentive scheme for once he has left prison – neither carrot, nor stick. Job Seeker's Allowance begins to bite after a while, but by that point he will probably be making money the only way he knows how. There are other problems: a family might move on while someone is in prison, and not wish to help. There might be domestic violence. The family might be a criminal influence. If someone leaves a prison with a drug addiction, it can take weeks for a substitute drug to be arranged.

Nathan stops. He's been talking quickly, expressively and angrily for the last fifteen minutes without a pause. He looks up, and says quietly: 'Hackney and Tottenham has taken so much blood from these ends. How much more? My nephew? My mother? There's no more blood to give.'

Since the early 1990s, the historical rivalry between Hackney and Tottenham has developed from isolated incidents and a general mutual dislike into organized and deadly war fought between groups of the most dangerous Elders and Youngers. No one really knows how the battle started. One of the earlier catalysts was the murder of a sixteen-year-old boy, Guy Dance-Dacres, who was killed at Chimes nightclub in Clapton in 1997. He was shot in the head by two Tottenham men, who fired into a crowd of partygoers as a display of force. The bullet passed through his head and hit a girl standing behind him, who was lucky to survive. In response, another youth, whose street name was Popcorn, was chased down by six men who beat him half to death and then shot him in the stomach. The tit-for-tat killings escalated – two of the six convicted would themselves be shot dead in years to come.

A key player at one time was Mark Lambie, who was finally sent down in 2002 after he kidnapped two men and tortured them with an iron, a hammer and by pouring boiling water on their genitals. Lambie, the 'Prince of Darkness', terrified everyone. He headed up the Tottenham Man Dem (TMD) and was known as 'Devil Man': those who knew him thought he was untouchable. They fought primarily with the London Fields gang from Hackney. After Lambie went down, many thought the war would be over, but nothing has changed: the TMD became Hackney North Star, and lives continued to be lost. People talk with reverence of one of Lambie's associates, a man whom they claim has murdered at least three Hackney boys, yet the only time he's been in court has been when he's given evidence against their crews. The territorialism transcends time and lifestyle, like that between Irish Republicans and Loyalists. In 2003 the successful rapper Dizzee Rascal was nearly stabbed to death in Ayia Napa: – he is from Bow, and his alleged assailants were Tottenham men.

We head to Nathan's estate. Like many in the area, it seems to come alive only at night. There are people everywhere, music playing from open windows, shops open nearby. And there's a group of children in the corner of one of the courtyards. Nathan calls one of them over. It's a Younger, Fabian, who's fifteen. There's a disturbing appearance to his face, which is expressionless a great deal of the time, but his eyes are constantly shifting around. He appears to be in the psychological state of frozen watchfulness, most common in victims of domestic abuse. In days to come, he will tell me his life story. For much of his upbringing, Fabian was brought up by his grandfather. His father was in and out of jail and his mother was a crack addict. When he was nine, his grandfather died. His father was finally released from a long sentence. He told Fabian he had to move back in with him and his mother. They were going to be a family.

But when Fabian was ten, his father upped and left again. However, he was free from his beatings.

The apprenticeship for many gang members is served in the home. If you are constantly on the alert for danger, and equate any show of emotion with violence, you are damaged in such a way that serves as an ideal preparation for gang life. You become a machine. And this is Fabian now: a walking, talking, twitching set of senses.

He and his mother lived in squalor. Often there was little food, unless one of the many men that came in and out of the house left them something. She was always high on crack. Fabian had spent a lot of time on the street when his father was still living with his mother. Home wasn't safe, but since he'd moved to his parents' flat, neither was the street. Fabian had been walking down Lower Clapton Road, and some boys had asked him which postcode was his. He'd lied, but they'd known – so they dragged him into a side road and beat him up. The first punch winded him. As he slumped on the floor, he was kicked in the face. He lost a tooth. Since then he'd tried to avoid leaving the estate: he was vulnerable, a target. He made friends with Chris, one of the boys from their estate. Like Fabian, Chris hadn't ever seen any point in going to school. Like Fabian, his mother was on crack. Chris and his friends would just hang out; they'd play football or rap together, or head off looking for adventure.

One time they headed straight into the Pembury Estate and stole a load of things from a van. Among them was a whole bunch of fireworks so they took them down to the canal and set them off. They found a boarded-up house and set up camp in it – it was their little base, where they could smoke spliffs and chill out without anyone noticing, even if they were right next to it. Chris looked after Fabian. He'd lend him money – never had any trouble with that.

Fabian is with a group of other boys when Nathan beckons him over. I ask them if they are in his gang. 'They're from E9,' he says. 'So they're in your gang?' I ask. 'No . . . they're just from E9,' he replies.

The battle between Tottenham and Hackney's gang men has been recounted numerous times in the media. What has been less reported is the way that its example was reflected back on a smaller scale within the borough. As the beef between the two areas grew, it meant that residence and affiliation became the same thing. Anyone gang-involved, even to the smallest extent, would be taking a risk if they slipped into the rival area. The same process has been seen on a smaller scale within Hackney. As the reputation of various gangs took off, it was hard to distinguish who, on any estate, wasn't a gang member. The resulting phenomenon, the 'Postcode War', affected the Youngers, but large-scale rivalries did not do the Elders any harm. If violent youth battles and general anti-social behaviour put fear into a community, the Elders are free to get on with the real business of selling drugs in the background.

These wider area rivalries do not translate to any kind of internal order. As in Waltham Forest there is such a complex machinery of rivalries and allegiances that it is impossible to keep track. Many of the lives lost on the Hackney side of the battle with Tottenham have been members of the London Fields gang, who originally hail from the estate around the park of the same name. London Fields lies within the E8 postcode to the south of the borough, and as such this gang also has bad relations with gangs in the E5 area (the centre) such as Pembury, who themselves do not always tend to get on with gangs in the E9 area to the west. However, London Fields also has a long-standing feud with the Holly Street Boys – who are in the same postcode. And one of the scores of recent crews established in the area is called 9 to 5 – a gang set up by people tired of the warring between E9 and E5. The gangs' fortunes are often influenced by the whims of just a few individuals. While everyone in Gangland knows that Hackney hates Tottenham, there are few certainties beneath that. There are patterns of behaviour – bloodlines, perceived postcode or borough territories – but no organized structure to the relationships.

After Fabian had been beaten up for the first time, he never left his estate without Chris. Chris gave him protection. No one on the estate messed with Chris, because they knew his brother was an Elder. Chris gave him respect, and something to which he might aspire: he was essentially a surrogate father. But Chris moved to a neighbouring borough. It transpired that his brother had beaten a man up over the theft of his watch. The man did not have the courage to retaliate directly, so he and several others had decided to attack Chris. They'd called Chris's brother, and told him they would do it. He didn't believe them. In their rage, they had assaulted Chris with such violence that he had ended up in hospital with fractured ribs and a broken arm. Upon his return his mother had sent him to live with his aunt.

Any older gang member that uses Youngers, even if there are blood links, is playing a dangerous game. Like Chris's brother, they are endangering them – although in many cases they don't care. The danger is also on the Elders' side: on the one hand, a senior gangster wants the Youngers to be as rowdy and violent as possible – under a cover of fear, they can make as much money as they want. But there is a flip side: if the Youngers fail to show respect to them, or begin to attract too much police attention, their purpose is negated. An Elder who connects himself to the Youngers is always walking this line – particularly the first risk. Some of today's killings are born of the resentment felt by Youngers at the tasks they have to do. They have been given the gun, and now they want the power. They operate at the coal face, sometimes on the behalf of others, and sometimes of their own accord. The youths who die in our cities are not necessarily a gang's Youngers. They might be Wana-bees, copying the behaviour of the Youngers of a larger gang in their area, or they might simply live in a rival area and be a target for that reason.

Fabian narrates all this in an alarmingly calm and quiet way. He took Chris's place, and began to work for his brother. His brother knew Nathan, and when he was sent to jail, Nathan took over. This might imply a structured criminal career ladder, but just as there is little order to the relationships between the gangs, so there is little between Youngers and Elders. It is a personal relationship, a long way from joining a company as an apprentice. Fabian says: 'I'll do stuff for Nathan, and he'll look after me. But it ain't that tight. I do my own shit most the time. A guy I know got beaten cos he went rolling with another Man Dem – wouldn't be a prob-lem 'cept one of them had raped his Elder's sister. Thing was, he had to roll with that click because one of them was his cousin so he had kind of a responsibility. Look at the Youngers in E9, most of them hate on the Elders, and there's always more and more aggro between them.'

Again there are certain patterns. One youth worker said: 'Most gang allegiances come through bloodlines – so a guy might be allied to a gang but because of his brother he's safe in the eyes of several more. You know what really hurts me? It's the fact that you can do all this work with the most damaged people there are, trying to get them back on the straight and narrow – and then suddenly, because people see what's happening to him, they try to destroy it. Usually they'll target one of their siblings. You can't ignore that – you have to go back down to their level. And then they're back in trouble. It hurts so fucking much. It's the legacy of the dispossessed – keep everyone around you where you are.'

Fabian loves his ends; would, he says, die for them. He sees nothing beyond his estate. I ask him if he has ever been on the

London Eye. I ask all the Youngers this and, wherever they are, a variation on the same response usually comes: 'Nah man, I don't go down them ends.' Would he like to? He would – he speaks of it as he would a holiday abroad. So many of the Youngers inhabit this strange cognitive landscape – when the peer group is all that provides safety, when there is none at home, and even less when they travel out of their area only to encounter grave danger, it is unsurprising. This is how many of the gangs evolve; from a playgroup, from boys looking for adventure, to crime, to a siege mentality.

Fabian is one of thousands of boys in this country who dare not fantasize in the conventional way, whose life is reduced to the daily dramas, conflicts and resolutions taking place within their immediate surroundings – one of the many boys who, brutalized into territorialism, sees only danger when he looks outside of his territory. It's as if these boys never grow out of the narrow worldview of early childhood: imagining unforeseen dangers outside their immediate environment and romanticizing their surroundings.[1]

This is the world of gang-involved children; where everything appears normal, but is not. Where the houses are new, where they may find love and respect of a kind from their siblings and peers, and where the natural human craving for protection is satisfied, but in a way that is skewed enough to endanger them. Soon, this cloistered mindset develops into something that is a great deal more dangerous.

In Queensbridge Road, a busy wide street that runs south from Hackney to the City, you might be standing right next to a gourmet restaurant without being in any way aware of the fact that it's the boundary between the territories of London Fields and Holly Street. You might walk two blocks to the left, to Holly Street itself, where a building site has supplanted the old council estate and only a few grey, stained slabs with sickeningly bright-orange balconies remain as a memorial to the urban blight of the area. On the other side of the road is a set of new terraced houses with beautifully tended gardens. You might walk a few blocks to the right, to London Fields, and pass row upon row of elegant town houses without ever being aware that this is the gang's territory, into the park itself, a picture of secluded urban bucolia, fringed as it is with tall oak trees. There are still signs; the old estates tucked away behind it give clues just as the carcass of Holly Street's estate remains, but Gangland is mostly found in the brand new, low-rise housing around it.

To envisage the gangs' areas, the mind's eye must rise above Queensbridge Road. As the view pans out, to the west one sees neat and dainty Stoke Newington Church Street, all expensive restaurants and bars, and surrounding it the mess of council flats that makes up the N16 postcode, with Live or Die (LORD) the pre-eminent gang. Just to the east lies the centre of Hackney, E5, with the sprawl of curved red buildings that make up the Pembury Estate which lies at its heart and, as one drifts ever higher, The Mother's Square, a little further to the west, a brand new close of pretty terraced houses which is rarely without its crew hanging around the centre of it, incongruous in the midst of the novelty. Beside it lies a small NHS day-care centre, now closed down, which was used as their base: while it was boarded up they set up Playstations, mattresses, and covered it with graffiti of children killing each other. There are bloodstains on the floor, presumably the result of abductions. And as the camera drifts back further the Lower Clapton Road – Murder Mile – comes into view; it runs to the top of the borough, where the crews in areas like Manor House and Stamford Hill are battling it out.

More of the city comes into view – Tottenham, its urban sprawl perched beside the stirring Lea Valley, and then Lordship Lane, the gang boundary on Tottenham's north side appears – for Tottenham fights the gangs from Wood Green, too. One thinks of David Gaynor, a Wood Green gang member who blew half a man's head off with a shotgun in front of his family, because he dared to challenge Simeon Szypusz who had crashed into his car – Szypusz had been disrespected and Gaynor evened up the score and wrote rap lyrics about it: 'I will kill you in front of your family.' In fact it just left his victim brain damaged, and the attack left a message, so soon forgotten, that this is the price you get for disrespecting Wood Green.

One thinks of Andre Linton, the man from Tottenham shot dead in his car with a converted starter pistol by a member of the Money Over Bitches crew, his killer later making gun signs and smiling at his family while still in the dock. Keep going higher still, so that to the southwest Highbury has appeared, the gangs of which are allied with Wood Green, and to the northwest there's Alexandra Park, which is LMD's, another Wood Green mob, and to the east, Edmonton (allied with Wood Green) is visible, and still further in this direction the Banbury Reservoir, and past that Chingford Hall, the home of Piff, slides into view, and beside that Highams Park, which likewise has its own little clique, and still higher until north London seems not so much one place as a collection of sharply defined areas of varying sizes, all of which are at war with each other and within themselves.

And in every area it's the same set-up – a few dangerous, brutalized men who have spent time in jail building up their contacts and learning their trade, and beneath them a small set of impressionable teenagers, willing to do whatever they're told. The impact of the two groups is too vast to understand. To make some sense of the situation, we need to return to our specific area.

Lisa is an attractive black girl in her mid-twenties. She is petite, and has a huge grin that seems to encompass half her face when she smiles. When she laughs, she throws her head back and screams, and when she becomes enthused her eyes flicker with a bright fervour. Her face bears no marks of the life she has led.

Lisa was the sister of a senior gang member. As such, she was a Gangland Queen. Most evenings her brother and his friends would go out and Lisa would be with them. They would take a limousine from one of her brother's flats to a rave, and she'd be treated like royalty. Every night they'd drink £200 bottles of Champagne. She'd spend £500 a week on clothes. The year she really started hanging around with her brother and the other Elders, she completed her GCSEs. As a sibling, Lisa's relationship with the gang members was different to that of other girls: 'My brother had five or six girls. But he shared them with the other guys, and they shared theirs with him. It's just how it is – after the club I'd go to bed, and there'd be three or four of them with one girl. They'd treat them like dirt. But that's how they expect to be treated; they're the kind of girls that follow those guys around.'

These girls are often taking huge risks. They can quite often be the people who facilitate hits, because they can be connected via sexual relationships to opposing gang members. Lisa had been arrested for robbery before: 'Most of the time I'd hit the same people as my brother. I was like a fully paid-up gang member: no one would snitch because of who I was. No street robberies. I don't respect people who hold you up in the street.' But she was finally sent down after one of her brother's friends was shot in the leg: 'I knew how they'd found him. It was one of the girls; she'd told them where he'd be. These girls – you offer them money to tell you where a guy is, she'll tell you. She told them he'd be around one night off the Clapton Road, and they tracked him down and took shots at him. He managed to stagger into the main road, and they ran off. I saw her a few days later, and I beat the shit out of her. I scratched her to pieces.'

Lisa went down for ABH. She didn't mind prison: 'All those years, I knew it was coming, that I had to pay for the life I'd led.' When she talks of the parties and the money, it is without a hint of pride. But what Lisa clings to, will always swing the conversation to if given the chance, are her educational achievements: 'I got eight GCSEs, none of them lower than a C. If I hadn't gone to jail, I'd have been a physicist.' She looks down at her nails: 'The guys in my ends . . . it means something for a girl to achieve what I did. You know, a lot of the Elders like that in a girl – she'll get a lot more respect if she's done well. They like to be able to say to the other people in their crew: "My girl's at university." It's something different.'

The social worker who introduced me to Lisa has seen the worst aspects of gangs and women: 'It's not just university girls an Elder likes. Many of them are going out with white professionals. These kind of women like a bit of rough, and don't know what they're involved in. The Elders like it because these women aren't like the ones on their estate . . . I've known women who'll take a thirteen-year-old girl over to an estate in order to be gang raped, because that girl's said something she shouldn't. They don't even call it gang rape: "Man's got needs," they tell me. No, he fucking doesn't. They beat up a girl, slash her with a knife because they think she's been dressing provocatively and flirting with their men. And how old is she? "Oh, twelve," they say. And they don't think they've got issues. What can you do? It's the way of life – you keep everyone around you down. Make sure no one has a better life than you.'

This is the Orwellian view of Gangland that many of the professionals who work there see every day in the likes of Nathan, Fabian and Lisa: a boot perpetually stamping on a human face. How did things get this bad?

*

Hackney is changing. It was always ripe for redevelopment: the Georgian terraced houses that line its streets have a scruffy attractiveness. Now many of them sell for millions, and like the rest of London, its property market has exploded. Run-down drinking holes have given way to pricey gastropubs. Where once there were fish and chip shops and fried chicken joints there are a few gourmet restaurants springing up. Its parks are well tended – Victoria Park, which sits by the canal with its nineteenth-century statues and elegant bandstand, is beautiful. The news that it will soon be serviced by a tube has increased the number of wealthy City workers moving there, eager to buy property near their place of employment. Yet beneath all this glitter, Gangland remains. The reduction target set for gun crime by Hackney police is 5 per cent annually. But in 2005/06 the borough saw a 34 per cent increase.[2]

The gentrification of areas in the borough of Hackney give as good an example as any regarding how Gangland developed. Teenagers do not start murdering each other out of the blue: the situation has been a time bomb ever since the 1980s. During this decade, the gap between rich and poor reached a level not seen since the Second World War. This was a global trend, but the pace at which inequality increased in the UK was faster than any other country except, curiously, New Zealand.[3] Spurred on by the writings of right-wing economists, the Thatcher government's policy towards unemployment changed the face of Britain. The increase in the number of jobless was in part due to industrial forces beyond governmental control, but there was a simultaneous drive to increase the productivity of manufacturing industries, and to choke inflation out of the economy with high interest rates. It meant jobs had to be cut, and during the 1980s incomes of the bottom 10 per cent of the population had declined in real terms by 17 per cent, while the incomes of the average had risen by a third.[4] At the same time those in jobs were earning comparatively less: after 1978 hourly wages for the lowest paid men hardly changed in real terms, but by 1992 were lower than in 1975. Median wages grew by 35 per cent; but high wages grew by 50 per cent.[5]

The welfare state was also being slimmed down. Norman Fowler, Secretary of State for Social Services, reviewed the social-security system and cut death grants, maternity grants, pensions, housing benefits, all benefits to those under 18, and some to those under 25. By 1992 the budget for crisis benefits had fallen from £504 million to £91 million. In the time of a crisis the poor's final safety net had gone; a crime, an illness, an unexpected bill – and they were unable to support themselves. Supplementary benefit was scrapped and income support was introduced; this was thrown out and the job seeker's allowance came in. Benefits were cut to the unemployed if they were aged between 18 and 24, among other groups.[6]

These changes, momentous though they were, did not create Gangland. The factor that really brought it into being was the manner in which this newly deprived underclass ended up living, in some part due to the housing policies of the time. Poor, rich and average households became less and less likely to live next door to one another between 1980 and 2000. The Joseph Rowntree Foundation has demonstrated that this trend was, again, a reversal from the 1970s, when Britain's population became substantially less concentrated in areas of high or low household poverty. The reversal of this trend continued throughout the 1990s.[7]

Professor Pitts cites Malcolm Dean of the Joseph Rowntree Foundation in his report on Waltham Forest. Dean described two distinct communities within the social-housing sector: 'At one end there are the established elderly residents, who have lived in social housing all their lives and who remember a time when having a council home was a desirable goal. At the other end are the new, younger residents, frequently suffering from multiple problems: unemployment, poverty, poor work skills and perhaps mental illness and drug abuse as well [. . .]. This happened despite the warnings of housing professionals about the problems which public housing projects generated when they were confined to the poor, the unemployed and the elderly.'[8] As Pitts argues, the Right to Buy and Tenants' Incentive Schemes served to exacerbate this, as the 'economically active' vacated these estates.

The Joseph Rowntree Group was particularly worried about the problem of geographically concentrated poverty in 1995. It stated: 'The Inquiry Group's prime concern is with the overall social effects of the changes in distribution, which impact on the whole community; with the accumulation of problems in particular areas; and with the long-term economic costs.' It continued: 'The way in which the living standards of a substantial minority of the population have lagged behind since the late 1970s is not only a problem for those directly affected, but also damages the social fabric and so affects us all.'[9]

While the amount of benefits available gradually increased, these general trends have not been reversed and the end product is Gangland. Within these communities there is a paucity of hope and opportunity. There is little *absolute* poverty in Britain – few people are starving – but research has shown that there are many poor people who are depressed, stressed, and riddled with worry and debt.[10] When Gangland was born, the choice for Britain's poor was clear: scrape by on reduced benefits, encased in rigid self-discipline, or become participants in what might be politely termed an 'informal economy'.[11]

It was an economy in which, mostly thanks to the growing drugs market, it was becoming increasingly easy to find work. It was not an economy that is properly regulated or measured. We know certain simple facts, such as a block of hash or a rock of cocaine costs less than it did twenty years ago, regardless of inflation. We also know, thanks to the British Crime Survey, that between 1981 and 1991 the general crime rate increased by 3 per cent each year. This is not an economy that has struggled, and in parts of these communities it has been accompanied by the growth of hyper-masculinity and a mood of self-sustaining detachment from the mainstream.

Two groups grew up within Gangland during those years. At one end there were teenagers and young men who were developing into successful criminals – well connected, and with a growing sense of how money could be made. At the other end were children born into Gangland, some of whom, were they unsuccessful in conventional social structures, would be susceptible to the influence of the first group.

Any area's gang will usually be ethnically representative of the area from which it is drawn. In Waltham Forest the gangs are a mishmash of different ethnicities, predominantly black. In London the black population increases with the level of deprivation, so it is not surprising that Hackney's gangs mostly comprise black men. These members still make up a tiny minority of the area's black community, but their effects are felt throughout it. The 2007 Home Affairs Committee Report entitled *Young Black People and the Criminal Justice System* placed social exclusion as 'the key, primary factor' behind black people's overrepresentation in terms of gun crime.[12]

It stated that black people make up two and a half times as high a proportion of the population in the most deprived areas of the country as for England as a whole. Eighty per cent of Black African and Black Caribbean communities live in Neighbourhood Renewal Areas, which are identified as England's most deprived areas. Black people, on average, experience significantly higher unemployment and lower earnings than white people. And as the report again made clear, this is a longstanding poverty within our country. It stretches back to the immediate post-war period, when the first settlers in Britain from the Caribbean were forced into ghettoes because of racial prejudice and restricted access to accommodation, resulting in them being stacked in places where schools were substandard, employment opportunities were minimal and long-term prospects of holding the family together were limited.[13]

Poverty is not an easy thing for a community to grow out of. Rather, as a series of witnesses to the Home Affairs Committee Report argued, it perpetuates itself. The first generation of ethnic minorities in the 1970s suffered higher rates of unemployment than British-born whites of the same age. The most disadvantaged group were black Caribbeans, with an unemployment rate twice that of whites. By the 1990s the next generation's unemployment rate had risen to nearly three times that of white men.[14] Two-thirds of black people live in London – young black Londoners under 18 make up 15 per cent of that age group, but represent 49 per cent of remand decisions, 43 per cent of custodial decisions and 30 per cent of those dealt with by Youth Offending Teams. At Feltham Young Offenders' Institution, 42 per cent of inmates are black.[15]

As we saw in the previous chapter, it is as if Britain is two nations, with each completely unaware of the other. The crime that happens in one nation does not concern the other, even if they are right next to each other, which in London they more often than not are. There is no question that in terms of gun crime, black people's overrepresentation is indeed high: they make up 2 per cent of the population but a third of gun crime suspects. Yet at the same time they are also more likely to be victims of violent crime. They are seven times more likely than white people to be a victim of homicide, three times more likely to be raped, nearly three times more likely to suffer violent crime and nearly twice as likely to be victims of robbery. More tellingly, they make up nearly 75 per cent of those murdered between the ages of 10 and 17.[16]

In April 2007 Tony Blair was, in his own words, 'lurching into total frankness' as his premiership ended. At a Callaghan Memorial Lecture in Cardiff he said: 'When are we going to start saying [gun crime] is a problem amongst a section of the black community and not, for reasons of political correctness, pretend that this is nothing to do with it?' Blair said there needed to be an 'intense police focus' on the minority of young black Britons behind the gun and knife attacks. The laws on knife and gun gangs needed to be toughened and the ringleaders 'taken out of circulation'. Answering questions later Blair said: 'Economic inequality is a factor and we should deal with that, but I don't think it's the thing that is producing the most violent expression of this social alienation.'[17]

It was an odd speech, which completely contradicted the Home Office's findings of the same year. Blair's statement was like a doctor telling a measles sufferer the fact he'd never been vaccinated didn't matter: he could just have plastic surgery to cover the spots. There is an intelligent evasiveness to the phrasing of his statement, because as we shall see, poverty is not quite the direct cause of the problem: there are reasons beyond the economic that encourage 'the most violent expression' of social disaffection. The Home Office report found that these 'compounded' the problem of black people's overrepresentation. But economic inequality forms the background to this type of crime, and it is not something that can be just 'dealt with': the other factors have to be seen within the environment of disorganized, and traditionally poor, neighbourhoods.

It does not mean that gang members are all drawn from poverty-stricken families. I met several whose family unit was stable but whose parents were busy professionals who worked for local councils, or hospitals, or ran shops – and as such they had little time for their children, who were attracted to (or lured into) gang life. Many of them were every bit as violent as others from tougher backgrounds: they had a point to prove.

Moreover, while black people are clearly overrepresented in terms of gun crime, the accusatory tone lacks perspective. In total, 2,653 homicides were recorded by the police in the three years 2002/3, 2003/4 and 2004/5. Three-quarters (1,923) of the victims were white, and 9 per cent (242) were black. Eighty-eight per cent of white victims were killed by suspects from the same ethnic group. The corresponding proportions, i.e. suspects being from the same ethnic group, were lower for Asian people (64 per cent) and black people (74 per cent).[18] The implicit equation of race and violence is a misleading assumption; Blair's statement and the casual use of phrases such as 'black on black gun crime' imply that gun crime is simply not a problem within other communities. It is hard to explain his willingness to blame the black community's culture for its problems. The most likely reason is that it is born of an outbreak of poor thinking among party analysts: that instead of looking at the structural reasons behind this type of violent crime, they have pathologized their study. They have confused symptoms with causes. We will see later in this book that this tendency within Labour's thinking also applies to its take on white working-class neighbourhoods.

Junior is another member of Nathan's crew in his early twenties; short, wiry and full of energy. I take him out for a burger – he waves it like a police baton, spraying food everywhere. He is no stranger to violence, and he doesn't like me much. He's only talking because Nathan told him to. 'It always happens in the club. We could get a gun in anywhere. The point about the club is it's where you prove to everyone – everyone – that you're a player. You're sitting in the corner with your boys, you're all drinking Champagne, you've got all the ladies with you. And deep down, you're scared. Because deep down you know any nigger can walk straight in, clip your wing, smash a champagne bottle to hide the prints, and be straight out. No running, just walk straight out. You know what, you ask that man sitting in the corner if he's really happy, and he'll tell you, if he has to be honest, that all he's doing is keeping himself safe. It's like the markings on a wasp – don't fuck with me. That's what all that gear's about. Plus, I don't know, there's just something in our culture about that stuff. Don't ever step on my trainer, man.' He laughs. 'Black people just love their trainers.' He's referring to murders such as the 1998 killing of Daniel Brown, twenty, in Birmingham's Plazza club; he was shot dead after treading on his killer's foot.

The nightclub murder that is said to have sparked the Tottenham/Hackney war was a typical show of strength. Nightclubs are where crew members will display their wealth and power. They are places where any challenge to someone's respect will be taken the most seriously. Hackney has seen its fair share of violence at these venues. Masculine honour causes fights in pubs and clubs across the country most Friday and Saturday nights. But in certain venues where there are a high number of criminals, there are always going to be fatalities.

The Palace Pavilion nightclub in Lower Clapton Road was shut down in 2006 after a string of violent incidents. The last was perhaps the most horrifying: Barrington Williams Samuels, nineteen, was out with his sister and his friend, and drove there early one Saturday evening to see if they could gain admittance. There was an altercation on the steps, and Barrington and his friend turned away. They went to a nearby takeaway for food, and then rejoined his sister in their car. They were preparing to drive away when two men approached the car from behind and fired a machine gun through the rear window. Williams-Samuels screamed his sister's name and leapt across the seat to protect her as the bullets ripped through the vehicle. He succeeded; both she and the friend survived the attack, but a bullet hit him in the head, and he died in hospital the next day. Williams-Samuels worked as a barman in J D Wetherspoon's. It was a simple case of mistaken identity.

Junior doesn't want to talk about home: 'The fuck you think it was like, bruv? Mum living off benefits, me and my sister . . . you do what you got to do. I dunno – maybe not even what you got to do, just what you think you got to do. Mum knew what I was doing . . . just didn't want to ask. We've grown up seeing those brothers with the flash cars with satellites outside their Mommas' flats . . . we know what's possible. One cat across my way's got a Porsche. A fucking Porsche Carrera. How many fucking doctors can afford one of those? Every night, in I come. Bang – a couple of hundred on the table. Yeah, I'm sleeping with a gun under the pillow, yeah I go out and every night Mum doesn't know if I'm coming home or not, but you do what you got to do. It's that or . . . having fucking nothing wears you down too. But I ain't. I'm earning serious P's every week. I dunno what I'm gonna do with that money; it's all under my bed, the paper I'm not spending on bitches and booze and gear . . . till one day I'm gonna be pushing a Porsche too. And you know what? Most use the other guy's got was driving round the estate shotting crack. That thing must've eaten petrol even in first.

'School? School just didn't appeal to me. Let me break it down for you as simply as I can.' Junior's eyes fix me with a deep stare. With every word he bangs his knuckles on the table. Everyone in the fast-food restaurant is looking at him, but he doesn't notice.

'That . . . cat . . . with . . . the . . . Porsche . . . was . . . my . . . fucking . . . education. How many people in my ends made it through school? Fuck all is how many. All I saw is guys with their cars, their clothes . . . that ain't gonna come out of exam grades. Least, that wasn't how I saw it. Now, now maybe I think different. But it's too late now, isn't it?'

ONE BLOOD

In weeks to come I will see Junior more and more, and begin to build a relationship with him. One day, I ask him if anything he told me the first time we met was a lie. 'One thing, bruv,' he replies. 'I don't make half the paper I made out.'

One shooting victim narrowly escaped with his life after falling out with gang members from both Hackney and Waltham Forest. He was at a house party when a group of Hackney men began to fire at him from outside. As he escaped out of the rear of the house, he was met by a hail of bullets from a second group of men. He knew trouble was coming, and was saved by his bullet-proof vest. The interesting detail about the incident is that the Waltham Forest men had not shown up in person to kill him. The second group of men had been hired from south London, and they would have prepared for the night in a manner regularly practised by Gangland's hit men.

THREE

South London

Sir Toby Belch: For I am now so far in offence . . . that I cannot pursue with any safety this sport to the upshot.

Twelfth Night, Act IV Scene II

Most gang members don't want to receive the call. When you receive it, your stomach sinks. It is like being suffocated by a force that, however hard you fight, you cannot restrain. You panic. You hold your head in your hands and scream, praying for a higher power to save you. Your prayers seem to last an age, but you are nothing; an infant crying for the light. Eventually, you see there is no way out.

The first thing you need to do is roll several joints. They have to be skunk, and they have to be packed. You place them on the table in front of you. Then you put on headphones, and light the first. You are not trying to allay your nerves. Your heart will not stop racing, and your breathing will not become any less deep. What you are trying to do is make use of the adrenaline.

The music coming from the headphones is not rap – it's grime. It has a thumping, fast beat and intense, aggressive lyrics. The rapper says that anyone who beefs with him will be killed; he'll merk anyone. You toke on the joint and, still trying to control your breathing, you inhale. The hairs on the back of your neck are bristling. You carry on smoking, the dull rhythmic tramp in your ears pounding and pounding. You are a soldier; you are all soldiers in the struggle. A hideous ecstasy of fear and vindictiveness begins to rise within you. It's impossible not to feel it – the terror has given way to rage; an uncontrollable urge to destroy your enemy. If you do not destroy him, then you must die. And yet this rage is still an abstract, undirected notion – a blowtorch you find yourself directing at someone you barely know. You smoke another joint, and perhaps another, and carry on, the anger and fury building and building, the weed allowing you to experience it, as it were, in a state of ecstasy, outside yourself.

The time to stop comes naturally. With a gasp, you put the headphones down, and stub out the last joint. Full of wrath, devoid of any other emotion, you pick up your gun and walk out into the night.

This depiction of a horrific, quasi-martial preparation was related by a senior gang member to a youth worker I interviewed. It is a received wisdom around the most heavily involved gang members of south London; what some of them will do prior to a killing.

The signs as to the changing face of south London's Gangland became clear after the murder of Damilola Taylor, stabbed to death by two ten-year-old boys in the North Peckham Estate in November 2000. One report in the *Observer* described how a fourteen-year-old was identified as a suspect and was taken in for questioning; given the high profile of the case, he had every right to be scared. With lawyers and social workers present, a detective constable asked him about the killing. The boy rushed forward and head-butted him in the face. As the detective fell backwards, the teenager sneered: 'Well? What are you going to do about that?' The *Observer* report continued: '. . . it was the first inkling that the investigation team had grossly under-estimated the intricacies of inner-city youth culture'.[1]

There is now a generation of young Britons who have the capa-bility to work as hit men. They are the first generation to be born into Gangland. In south London, they may be as young as ten: cer-tainly, children of that age have been arrested for firearms offences. The Metropolitan Police say that many of those arrested for homi-cide as part of Operation Trident are young teenagers, in contrast to the 20-, 30- and 40-year-olds when it began. The peak age for victims and suspects of Trident murders and shootings is nineteen. Fifty-four teenagers, one only fourteen years of age, were charged with Trident shootings over the two years to 2006.

These boys have suffered the apprenticeship of domestic vio-lence, or violence on the street, or have grown up with gang-involved siblings. Some have been left psychologically dam-aged by constant bereavements, in some cases at least once a year. They are desensitized to the act of violence. They have learned to bottle up their rage, never to show emotion – that can get you killed – and yet at the same time they have no tools with which to deal with the pain and suffering that they have suffered. The inevitable result is an occasional outpouring of violence. In 2007 a key worker with one of south London's charities was quoted in *GQ* magazine. He equated the experiences of some youths in the area with post-traumatic stress disorder:

'They've been at war basically . . . We see the same things in soldiers coming back from Iraq – anti-social behaviour, aggression, hyper-vigilance. We've brutalized our young people to the point where we have the highest amount of teenage pregnancy, sexual disease and drugs and alcohol abuse in Europe. We've just swept a whole generation under the carpet, as far as I'm concerned. These kids are damaged and they're programmed for collapse.'[2]

Again, this sort of violence is self-perpetuating. I was introduced to William, a ghetto Elder who was trying to turn his life around, in an outreach centre in Lewisham. A mountain of a man, he has a quiet and thoughtful way of talking, his deep voice slowly booming around the church hall in which we were sitting. He wears a wooden cross around his neck; a statement. Christ has replaced the bling. He had a simple take on the situation: 'Why are the young kids dying all of a sudden? Because now there are 25-year-olds who have grown up their entire life being robbed and being full of resentment. They're the first generation of adults who've lived their entire lives in this culture. And this is the first generation of kids who've not only lived it – they were born into it. So the Elders are quite prepared to make the kids' lives even worse than theirs were. [They'll say] "Yeah, sure, give them the guns, let them shoot each other to shit . . . can't be any worse than we had it."'

William has no fear of them: 'They're stupid. They don't know diddly. My average day involves getting up, getting in my car and driving round delivering packages. There's beef, but there's got to be a reason, and whatever it is has to be settled quickly, one way or the other. If you get popped, then, well, it's your time. But the Youngers? They're all about hype. They smoke people and aren't earning a fucking penny. If they scare us, it's only because they represent the fact that we're getting old.' Hype is a key word in Gangland: it means being loud, never backing down, instilling fear in those around you. As William continues: 'You give a twelve-year-old a gun and how the fuck do you expect him to behave?'

These chickens came home to roost in 2007, when several young boys were killed in horrific circumstances. The most notable were Billy Cox and Michael Dosunmu, shot dead in their own homes. Suddenly the headlines appeared and the country began to wonder what was happening to these boys. But the situation had been developing for at least two decades.

Modern psychology, and indeed such events as the Holocaust, has taught us that a figure of authority, in the right circumstances, can wield unfettered power over any right-thinking individual. A young teenager can be dispatched to kill as easily as the subjects in Milgram's famous experiment were prepared to give people lethal doses of electricity.[3] In several shootings in south London, many of them unreported, they have. Many of the Youngers have seen what the Elders possess and, being young, being tired of being victimized, and being armed and thus in as much of a position of power as their masters, they want it. The criminologist Steve Shropshire has described the phenomenon: 'The more desensitized they become the more violence there is, in turn desensitizing young people further. The young teens in today's gangs and crews are more violent than those gang-involved individuals now in their twenties who were becoming gang-involved in the late 1980s and early 1990s.'[4]

There is a growing unease, especially in the borough of Lambeth. Walk out of Brixton tube on a Friday night, turn left, and walk up the main road. As you turn the corner into Coldharbour Lane, by the huge KFC, you see them. As in the main road of a developing nation, every other face is offering something – wants something. Brief eye contact, muttered words: 'Skunk, Mista? Ay, what's up, skunk . . . skunk.'

This is where middle-class London comes to buy its weed of an evening. Look at the faces offering it to you. Where once there were grown men, now they are all young teenagers. Age is now no barrier to the lucrative Coldharbour Lane market: the Youngers have as much power as anyone. A youth worker who pointed out how this market had changed said: 'When you put a gun into someone's hands, however old they are, you give them a power. However old you are, it's the ultimate power – felt more keenly than any other, be it economic or sexual or whatever.' And as Professor Dick Hobbs of the LSE puts it: 'Apprenticeships into adult deviant groups are no longer necessary: the youth group itself can now evolve into something more substantial.'[5]

Not much research for this book scared me. Not one of the gang Elders ever saw me as a threat: I wasn't. If we disagreed, they could be reasoned with; in fact many of them enjoy the process of a debate. But if ever I met Youngers in a group, there was a temptation to be aggressive towards me, just to prove a point to their peers. They could not be reasoned with, and they had no respect for anything. As with much of Gangland, it is a grotesque mutation of everyday circumstances. I have worked as a teacher, and know that thirteen- or fourteen-year-olds are desperate to show off to their friends, see adults as clueless and yet want the same things they have. But they are not prepared to kill to get it, and their bravado has a limit. Not in Gangland. Many of them have been brutalized into leading a life they do not wish to lead. Some see no other way to live; others see it but are held in check by their peers. And many of them have reached a point where the only way they know how to make an impression is through violence.

I met one in an outreach centre. He clocked me, and walked up: 'So, you BBC or newspapers?'

I'm writing a book.

'Who you gonna talk to?'

The head of the centre.

'Why do you guys always talk to that mong? He knows fuck all.' A pause. 'I shanked a guy last week. Want to know more?'

No.

'I could shank you. If I had a knife, I'd walk up to you and shank you in the guts, like this – what you think of that?'

Silence.

'I might just shank you, if you turn your back. Don't turn your back on me, big man.'

Telling him to go away would be to initiate the escalation he wants. So I nod. He's laughing and shouting to his friends, telling him the big journalist guy's scared of him. All of a sudden I'm the one filled with rage, the one who wants to smack this boy about the head, to teach him some respect and some discipline. There would be no point. Already violence is nothing to him. And that feeling tells me more about Gangland – that I wouldn't do well there – than it does about him, as he is led away by an outreach worker, slitting his throat with his finger while staring into my eyes.

Outside Stockwell tube station there is a memorial to Jean Charles de Menezes. Across the wide, busy Clapham Road, in the foyer of Cassell House, a huge block of flats which overlooks the road, another shooting took place in 2007. Abukar Muhamed, sixteen, was chased here by a pack of youths on mountain bikes: he died of a single bullet wound to the neck.

The Stockwell Gardens Estate, of which Cassell House is a part, does not look threatening. The first section of the estate looks like the quad of an Oxbridge college, with a playground in the middle. All of the windows are PVC. By day it's quiet, set aside from the noise of the Stockwell roundabout. Notice boards around the estate proclaim youth-group activities for the children over the school holidays – still others prohibit them from playing football in the forecourts. The cars are all new. The atmosphere is pleasant. You walk out of this section and into St Michael's Road, which heads on to Stockwell Road, which splits the estate in half. On the other side of the road is Cassell House. Stockwell Road is a limbo, nothingness. It lacks the vitality of Brixton – there are few shops, restaurants or even pedestrians: just endless streams of traffic passing through. It is flanked by row upon row of estates and houses.

Rather than take this road south to Brixton, it is better to head west, back up St Michael's Road. Suddenly, Gangland stops. The road takes you to Stockwell Park Crescent, a leafy enclave of spacious Victorian houses which face on to a large park. This aesthetic oasis is incongruously juxtaposed with the Stockwell Park Estate, the hinterland that runs alongside the road to Brixton: a mish-mash of different blocks of flats, some high-rise and some bewilderingly squat. There are several places in London where the discrepancy between Gangland and affluence is not defined by degrees; this is one.

Slightly further to the west lies the A23, the Brixton Road, and on the other side of that lies one of the hearts of Gangland. Angell Town, formerly a hulking grey estate built in the 1970s, has been regenerated. Over the last ten years it has been rebuilt into a series of shining yellow-brick units, each of them a couple of storeys high. The road surfaces are new. Its newness is intrusive; every angle is sharply defined, everything so fresh and contemporary that the gang of Youngers speaking to an Elder in his bright purple BMW looks completely out of place.

The words of a policeman who has worked in the area for a long time echo around my head: 'It's the thirteen-, fourteen-year-olds, even younger than that, that scare me. About ten years ago it seemed using a gun was a big thing. If there was a fight, it was fist on fist. Now getting a gun is not a problem, and they are fearless. There are no more hard men left; which means the rules of the game have totally changed. Any teenager can pop you if they don't like you. Prison, the risk of getting shot: it's not a deterrent. If anything, it's a rite of passage. They have no respect for anything other than their peers. They don't see beyond their estate.'

The more I spoke to him, the more I felt he suffered from the same sense of hopelessness as everyone else: 'How are you supposed to deal with a ten-year-old who won't say a word to you until he has his brief there? What kind of world is this? The gangs have such a hold on the kids. We've tried everything – intervention programmes, initiatives, amnesties . . . and it's doing nothing. Very occasionally they leave, but quite often they rejoin and are more eager to prove themselves. It's hopeless.'

One night I am in the area to set up a meeting with one of my contacts. As I walk away from the estate, a couple of the Youngers spot me. They are told by the Elders to keep an eye on people enter-ing the estates: I'm no threat, but they want to know what I'm doing. I'm 50 or 60 yards away from them, and I have my usual story ready – I'm working on a book about police corruption. But I don't want to take the risk this evening; not when I can avoid it. I begin to walk away, and they call to me: 'Hey, you! Yes, nigger [I am actually white], yes, you!' I carry on walking. 'Hey, you!' I turn one sharply defined corner, then another, then another. I know that if I keep heading west I will be safe. I still hear footsteps and shouts. I don't know if they're following me, but I turn one more corner, and I'm running, and I'm gone.

I run into Loughborough Road, where poverty suddenly shows its ugly face; the truth that was lying behind those low-rise, crisply defined housing units. There are huge, multi-storey blocks of flats on either side.

At a nearby youth centre a woman I met told me about how she watched one boy trying to shoot another, where he kept shooting and shooting and the boy kept diving left and right: it looked like a strange comedy routine, the one unable to hit the other despite being only ten yards away, until suddenly his target crumpled to the floor with a shattered femur. Like so much of the violence, unreported. A little further south, under a railway bridge, lies the hulking neo-brutalist horseshoe known locally as the Barrier Block that forms the facade to the Moorlands Estate, its different levels jutting out at sharp angles so that they form a zig-zag across it between the tiny turret windows. Around the corner is Coldharbour Lane and the lights and tin drums and smell of frying meat of Brixton centre.

There are scores of interrelated cliques in south London – some larger, like the South Man Syndicate, many smaller, like the Roadside Gs and Paid in Full. One could write about the Wildcats in Catford, the SUK, T-Block, Kids on the Hill, the Brockley Boys – the list goes on. It is more productive to concentrate on a smaller area. Most of Brixton's Gangland consists of two estates: Angell Town and nearby Myatts Field. For many years the predominant gang in the area was the 28s. Members left and the power shifted to the Peel Dem Crew (PDC), many of the original members of whom were drawn from the 28s. In recent years the PDC began to split. The members who lived in Angell Town remained PDC members. What happened in Myatts Field is a story for later. The PDC has now begun to legitimize itself; the founder, Elijah Kerr, has set up a music business and the videos which the crew put out can be found all over the Internet. PDC now stands for Poverty Driven Children, or Pray Days Change. This is not to say that the gangs in Brixton are no more; rather, they partitioned off into smaller cliques; one of the more notorious is called Organized Crime. The most obvious divisions within Brixton are by area: gang members wear different colours to show which estates they belong to: purple for Angell Town, green for Myatts Field. There are also gangs around Clapham to the east, the most notorious of which is G-Street, whose members wear red.

You can walk in a straight line from Brixton to the east to take in the major south London territories. Head up Coldharbour Lane for about a mile, past Loughborough Junction, and you are now in the borough of Southwark, at the busy but dilapidated junction of Camberwell Green. Litter-strewn with the detritus of numerous fast-food outlets, it can be a menacing place after dark and seems to be a magnet for vulnerable people, many of whom attend the Maudsley mental-health unit on Denmark Hill.

You head east to the regenerated pleasantness of Peckham High Street. For a busy road it's fairly quiet – the buildings, from the tasteful, neo-classical Southwark Town Hall to the inverted steel modernity of Peckham's library, all seem to fit. Gangland lurks behind it to the north, in what was the North Peckham Estate and its environs; now reinvented in red brick and blue modernity. Sumner Road and the Aylesbury Estate are a little scruffier. This area belongs to the Peckham Boys.

Continuing to the east for a mile, past more busy normality – petrol stations, shops, a few tidy houses – and you reach Pomeroy Street which heads north, and Lausanne Road, to the south. This area is a literal division marking the boundary between the boroughs of Southwark and Lewisham, and a division in Gangland terms. This is the boundary between the Peckham Boys' area and that of the Ghetto Boys, in New Cross. As before, Gangland is hiding away to the north. It is a great deal shabbier than the Peckham Boys' territory. It's a maze of different estates; Milton Court is nondescript, a mash of low-rise flats in varying states of repair. Evelyn Estate, a sprawling territory of looming eggshell-blue blocks and low-rise flats, wears its poverty more obviously. Cross Evelyn Road, the road which leads back to London Bridge and prosperity, and head further north, and you're at the Pepys Estate, a huge area flanked by high-rise towers. It has its own shops and a main road running through it, Grove Street. Head up this main road and suddenly, between the blocks of flats, the Thames appears, the gleaming lights of Canary Wharf shining across the water, an abrupt stop to Gangland, as if to say this perpetual urban sprawl must end somewhere; will only stop once it runs out of land.

*

If we ignore the smaller cliques and the areas to the south of the boroughs, we can, then, see three clearly divided territories spread out over a few miles – from east to west, the gangs of Brixton, the Peckham Boys and the Ghetto Boys. Three large, warring institutions, or so it would seem.

Wilson's gold jewellery looks absurd on his young frame. The huge ring, the gold chain, all these mark him out as a gang member, yet his brittle-looking arms and legs betray the fact that he is only fifteen years old. He never knew Dad. Mum knew he was up to something, but was tired, stressed; it was only when they called at her home, a basement flat in a quiet and leafy road in south London, that she knew something was wrong. She showed the two policemen into the living room, decrepit television and carpets and clutter all around, a bong perched by the window, incongruously beside Wilson's under-12 football trophy. It's here I meet him. Mum brings me a cup of tea: elegant, neat china, that doesn't seem to belong here. She smiles and leaves the room. Wilson had stabbed someone in the leg. It was in retaliation for when they beat his friend, twenty or so of them, punching him and kicking him until two of his ribs were shattered, and his face an unrecognizable mess. He's still living with her. She's attempting to make alternative arrangements for his education.

I ask Wilson about a recent battle which took place between the Ghetto and Peckham Boys. What sparked it off? How had it been organized? Had it been planned a long time in advance?

'Yeah, I think I remember that. It was something to do with a robbery. I think one of the older guys round these ends had a chain stolen or something, so he went to have it out with the guy, innit – course, he gets the shit kicked out of him. So he's back in Peckham and rounding up the other Elders. My breds are back there, and they say to them, "You wanna go and fuck up some Ghetto mans?" And they ain't gonna say no to them men. Sooner or later there's like a whole mob of them, cos they call their friends – they know shit's gonna kick off and they don't know what they're getting into. Next thing you know there's a load of guys all getting down with it; wanting to go and smash the place up. I missed the whole thing, cos I had to see my counsellor. Anyway, it wasn't like you asked, like Peckham Boys against Ghetto Boys . . . it was just like . . . I dunno . . . mob justice or whatever it's called. These ends just don't get on.'

On 22 August 2007 a man named Marlon Granderson was sent down. The *South London Press* story opened: 'One of Britain's most feared gang generals, the leader of the notorious Peckham Boys, is facing life behind bars today.'[6] He was caught after officers found a Mac 10, three Makarov handguns, two silencers, 379 rounds, 62 hollow-point bullets, gunpowder, 60,000 fake ecstasy pills and a solid block of cocaine worth £2,000 in his car. All three handguns were linked to six separate shootings between June and August 2006: most of the victims wouldn't help police with their enquiries, including a woman who was shot in the stomach. No one has been charged for these incidents. When he was arrested he was carrying £1,000 in cash. The story continued: 'A police source said: "Granderson was really the top dog, the high-level criminal we had been looking for. When we realized we'd got him our officers were overjoyed."'

I ask: 'Tell me about Marlon Granderson.'

Wilson looks bemused: 'Who?'

'The Peckham Boys' leader.'

'What?'

'Marlon Granderson – he was caught with a load of guns in his car. You must know him, you're a Peckham Boy, and he's . . .'

'Oh! You mean Raver. Yeah, I heard they busted him. Dunno what you mean by leader. He was rolling pretty heavy, like, a real serious player. We don't have a leader; we just like . . . we just do what we do.'

'But you have Elders, you have . . .'

'Yeah, but that's . . . look, if an Elder asks you to do something, it's like . . . you do it, yeah. Or if you need something from him. But that's it really. It's not like we're the fucking cops or nothing. I mean, what is the Peckham Boys? Half of them hate the other half . . . in fact there's more beef than that.'

Through conversations such as these, and clues here and there, the gaps in the jigsaw begin to be filled in, and we are able to complete our understanding of how gangs work, showing how they can be at once hierarchical in terms of their drug dealing or other crimes, and disordered in most other ways. It will inform the rest of this book, and retrospectively colour what we have seen.

Looking at the various stories in retrospect, there's a cloying sense of inevitability about them, as if you are stumbling upon what was always known, but only tacitly acknowledged – that they are contradictory. Contradictions were in Fabian's story, when he was talking about the relationship between a gang's Elders and Youngers, which seemed to have no code of practice at all; they are evident when you look at how chaotic the relationships are between gangs in each postcode, let alone each borough. It seems contradictory that the Ghetto Boys allegedly number 200 yet are still able to organize their activities. Do they meet in a huge rented boardroom, or are jobs franchised out via email? It doesn't seem to fit. Likewise, when the Peckham and Ghetto Boys' battle turned out to be a personal vendetta that escalated into something larger; and when Wilson had never heard of his own gang's alleged boss.

The problem is not the gangs. In some cases they barely exist at all, except in the way chemical reactions exist: a mixture of dangerous elements that occasionally react and then disappear. Being a gang member at the lower levels is less a question of daily enterprise and more a question of how your peers perceive you. The gangsters certainly exist: theirs is a way of life that has spread throughout the country, through blood relations, time spent in prison, down to the Youngers, via the Internet and beyond. They share patterns of behaviour, language, culture. Despite this, the problem still isn't gangs at all: the problem is Gangland.

In 1927 an academic at the University of Chicago, Frederic Thrasher, decided to undertake a survey of over 1,000 gangs in the city. He found the word 'gang' a difficult term; his study included everything from institutionalized sports clubs to little cliques of drug dealers and violent street robbers. But the theory that Thrasher espoused is still relevant today. He argued that Gangland was what he called an *interstitial* area: a poverty belt 'isolated from the wider culture of the larger community by the processes of competition and conflict which have resulted in the selection of its population'.

Interstitial areas are parts of the city that exist between sections of the urban fabric. They are slum neighbourhoods typified by social breakdown and disorganization, which was filtered through the experiences of successive waves of immigrants. For Thrasher, youth gangs are manifestations of: '. . . the disorganization incident to cultural conflict among diverse nations and races gathered together in one place and themselves in contact with a civilization foreign and largely inimical to them'.[7]

Criminal behaviour, for the gangs that Thrasher researched, was no more common than among other adolescents in the slum. Thrasher and subsequent gang studies describe a delinquent career that begins as a form of play, which brings the youth into conflict with the community and the family – and in working-class life the latter has often lost its cohesion. The gang becomes an alternative family where criminal careers are nurtured. There are some differences between Thrasher's subjects and Britain's twenty-first-century gangs. Arguably, fewer people in Thrasher's Gangland had the chances that Britain's Youngers have. At the same time, there was no crack market for Thrasher, and less access to guns; two of the factors that mean gang members are more likely to commit crime than others in their area. But both sets of gangs are born of marginalized areas, areas whose primary relationship with the state is when the police enter them to make arrests.

The key point is that the crime will always be there, and people use the idea of the gang to give it cohesion, so when there is crack that needs to be sold or if an older criminal requires assistance in some other way – perhaps a fight – the jobs of Elder, Younger and Shotter all fall into place. On duty, they have roles, but off duty, the relationships and antagonisms are more random, informed by territorialism, bloodlines or other obvious factors. Being a gangster is less about being part of a solid street unit, and more about a choice of lifestyle, a template for living in Gangland.

It's easy to see how the common perception of gangs as organized criminal bodies is perpetuated – gang members themselves often like to claim their crews are more organized than they really are, so that as individuals they are more feared by their association with them. I remember the first time I ventured into Gangland and saw a man drive up to a crowd of children to deliver some drugs to them. I saw Elder, Younger, Shotter, but what I didn't appreciate was that those roles were as temporary and unfixed as the moment itself. These moments happen on a very regular basis; it is certainly not the case that there is no stability to the relationships between those involved. But it is not quite the same as an organized, permanent institution.

It is nothing new for there to be territorial rivalries, such as Tottenham and Hackney or Peckham and New Cross (Ghetto Boys), but their real relationship to the drugs trade is the fact that they too provide order, and that the same people are usually involved in the violence. And a great deal of the time this violence is motivated by personal rivalries and needs, which can drag other people in: the same as it would be were there no gangs. As Professor Hobbs puts it: 'When these webs of relationships are untangled, violence is often exposed as the expression of personal disputes and conflicts, as opposed to structural characteristics and aims.'[8]

Look at the crimes detailed in this book so far: the fact that the victims and perpetrators are gang members only matters in terms of the general violence associated with the lifestyle; in fact, many of the battles are between members of the same crews. It does us no favour to use the phrase 'internal beef' in these circumstances – rather, we should simply see them as battles between two people who live hyper-masculine, violent lives. Occasionally there is a breakdown in trust in the drug market and it is resolved through violence, but no gang member to whom I spoke ever felt that they were in a turf war with another gang for control of business – if they fought another group, it was a longstanding rivalry.

It is a different story at the top levels, where disputes over business interests are settled quickly and lethally. Until certain recent cases these murders have always involved people who have reached such a point in their careers that they should be seen as criminals as much as they are gang members. Some claim allegiance to or have influence within a gang (in which case we might dub them the theoretical Faces – or some Elders – of the first chapter), but their dealings often stretch far beyond the remit of most street-gang members. When the press talks about feared drug gangs battling for territory on the streets they are quite wrong. Usually they are describing historical territorial battles between groups that are involved in crime, which is a subtle but important difference.

With this theory in place we might return to the rivalry between the Peckham and Ghetto Boys as an example. Locals who have lived in the area a long time say that the friction between the two began to pick up in the 1980s. Many of the estates in Lewisham (Silwood, Honor Oak and Greater Pepys, for example) were Greater London Council estates, but this changed: they began to straddle boundaries between the boroughs. People who lived on them were technically Lewisham residents but it was easier for them to shop in Peckham. From the mid-1980s onwards there was tension between the youths – but by the mid-1990s it was becoming defined as Ghetto Boys against Peckham.

The interstitial areas, for Thrasher, are parts of the city where there have historically been a high number of people moving in and out. Brixton, Hackney, Peckham – all of them have third- or fourth-generation immigrants living in an area that, because of the cyclical nature of poverty, low expectation and cultural differences, feel economically and socially distanced from the rest of the country. The economic changes in Britain's cities described in the previous chapter exacerbated the problems, but they also demonstrate that, in terms of how gangs develop, immigration and cultural distance are lesser issues than poverty itself. Today's interstitial areas might have Asians, blacks, whites or all three living in it, but they still fit into Thrasher's definition of detachment from mainstream society.

It is only natural for our world to try to impose order upon the chaos that is Gangland; in most of our daily activities we encounter a hierarchy and a social structure of some sort. It is only natural for the authorities to paint a picture of the enemy, far simpler for the media to accept that image. But while the dealing of drugs or violent crime can provide a momentary order, the lives of gangsters rarely have the structure ours have.

Heavily involved gang members are like freelance businessmen, and like any business people, they find loopholes in the law. When a tougher sentence (five years) for the possession of firearms was imposed, one obvious answer for the Elders was to give them to the Youngers.

Many of the youth workers and community figures I spoke to felt that the rising use of guns (from 13,874 offences in 1998/9 to 21,521 in 2005/6)[9] had to be explained by an influx of them into the country, and wanted to know where they were coming from. The routes from overseas have been covered in depth by the media: on ferries from Eastern Europe, by soldiers from war zones (in October 2007 two soldiers were arrested for smuggling weapons back from Iraq) and even from the Internet (in 2006 a man from Reading was jailed for buying guns from a US website). A 2005 Home Office report felt that the vast majority of guns have been here all along: there just hasn't been the demand for them before.[10] The report felt that this is what lies behind the drop in their price, and not a sudden rise in supply. The NCIS does not think that the UK market is being flooded with guns, but there is significant evidence to suggest that a great number of guns are being converted. Most guns in Gangland are kept in circulation – they are used for a crime and sold on.

All prices vary according to where the gun is bought, and from whom. A shotgun will cost between £50 and £200. Many of them have been stolen from rural burglaries. It is, however, not a practical weapon, being hard to conceal. Most gang members will choose to buy a pistol instead – usually a nine millimetre. The key issue here is whether it is 'clean' or 'dirty'. As guns are kept in circulation, they can chalk up a considerable number of crimes before they are bought. A brand new gun could cost about £1000, but one that has a more dubious provenance could cost as little as £150. The cheapest way of getting hold of a clean pistol is to buy a converted starter pistol, which could cost about £400 – a 'converted rebore' is the most common (it is perhaps the prevalence of these that gives the commonly held impression of areas being flooded with guns). However, with these you are running the risk of owning a gun that does not function properly, and even if it does, it will have a low level of accuracy and will begin to break down after it has been used a few times.

The most expensive option for a pistol is an automatic, which could cost up to £4,000. However, while one of these will give you more firepower, it will also leave forensic evidence in the shape of shells. A machine gun such as a Mac-10, the 'spray and pray', is relatively uncommon; it costs at least £5 per bullet, which means one spray will cost you £150. Whatever your choice of firearm, the limiting factor is ammunition. It can cost £2,000 to £3,000 for a box of ammunition for a pistol. However, many criminals are starting to make their own ammunition; it is not against the law to own the constituent parts, only to put them together. One of the easiest ways for any young gang member to earn money is by robbing the dealers in another gang; a type of crime which provides an obvious reason to carry a firearm.

A stocky man in his mid-twenties, Danny runs his fingers through his cornrows and shakes his head. His bright-blue eyes gleam as he boasts of his exploits: 'Some days, we'd head on down to Herne Hill and rob the Shotters. Same guys, every day. They'd never see me coming. Slam them up against the wall, and it's "give me your money, nigger". They know I'm strapped. Day in day out, gimme the money, the jewellery, their phone – anything they had. Who they going to tell?

'If we knew where there was a crack house, we'd go in and clear the place out too – but there aren't many these days. In a crack house, no one's packing – no one wants to be caught with drugs and a gun for no reason, and those places are supposed to be secret. You just stroll right on in, and everyone's too fucked to argue. I'd be in and out in five minutes. But you got to be strapped. You *got* to be strapped. You turn up there with a knife, you're taking too many chances. And you got to be strapped all the time. Because they'll tell their crew what you done. Thing is, whatever they can do to you – it ain't any worse than doing time.

'I guess I did feel bad about it, but never too bad. That's the thing about gangs – you know that the players you attack are doing the same shit to other people. It's kind of like – this is the road – this is how it is. You don't like it, get off the road.'

It is all about humiliation, and all about power. One researcher I spoke to had been interviewing young people in one of these boroughs for an academic survey in the weeks before he met me, in 2006. He made contact with a fifteen-year-old boy, and met him in McDonald's. Midway through the interview three men walked in. 'I'll rob anyone,' said the boy. 'Those three over there have been done by me.' The boy looked across at the men who stared back at him. Nothing was said, but the atmosphere was intimidating. The researcher asked the boy if they should leave. 'Nah, they're pussies,' said the boy. A few days later he was murdered. His death was followed by extensive media coverage – why should an innocent die? In fact, his actions made him as subject to the rules of the street as anyone: you live like a man, you die like a man. Without the reputation, there is no chance to make money. The Shotters always know who the people are that will rob them; often they know them well.

A 2007 Home Office report by the University of Portsmouth quoted one gangster who described his fury at a dealer who had told the police about his actions, which lead to his arrest: 'It's like he's broken the laws of the street.' The same report showed how gang members are coming up with other methods of making money in saturated markets. One interviewee worked with a drug dealer to rob his clients and also lured dealers into attacks: '. . . he would basically sell about . . . three grand [of drugs] to somebody and phone me up and say, look, I will be here and I am doing a deal and blah, blah.

ONE BLOOD

And basically, I would jump in there and take the money, and take the gear and then we would meet up later to carve it up.'[11]

There is evidence to suggest that the robbing of drug dealers in recent years has been on the increase due to the saturation of the drug market in certain areas. The growth of this type of crime has made Gangland's rules very simple. Reputation is a gang member's life blood. If you are threatened and respond but are seen not to carry through with your threat, you only serve to make yourself a target for more intimidation. The rules of engagement are simple; it's like a poker game in which you can only ever raise your opponent – there is no option to stick, and to fold would make you a target. For a gang member, to be mocked is to be issued with a significant threat: to disrespect someone is to undermine the very sustenance on which they survive. This is why a dispute over what seems to be very little can quickly escalate into a fatal disagreement – a threat is made; will your opponent back down? If he doesn't, you must make a more serious threat, or you're not safe. He must choose whether or not to respond to each development, and the stakes become more and more serious, until you are both embroiled in a game you never wanted to play. Finally, with both of you all in, the cards fall.

In Peckham I meet a number of former gang members to talk about the death of their friend Marcus, several years ago. He had been a heavily involved gang member, but had begun to turn his life around. He had a full-time job and in his spare time was starting to help out at a local youth centre. He was something that the young community around his estate desperately needed: a genuine role model. This was a man who had seen and done much of what the worst offenders were doing, but who had managed to stop it all. Some found the fact that he earned this respect, and worse, proper money earned through proper work, money that you could actually feel proud to spend, galling. But for the most part, he was admired.

One night, Marcus was at a house party in south London when a gang member from one of the neighbouring territories began to drunkenly threaten him. Marcus had known the man for years, but in the light of his knowledge of the gang culture, his response was foolish to say the least. He refused to play the game. He shrugged, disregarded his aggressor, and simply said, 'Whatever.' He didn't back down, or threaten him back. In front of everyone at the party, he just ignored him. Maddened by his humiliation, this person left the party and returned ten minutes later. He had a gun. Again, Marcus would not play. He did not concede respect to him; he merely looked away. If he wasn't playing the game, his opponent still was. All his jealousy, bitterness and pent-up rage were released as he pulled the trigger.

This is the curse of these individuals: the compulsion to tear down those who are doing better than you. It may not help your cause, but you will feel better for it. As one of Marcus's friends said to me: 'Why is it that the good seem to die young around here? Because there is a lot of resentment – a lot of young people who realize that, aged seventeen or eighteen, they have been sold the wrong dreams. They won't be rappers. They won't be footballers. You can still hear twenty-five-year-olds talking about how their album's going to be the bomb, how they're going to get signed to a Premiership club. A lot of crew members were good sportsmen who never made it, looking for the respect they had when they were young. No one's ever managed their expectations.'

In the road opposite the house, one more little memorial had been erected. 'RIP Marcus' was written on the wall in foot-high graffiti. There were poems written by friends which have been stuck to the wall where he died. There was a favourite CD. Flowers. His favourite T-shirt. Marcus's shrine sat quietly aside from the stirring world. It was here, a few years ago, that I met a sixteen-year-old, standing beside it, his eyes lowered. 'Everyone knew who shot Marcus,' he says. 'Half of us were there when it happened. He ran off, and we were going to get him. All the rats that crawl out the woodwork when someone dies were out there talking to the press . . . all we wanted was revenge. It was us or the feds were going to get him. About twenty of us set off looking for him. Fortunately for him, they got the bastard first.' The anger still burned in his eyes.

In August 2007 the American civil-rights leader Jesse Jackson was visiting Britain. In a public statement, he said that the UK's gang problem was rooted in 'the economics of desperation'. In response, the Justice Secretary, Jack Straw, was quick to move the blame away from black families' circumstances, and towards their make-up: 'Black boys go backwards when they get to secondary school. It's a cultural problem. It's the absence of fathers who are actively involved in parenting. And as we know, lads need dads. Of course they need their mums as well, but there is a particular point in teenagers' development, of young men, where fathers are very important and they are more likely to be absent in the case of the Afro-Caribbean.'[12]

Once again, the problems had been shifted away from the economic and towards the racial. Black children are certainly a great deal more likely to grow up in single-parent households than white children – nearly 60 per cent of black Caribbean children are brought up by one parent, as opposed to 22 per cent of white children.[13] We cannot say for certain how far the number of black fatherless families in these areas is a representation of poverty rather than race. We know that the majority of lone mothers are in the bottom 40 per cent of household income, but we do not know how regularly this is due to the marital break-up.[14] However, given that the father should be paying child support, it suggests that most of them may have been in poverty beforehand.[15]

Whatever the reasons, there are plenty of black single parents in Britain with control over their children; and the difference here is very definitely an economic one. Poor single mothers work long hours and multiple jobs to make ends meet, creating very little time for effective parenting. In the absence of economic prospects and family ties, it isn't surprising that a gang can become a central source of identity and wellbeing. As we shall see in the next chapter, Straw was perhaps not incorrect in making a connection between absent father figures and gun crime, but in doing so he was deliberately missing the wider picture: the context of disadvantaged neighbourhoods in which the majority of gang-related behaviour must be placed. As the Home Office report made clear, this was an issue which 'compounded' the problems within these communities.[16]

The journalist Melanie Phillips has written in her *Daily Mail* column of 'whole neighbourhoods where fathers are nonexistent, resulting in violent children, uncontrolled juvenile crime . . . It is certainly true that at the core of juvenile crime and anti-social behaviour lie the indifference or even active connivance of grossly irresponsible parents.'[17]

It is a common view. But the more time you spend in Gangland, the more you realize that, whether divorced or not, parents are not always to be blamed for the problems. They are aware of the gang problem, and aware of the assumption that it's a product of poor parenting. Nowhere is the gap between the two nations drawn into sharper relief. The fallacy of autonomy, the idea that we can separate parenting ability from the circumstances in which parenting is undertaken, is the cruellest misconception about gangs there is. As one social worker put it in Professor Pitts' report on Waltham Forest: 'Telling these families to take responsibility for their kids' behaviour is like telling them to take their kids into the jungle and take responsibility for not getting eaten by lions and tigers.'[18]

Where Straw might have made an overlooked point is regarding the impact of broken marriages on the fathers. Given that they look after the children, the women take the house tenure; the men are left to circulate around the community, their days filled with hanging out and discussing the latest beef, trying to make money in their own ways – a perfect recipe for creating gangs.

The issue regarding absent fathers is often conflated into one of absent role models. It should not be, because the latter is more complex and more worthy of consideration. A vast number of children who go on to become Youngers do not grow up with role models. They are surrounded by adults with little hope and low expectations. You see it in the community leader who everyone knows has a son who is a gang Elder, and who gives sermons at every peace march on how it is possible for 'his people' to live without violence – not without gangs; without violence. You see it in the community figures who insist, when I speak to them, that there are no gangs, only positive stories to be related – as if, by ignoring the problem and focussing on the fleeting instances of success, the damage of the last few decades can be undone. The gang Elders are the ones who take the role of a father figure. It is only natural for a teenage boy to want approval for what they do, and the Elder can provide other things a father might – protection, and something to which they can aspire.

The relationship is sometimes reciprocal, but it can be exploitative. A woman in one of these boroughs approached the police because she had found drugs in her boy's bedroom. The police took them off him, and issued him with a caution. However, neither the police nor the mother realized that they were in the boy's room because he was planning to sell them for an Elder. The standard deal for a Shotter is that if you are arrested by the police with a bag of drugs then you pay the drug dealers back twice over – for the lost drugs and the money you would have made. The boy could never raise that money, and became increasingly agitated. Underestimating the situation, his mother decided to take a firm line, and tell the police who she thought he'd got the drugs from. A day after she did this, the boy was beaten up and put in intensive care. Worse was to follow. She was gang raped. This story is not here to shock, or to lay blame on the police; the point is simple: protecting your children in Gangland is hard whether you have a firm hand or not.

The son of a white Irish family living in one of the estates was being victimized by one of the gangs. The gang, seeing a stable white family unit, also saw potential victims. They attacked one of the family's younger members and robbed him. What the gang didn't know was that the family were as mired in criminal activity as they were. The family members piled into a van, drove to the house of a gang leader and stabbed him to death. It was only in the aftermath that they discovered they had stabbed the wrong man – an innocent. Stable family units in Gangland do not always equate to the passing on of good moral values.

In 2007 there was a great deal of talk about the need for positive role models for black children, and of the fact that children are regularly confronted with negative images of black males in popular culture. Rap music, films and video games do glamorize violent, criminal lifestyles. Perhaps they have a special impact on children without a reasonable level of resilience. Gangs produce and submit videos on digital musical channels which advocate violence against their rivals. In short, it seems to be a cut-and-dried case – these images are forcing children into criminal activity.

Gang Elder William, whom we met earlier, doesn't believe a word of it. 'The way I see it, people been banging for years. These studio gangsters, like 50 Cent, making money out of the pain that people like I've suffered; all that pain, all that loss . . . fuck all that. If he did the kind of shit he says he did, ain't no way he'd have had time to have a rap career. And anyway, how many people in my crew listened to 50 Cent? I don't think any of us liked that stuff . . . most of the boys I know listened to garage – most shootings were at garage nights. And OK, some of the younger kids do listen to that, and yeah, they do have the video games, but you're telling me they wouldn't be banging if they didn't have rap music? These guys are rapping about something that's real – you live in the ghetto, you need to make your P's somehow. Ain't no surprise they're listening.'

Art holds a mirror up to reality. There is no conclusive evidence that any of the often criticized media portrayals of criminal lifestyles lead to criminal behaviour. More likely, like the *Scarface* speech, gang-involved youths latch on to them in order to justify their behaviour to themselves. While the talk of negative role models is a pathologizing of the gang problem, it is still an issue worth addressing. A young man born into poverty, with little education and few positive role models in his background, risks being seduced by whichever cultural narratives come his way.

This point brings us to the aforementioned PDC members who lived on Myatts Field. A strange occurrence indeed: they began converting to Islam. Soon the trend spread around the borough. But this was no version of Islam recognizable to any true Muslim. This version of Islam is taken from the passage in the Koran in Sura Eight where Mohammed robs a set of caravans; this validates any of gang life's crimes, as long as there is a visit to the mosque afterwards. The newspapers portrayed the trend as the birth of another gang, and taking their cue from a throwaway police comment, came up with a title for them: 'the Muslim Boys'. The Youngers in Brixton were recruited with the chilling exhortation: 'Get down [to pray] or lay down.' In 2005 the *Evening Standard* interviewed a 'member'. He said: 'Knives is f*** all. Later, my bruvs will be back from their robberies with our skengelengs [guns] and cream [money]. Later there be MAC-10s [sub-machine guns] all over the floor, laid wall to wall. And moolah! We count it – 10 grand, 20 grand. Then, after midnight,' he adds, 'me and my bruvs go to mosque to pray.' The Muslim Boys, the *Standard* alleged, were potentially behind a 'national crimewave'.[19]

Adrian Marriott, a 21-year-old accountancy student, was made to 'lay down' in June 2004. Reports alleged that members of the gang turned up at his house with DVDs and copies of the Koran for them. It was said that his sisters Jade and Tara agreed to wear the hijab, but Marriott didn't take the gang's demands seriously. He was shot in the head five times near Angell Town, his body dumped in a nearby park. Three men appeared in court accused of his murder: Marlon Stubbs, Marcus Archer and Aaron Irving Simpson. The information that emerged during the trial painted a more conventional picture of Gangland antagonism. Irving Simpson had been attacked by a friend of Marriot's, Nyrome Hinds, in West Norwood in July 2004. Hinds was tackled by policemen and found to be in possession of a Mac-10 and £13,500 in cash. It emerged that Marriot had known Archer and Stubbs for several years. The jury were told that Marriot had been threatened at gunpoint by Stubbs and two other men and £500 demanded from him. Marriot and another man had then 'accosted' Archer at Loughborough Junction train station. Stubbs had telephoned Tara Marriott and told her: 'Your brother is a little tadpole. He just messed with a big shark, a whale.'

The Old Bailey trial in the Marriott murder case ended abruptly: charges against all three defendants were dropped. However, due to a former arrest for possessing an illegal firearm Marcus Archer was jailed for eight years. Marlon Stubbs was jailed a year later for possessing a handgun with intent to endanger life, after an incident in Battersea: a man named Marlon Crooks was showing his family a BMW convertible outside their home when a gang, wearing Muslim-style headscarves, had fired upon Crooks, his eight-year-old daughter, his mother, grandmother, sister and brother, who all managed to escape without injury.

Three more 'Muslim' gangsters were convicted after a killing in 2006. Charles Anokye had been stabbed to death on 1 August 2005. He had received 13 knife wounds in his chest and back after being attacked by five assailants. His attackers rifled through his pockets, and took his valuables as he lay bleeding to death. Anokye was at the Mass nightclub at St Matthew's Church, Effra Road, Brixton with a friend, James Idamakin. Both worked at the Rosedale Nursing Home in Tooting Broadway. Idamakin gave evidence to the court that Anokye had been dancing when another person had said to him, 'You're blocking my view'. He knocked another dancer with his drink bottle, and Idamakin had excused his friend by saying that Anokye was drunk, and had not intended that to happen. When the pair left the nightclub at 4 a.m., Idamakin said that he saw the 'Muslim Boys' running out of the club, and had to run for his life.

'Converting' to Islam does not seem to alter the gang members' behaviour: we know this much. But what is less clear is the organization behind this trend. The original grouping on Myatt's Field seemed little different to other gangs; a Trident officer told local newspapers in 2006 there were a few older individuals who were encouraging younger children to deal drugs. But a local policeman told me: 'Is it simply a movement which everyone's latching on to, or is there something more organized and sinister behind it? The truth is, we just don't know. What I do know is that it's spreading way beyond Lambeth.' The latter statement is definitely true: in the course of researching this book, I encountered several gang members to the south of Brixton, and further out to the areas covered in the next chapter, who claimed to have recently converted. When I spoke to them about why, they were reticent. It wasn't a gang, they said. They were still gang members; they just happened to be Muslims.

The likelihood is that, as always, there is little order to the trend. Contrary to the newspapers' reports, these are merely young men in search of a cultural narrative; like most adolescents, they have picked an identity off the shelf. Gang life is without routine or discipline, something the human spirit always requires, to some degree at least. Praying to Allah gives this to the gang members. In a way it is nothing new or surprising: in 1988 a sociologist in Milwaukee found that dozens of his gang-involved interviewees mentioned Al Capone, while hardly any mentioned Martin Luther King.[20] It's like *Scarface* and the many other cultural tags which gang members are prone to assimilate to confirm their lifestyles. But a quasi-conversion to Islam is not only attractive: it's the ultimate validation.

Recruitment seems to happen within prisons, so the level of organization remains unclear. In April 2006, in HMP Belmarsh, a prisoner was savagely attacked for his 'apostasy' after he said he did not want to be a Muslim any more. Eight prisoners cornered him in the lavatories, and 'punished' him with a severe beating, causing serious head injuries. Four prisoners from the gang received 'administrative action' from the prison authorities. Two leaders were transferred to other jails. Many members were sent to a segregation unit within the prison. The Home Office said the attack had not been a major incident. A leaked prison report claimed the members of the Muslim Boys were recruiting for Al Qaeda within the jail. Other prisoners claimed to be in fear of their lives after the gang attacked victims with razor blades attached to toothbrushes. A number of reports have followed in 2007 and 2008 describing violent incidents involving the Muslim Boys.[21]

This eerie perversion of a major cultural ideal, its followers robbing, dealing and killing before they head back to pray, might just carry a lesson. The rumours regarding Al Qaeda involvement have never been proved, but it is most likely another appealing aspect of the Muslim narrative: if the gang members see themselves as separate from the rest of the population, what better role models to adopt than an army that has fought the mainstream with success? Those who speak of role models might just be right – there is a spiritual gap in the heart of Gangland, with nothing to believe in, no one positive to emulate. If a few gang leaders can win over dozens of recruits with a simple rehashing of Islam, one wonders what possibilities might exist were there a way of making the gang a positive entity. It is something with which youth workers across the city have been struggling – how can a credible, positive identity be sold to Gangland's youth?

FOUR

Going Country

The square was silent; desolately silent, as only a suburban square can be.

Wilkie Collins, *Basil*

One of the biggest steps I made in understanding gang culture came when I was interviewing a senior gang member in Croydon. It wasn't anything he told me – it was a question he asked me: 'When did you last feel fear, bruv? Not worry, or stress, proper fear. Because you see, I look at you and I see a man who knows that deep down, whatever happens, you'll be alright. So what I'm asking you is, when were you last properly, properly scared? When did you have no idea what was going to happen to you or to a loved one? How did it make you feel?'

I think for a minute, and the memories come back: 'It was years ago, when I was about thirteen or fourteen. I went to a school in Portsmouth, a private school. About half the kids came in on the train from upmarket areas about twenty or so miles away, and the other half came from the city itself, from its nicer areas, or a few on assisted places. Portsmouth's a working-class city on the whole. So if you lived in the city, like I did, there were certain places you just didn't go in your school uniform.

'I knew about the fights that went on between the state schools, as a lot of my friends I'd known from before I'd gone to the private school would tell me about them. A friend from the Catholic school would tell me about the street battles they had with another school nearby – snooker balls in socks, bricks being thrown . . . I was quite a way from those two, being in the posh bit of town, where no one got caught up in that kind of bother.

'But then I remember, one night, I was with a mate up at our playing fields, and a bunch of kids from one of the other schools confronted us about 100 metres from the gates. One of them smacked my mate in the face. I remember how fucking scared we all were – they'd backed me and my mate into a corner. I remember my heart was pounding, absolutely pounding, my limbs were trembling, I wanted to be sick and I wanted to cry, and I said to one of the kids: "You and me, before you do anything, I need to talk to you alone."

'And to my disbelief, he said OK. We went away for a couple of minutes, and when we came back he said to the others: "Leave it, boys, they're not worth it." And of course my mate, who had tears in his eyes, asked what I said, and I didn't tell him. I liked the air of mystery. But I'll tell you what I said; I remember the words exactly. I said: "If you want to get leery with us, do. But I'm a fucking Grover. I'm at this place on a scholarship."

'My mate wouldn't have known what a Grover was – he came to Portsmouth from West Sussex, miles away. In fact, a lot of people from the posh end of the city wouldn't have known what a Grover was. But before I went to the private school, when I was at one of the state junior schools, everyone was scared of the Grovers. No one ever saw them; that was part of the mystique and the fear. We knew they hailed from the Paulsgrove Estate (the area that years later would become famous for the riots that followed the *News of the World*'s campaign of naming and shaming paedophiles) and that they were the scariest in the city by a long way. The state-school kids had heard all the stories – they killed people, they had guns, all the rest of it. It was a foreign world to most people at my school – our battles were on the rugby and cricket pitches against other private schools.

'Were the Grovers worse than anyone else? I guess so, but you'd read the local news and hear about violence, and not notice that it was all happening in the estate itself. What I definitely do know is that when I was fifteen there were no gangs. The kids from the Catholic school and the state school having their street battles didn't see themselves as gangs. No one saw the Grovers as a gang either. No one claimed they were an organized group; it was just a simple equation people knew – Grover equals hard. Parents and teachers didn't talk about gangs. There was violence, there were scary groups of kids, but there were no gangs when I was growing up.'

At the top of Gypsy Hill in autumn, the leaves are scattered around the pavement like crumpled playbills after a theatre show. The view encompasses the rows of tiny houses in Sydenham to the north, and the parkland of Dulwich beyond. The green scrambles out, scarred but untamed, from the architecture that is trying to swallow it. The houses on the hill are huge, mostly Victorian, with black iron gates in front of driveways. The shops and cafes of Central Hill, which lead off into the east along Westow Hill, are upmarket. Yet it was right here that 23-year-old Evren Anil was killed. He was in the passenger seat of his sister's car when two teenagers were walking past. One of them threw a half-eaten chocolate bar into the car. Anil got out of his car, at which point one of the boys produced a knife and hit him. He smashed his head on the pavement and Evren died of his injuries a week later. The two youths, who later pleaded guilty to manslaughter, ran off into the little chunk of Gangland hidden behind the plush houses on the side of the hill; the Central Hill Estate. The estate's gang are called Gypset.

Head east from Central Hill and the giant television transmitter of Crystal Palace Park strides into view. The park itself was once a glorious Victorian showpiece with elegant landscaping, boasting the famous Crystal Palace Exhibition building, which burned down in 1936. Head southeast from the park and you are in traffic-congested Penge High Street, a nondescript collection of charity shops and discount butchers yet to see any evidence of gentrification. Just north of here is true suburbia; the roads are quiet, the houses neat and large, the small blocks of flats tidy and well maintained. It is a huge circuit board of privet and red brick. There is a balance to this area; a lot of people live here, but at the same time it feels open and uncrowded. Walk through this, past the pubs and their beer gardens, the cricket fields, the elegant gates and driveways, and one comes to Southend Road, which runs from north to south through Beckenham. It's a busy main road, with orderly blocks of flats on either side, and nothing lurking behind them but a golf course on one side and a set of sports grounds on the other, and it's here where Ben Hitchcock, a white sixteen-year-old who went to nearby Kelsey Park Secondary School, was beaten and stabbed to death in June 2007. There are scores of tributes to him on the Internet; pictures of him with his white school shirt signed after his last day at school – and other pictures, of him posing with his gang, Penge Block.

To borrow a cliché, Gangland seems to spread out of central London like a cancer. Its lines of influence appear easy to pick out. If you head far enough south out of the three boroughs described in the last chapter the density of population decreases by degrees. Head south from Peckham and you're in Dulwich, which has fewer gang-dominated estates, and less violence. The Dulwich crews talk of their relations with the Peckham Boys, some antagonistic, some cooperative. They talk of how they would head into Croydon to attack young men there, which was why gangs began to form – and the gangs of Croydon say the same thing, but the role of aggressor is reversed. It's the same story to the southwest, where Gypsy Hill's gang talk of Brixton's PDC and OC, and to the east, where the gangs of Catford will tell you how they interact with the gangs of New Cross. South of Catford there are smaller crews around Beckenham and Penge. It seems that man hands on misery to man, that the culture is spreading out from the inner city and into the suburbs: that a group of young men that presents a threat to another group of young men will inevitably lead to the creation of a new gang. But it's not always useful to take what the gangs say at face value. There is a strong tendency for self-mythologizing; how they perceive the gangs' conception and how it actually happened are often two different things. To understand suburbia's Gangland, one has to look at south London suburbia itself.

Crystal Palace is the hub where five boroughs, Lambeth, Southwark, Lewisham, Croydon and Bromley, all meet. Walking around the streets that surround it means repeatedly crossing borough boundaries. These political divisions should not have any influence on Gangland. But in a strange way they do. This area is ripe for territorial rivalry among its young men. There are plenty of small urban centres situated a few miles apart, perhaps ten or fifteen minutes by bus – south from the estates in Dulwich to the centres of Thornton Heath or Croydon, or from the flats around Penge north to the estates in Catford.

Territorial rivalries between young boys in these areas are nothing new. As one youth worker puts it: 'Kids have been coming into Catford from Bromley to get up to mischief for decades. It was getting in fights, then it was nicking mobile phones, and now it seems to be more violent.' If the last few chapters established that the cultural and economic infection at the heart of Gangland, its detach-ment from conventional society, means that the gangs are symptoms rather than causes, then this area is blighted by a different sickness. It is a malady that transmits itself through a variety of channels. In the previous chapters' Ganglands, there have been gangs for decades; the difference today is that those involved at a high level are becom-ing much younger. In this Gangland, there have been gangs for a long time too: the difference is they have only just begun to see themselves as such.

To understand why, we might look at the moral panic over football hooliganism in the 1970s and 1980s and its analysis by the academic Stuart Hall. He identified a phenomenon he called the 'amplification spiral'.[1] He said that the sensationalist reporting of hooliganism precipitated a call for tougher control measures, which in turn creates a situation of confrontation where more people are drawn into the conflict, which in turn means there will be more coverage.

A policeman in one of these boroughs articulated this phenom-enon during an interview with me. He had been involved in hooliganism as a young man, and said: 'It's quite simple; there were often fights between rival groups of fans, which weren't that well organized. But once it was possible to read about what your mates had got up to the next day, people got more organized; they had a reputation to maintain. So if society tells a group of kids who are just hanging out that they're not a group of kids, that they're a gang – is it any wonder that all of a sudden they become the "Wherever Man Dem"? And all it takes is a few individuals to give the semblance of control in order for a gang to be formed. In my day, a few blokes could stand outside the train station before we played Cardiff, get everyone's attention and tell them what we were going to do.'

Modern depictions of urban children in a negative light exacer-bate the very problems upon which they are based.[2] Terms such as anti-social behaviour, hoodies and dispersal orders are all relatively new. Young people, especially those who do not succeed in education, can find themselves distanced from economic and social norms, like individuals within the Ganglands of Hackney and south London. The ideal of the gangster lifestyle is then a suitable template. In terms of their peer groups, and the places in which they hang around, even the things they do, it does not necessarily have a huge impact. Where it can make a difference is in the importance of violence, and the lengths to which they feel they must go when carrying it out.

This is the untold story about the death of Ben Hitchcock. It was reported that he died in the battle between Penge Block and Young Thugs, their rivals. In one sense this is true, but the battle is an old one; a rivalry between two areas. A hundred yards from where he died, a bright-blue sign proclaims 'Welcome to Lewisham'. The borough was recently re-branded as the 'blue borough' – its bins, signs and council publicity are all coloured blue. This change in image was seized upon by the different youth groups in the area; the battles between the youths of Penge and Lewisham were seen as a battle between blue and green. This is why Penge Block wore green colours and Young Thugs wore blue towels over their heads. The gang colours show how they have adopted the practices of the inner city, but they also show that the battle is a re-imagining of an old territorial rivalry. It is a fatal re-imagining; a group of kids might get up to trouble, but a *gang* is something quite different. What do gangs do? They stab people, they deal drugs, they rap, they rep their ends. If those guys up the road are a gang – then I guess we must be too.

Penge Block's videos can be seen on YouTube – young boys rapping about violent acts. The tributes to Ben read much the same as tributes to any of the gang members in central London: 'Miss ya loads true Penge Block soldier', 'RIP our nigga Swipe' (his street name). In terms of what they signify, they differ in no way to the videos put out by more serious groups.

The fact that this phenomenon can be applied to the Ganglands of the previous chapter is extremely important. It means that we have more and more adolescent peer groups claiming to be gangs, and it can put them in real danger. In Hackney there are youths in Manor House who claim to be a gang at war with the Stamford Hill Mob, but the latter group are on the whole older and have better access to guns. If they see a rival gang then their antagonism to the former will intensify. It also explains a great deal about the relationship between Youngers and Elders. Just as I warded off my teenage assailants by claiming to be a Grover as a child, so a teenager who feels threatened can put himself forward as a Peckham Boy for the same reason. But once you claim to be such a thing, you have declared yourself open for business to everyone in your area, and have a reputation to maintain. It's not that organized criminal groups with a hierarchy and the ability to recruit younger members do not exist in these areas; but it is dangerous to portray them as the same as adolescent peer groups, occasional criminals and every other type of gangster in between. It means that certain areas do indeed become the mental property of these gangs, where once they were just the areas in which they operated. It is why, time and again, we hear older criminals who were once part of well-known gangs describe today's groups as 'hype among the Youngers' – for them the gang was about the criminal exploits it carried out as much as it was about reputation; for the next generation the latter carries far more weight.

This is why people who work in these communities are very keen not to mention the gangs by name, or indeed to admit they exist. It's not a case of burying their heads in the sand; once the devil has a name, he begins to exist. If we do not have the large-scale gangs that are found in America, this could one day change. As residence on an estate and affiliation to a gang become synonymous, the number of children who can be assimilated to the Elders' private business schemes becomes ever higher, and this ideal of the large, organized criminal group could be gradually borne out.

It's a near-unbreakable circle we are describing here. Yet in a way the media is right – the adolescent peer group at play is indeed where many violent groups find their origin; but this very perception only serves to perpetuate the phenomenon. You see it when you attend a gang member's court hearing and hear the litany of offences being read out – from possession of cannabis, to possession of cannabis with intent to supply, to possession of Class A drugs, to carrying a knife and onwards.

I meet Daniel in the Whitgift Centre in Croydon. He doesn't stand out from the crowd of shoppers, but by any accounts he is a man on top of his game – an Elder with his own Younger doing jobs for him, a man who makes good money from what he does. He is one of the bad guys; the senior figure behind the violence. He is also a pleasant, interested and interesting man. The two are not incompatible: gang life is the outline for how to live in Gangland – the violence and everything else that goes on there do not apply outside. He likes me. We talk about hip-hop, about how we both like Dilated Peoples and Dead Prez. We talk about how well Arsenal are playing this season. He notices my shorthand and wants to learn how to do it – I explain and show him the word 'biblical', an outline which swirls forever down the page, probably the strangest word in the language, and he laughs uproariously.

I like Daniel, and he likes me. When he talks about his territory, I realize there's a shrewd business mind at work – nothing more nor less than CEO material. He sits on the periphery of things, watches and observes, and makes stacks of money. And still there are people terrified of him, people he has no more reason to hate than anyone else. And still there is the same problem – he wants to go to college, wants some order and routine in his life, but knows that the reaction among his peers would be too fearful to contemplate.

Tessa Jowell was slated in 2007 for saying that gang members have entrepreneurial skills that need to be utilized. David Davies, the shadow Home Secretary, did not miss out on a chance to score points: 'The victims of some of these evil villains will recoil with horror at these comments. It's one thing to want to tackle the causes of crime, but it's another thing entirely to praise some nonexistent virtues of people who cause such grief and suffering to the communities they wreck.'[3] In fact she was correct in what she said; and what Davies neglected to mention was the fact that the likes of Daniel are a product of the very communities they damage.

The problem is that in a way he was also right: gang members do reprehensible things and make bad moral choices. They are not growing up in a country beleaguered by war and famine; there is no doubt that much of the injustice gang members face is perceived. If a gang member says he was starving and committed crimes in order to feed his family, more often than not it is his imagination running away with him. As mentioned earlier, poverty is not the only reason people join gangs and, even in the most deprived areas of the city, it is usually not about basic survival. But for a child who has been excluded from school and can see no obvious path to legitimate employment and little likelihood he could earn a respectable wage, the obvious role models are the self-sustaining gangsters in his area. The gang template is a pattern that spreads through young offenders' institutions and prisons, through popular culture and the Internet, through word of mouth from one disaffected youth to another. They need little persuasion to buy into this ideal.

At first, Daniel is all about hype – he spends the first half an hour of our time boasting of his gang's reputation and their deeds. But the more he opens up, the more the story appears to have been a series of influences over which he had little control. The progression from less serious, youthful crimes to fully fledged gang leader seemed to happen almost without his input.

'It started at age twelve, it was just stupidness among a little group of friends – we'd go to Dulwich, the West End, and some of them would just be robbing youts. No women. I got kicked out of school Year Eight, at aged twelve. Take the 312 to Dulwich. Them days was all hype. We'd just get on the bus and some of the people in my crew would be like – who shall we pick on? Then we started robbing phones; we had mad beef with Dulwich and Gypsy Hill. I went to a young offenders' institution and when I came out there were bare heads in the crew. All these people rolling, not repping their ends. Every time we went to their ends the numbers in the crew would increase. Every time I went inside I'd come out and find that the numbers had gone up.

'The next phase was that we started robbing the Shotters. We'd rob guys in Crystal Palace, take their decks, their speakers, sell it all and go to One Nation. Our original Man Dem had each other, but it was all about one man – my bred – who was drawing everyone to him – he's a Capricorn and he's just got that thing about him, you know? I'm now the one person in ends who started years ago. So every time I came out of prison there were bare strays. We'd started moving on with our scams, robbing twenty different Vietnamese DVD sellers a day. And we'd have other scams. A guy would go in the bank and read all the information leaflets, etc. – but actually he'd be looking for someone with their passport – because if you see their passport you can tell they're drawing out big money. Then you get on the phone and describe him to the others. I was lucky because every time I went to prison something crazy went on in the road. And it's at this time that the gang gets a title; people want to be a part of our crew for all the respect the name gets. I'm a leader of these guys, and I don't even want to roll with them.

'I realized that it was all getting out of control – all so far from what we'd got up to as kids. When you try to leave a gang people want to know why . . . what possible reason? Are you a snitch? It couldn't be for a positive reason. My bred robbed a PDC member, took his ring off him – soon he's phoning me up and telling me I'm done. Then he starts rolling with my bred, the guy that robbed him – and he sees me and says it's all good. What the fuck is going on? A bit later they gave me a Younger. I knew he needed to do an initiation, so I made him steal some shit – except, I knew it was easy to teef. They all thought he'd robbed some serious players, but I knew there was no one around. I can see in his eyes he wants what I have, I can see that if I give him a piece he won't just be doing my work with it, and I know how to use my mad side, but he's about hype . . . and I'm thinking here's how I should really look after him: tell him to get the fuck out of the gang. And take me with you.'

As we've already established, gangs are often disorganized, yet much of what they do is an attempt to create order. It is why there are the roles of Elder, Younger, Shotter; and it is why there are initiations. The initiation is the act that tells your peers you have adopted the gangster model for living – the 'thug life', to use Tupac's expression. The word I heard used most often about them was 'heavy'. They are an ordeal, an expression of the hyper-masculinity which drives gang culture. Several gang members told me they had to withstand a physical assault by the gang. One of them told how he had been beaten heavily, and then the gang leader attacked him with a broken bottle. He had to lie passive and take it. Another told me about a friend of his who had been found slumped behind the dashboard of his car, having been shot in the back of the neck. There were money and drugs inside, but they had not been taken. Why not? It had to have been an initiation killing: certain gangs expect its members to prove their bravery by murdering rival gangs' members. It may seem a contradiction that bodies which are so fluid, temporary and transitory can demand such sacrifice and loyalty. But once you see the gang as less of an organized group and more a pattern of behaviour, it makes perfect sense. It's not like a job interview; it's a personal statement on behalf of the young man to whichever peers are listening: that this is what I am now. It is the nature of hype.

It is worth dwelling on contemporary coverage of gangs a little more. Unsurprisingly, those who work with gang-involved youths do not want the newspapers or television companies near them. In the course of writing this book I have met those who have been offered money to pose with water pistols for national newspaper features, another youth worker who briefed a group of gang members to speak only about the positive things they were trying to do with their lives to a documentary team (not a word of theirs was used), and have heard how young people were paid to pose with guns in a documentary, an act which infuriated rivals in the area and prompted them to commit an assault after the programme was broadcast.

And at the same time, the media does not appear to be that interested in the killing of black adult gang members within Gangland: it happens too regularly to be a story.[4] If a child dies, it's considered worthy of coverage, often accompanied by opinion pieces that give the false impression law and order is declining in a uniform way across the nation. While the reasons behind this bias appear less to do with colour and more to do with how common the circumstances surrounding a death are, the overall effect is to cheapen the lives of those who live in heavily deprived areas, and it accentuates their detachment from the rest of society. The media also does not seem prepared to differentiate between the more organized and serious criminal gangs of Inner London and the peer groups of the suburbs – they are all just gangs, and this, it could be argued, operates as a factor in the latter group seeing themselves as just that. As we have seen, once the seeds of the gang ideal have been sown among an area's youth, the Internet can help to perpetuate them.

The horrors of gang life are available for all to see online. In 2007 the *Croydon Advertiser* found a video on a MySpace account of a terrified youth with blood oozing from the side of his mouth being forced to strip naked. He was then slapped, told to identify himself, and repeat the name DSN, which stands for Don't Say Nothing.[5] There have been other sporadic acts of intense violence: in 2005 sixteen-year-old schoolboy Stefan Persaud was beaten to death with a hammer, a baseball bat and a brick in South Norwood. The next year an innocent man had his ear partially severed after he attempted to stop a teenager being beaten in an apparent gang initiation.

The gangs of Croydon are of a similar ilk to others in the suburbs; young men who have only recently begun to draw upon the idea of gangs. Before gang culture hit the headlines, Croydon had the Dirty Thirty, which was a more organized and criminal group. Now it is about hype and territory and seeking to impose yourself. The two biggest are Don't Say Nothing and Shine My Nine (or Straight Merkin Niggas, or any number of variations) but there are scores – perhaps hundreds – of smaller groups.

Every local knows that Croydon has an emerging gang problem, and there are two reasons for this. The first is that, unusually, the territory in which the groups regularly battle is a very public place: Croydon town centre. This has led to a number of very blatant conflicts: in January 2007 at East Croydon station a sixteen-year-old was stabbed and put into intensive care. In April around a hundred gang members fought in Croydon High Street – weapons were brandished but only one person, a girl, was taken to hospital – and two months later another battle erupted in the Whitgift shopping centre: the two groups hurled plastic chairs at each other.

The second reason is that the gangs themselves are keen to make clear that Croydon has an emerging gang problem. SMN, in particular, has given a number of interviews to the local press. They have talked about having links to the dangerous Brixton gangs, that they dislike DSN because they 'go round robbing people for no reason', and that they have access to weapons, should they be required. The image they have sought to portray is of a fair criminal organization, one with its own moral code. In one article, which ran under the headline 'Society has failed us, but we are a success in a gang', one says: 'I'm trying to get out of this – but the system's made for us to fail.' Another added, 'The government is not giving me money, so I'm making my own money. When we get money we give to the young ones.'[6]

However, the more important quotes are elsewhere in the interview. The same interviewee says: 'SMN has been around since 2002. We used to go to school in Beulah Hill and Melfort Park and play football together.' Not so long ago, they were ordinary boys. What has happened to the youths in this area that has made them see themselves as a gang? Why did both gangs suddenly appear at the same time? Unlike the inner city, territory has little part to play. All the gang members are scattered around and not really divided by estate or postcode. There is some antagonism between north and south Croydon, but this can be seen as tension between haves (the latter) and have-nots (the former).

It is not simply a question of economics. The demographics of Croydon changed throughout the 1980s and 1990s. House prices in more central areas like Brixton began to skyrocket. At the same time there were young families wanting to buy houses. You could sell a house in Brixton or Battersea for £500,000 and buy something comparable in Thornton Heath for £75,000. There are no warring council estates here. Unlike the inner-city gangs they seek to emulate, few of them suffer from the deprivation that drives much gang affiliation – as one youth worker put it: 'I've been to a gang member's house and it's beautiful – Nintendo Wii on the floor, in better condition than mine. But there's a perception among them that they have it tough – in some cases it's literally as absurd as their mother not allowing them to play computer games.'

In Croydon the brash culture that children from the inner city brought to the borough did not sit well in its schools, staffed as they were by suburban teachers who did not appreciate the shift in demographics, and whose conception of discipline was at odds with the urban mindset. The end result was that Croydon's exclusion rates started running at twice the national average. Bored and lacking direction, these youths found a purpose when they hung out together.

Their claims such as affiliation to Brixton gangs are not all lies; several older people who claim affiliation to SMN have probably spent enough time in prison to network successfully, and then there is the crucial influence of blood relations. The key point is that their portrayal of an organized criminal enterprise does not stack up. For a disaffected youth – one who has failed in his educational career, who feels that the world doesn't treat him fairly, one who sees little hope for his future – the ideals espoused by SMN are very attractive. The gang narrative says territorialism and crime are OK; they're all part of a wider struggle, the same struggle that is embodied when they give themselves names like Capone and Soze.

Professor Hobbs has described: 'the notion of a distinct and homogenous environment of professional crime' which 'enables contemporary . . . criminals to inject a sense of retrospective order into their manic lifeworlds'. For Hobbs this illusion is sustained by the mythologizing of criminal figures from history.[7] Other academics have seen the gang culture, with its specific language and artistic, historical and cultural reference points, as being something like the

Skinheads or the Mods: an attempt by working-class youths to develop a culture of their own, to create an individual world which compensates for the fact that they are not a part of ordinary society. Like these movements, it is also about confrontation with the majority; playing music through their mobile phones at the back of the bus, the very notion of hype – these are ways of sticking two fingers up at a world they consider unfair.

The brutality and detachment from normality felt within inner-city Ganglands is very particular; they are unusual places. In the suburbs, the emotions felt by those affected by gangs come a great deal closer to home. One afternoon I found myself in a room above a garage in southeast London. I met a man who had separated from his wife, whose son lived with his mother in Totten Heath. The man would meet his son every weekend at London Bridge and play tennis with him. His boy was amazingly talented; a little black Roger Federer, speeding between the lines, delivering backhands and cross-court volleys with ever-increasing skill, yanking his opponent around the court, firing winners with no balance at all: a boy who was clearly special the very first time he picked up a racket.

The man knew his boy was popular, knew he played football at a club in Wandsworth. He knew nothing of any gangs. One Guy Fawkes' Night this boy went to Mitcham to watch a fireworks display. Some of his friends were in a Battersea gang – the Stuck Up Krew. The local Mitcham gang, Terrorzone, didn't want them in their area. They ran into each other and a fight ensued. Eyewitnesses say they chased them into Lavender Avenue. Four boys from the SUK were stabbed. Two came out of hospital the next day, one was put in a coma and recovered, and the man's son died on the spot.

It destroyed him, psychologically and financially. He could barely afford his funeral – no father expects to have to pay for one. The man was studying Law at Greenwich University and had to give it up. He looks at me, his head bowed, holding back tears: 'Every day it's like driving a car into a ditch. Every day you hear about absent fathers and how their children end up in gangs, and it makes me think it's my fault. But my son was my best friend. I saw him every weekend. The whole world comes down on you – press, TV – suddenly you're in the limelight. But if you're going to be in the limelight you want it to be for something positive, not something like this.'

The more people you speak to in the suburbs, the more you see that gang culture affects their lives. I took a train to meet some of the young people who live in Bromley, all of them between the ages of sixteen and eighteen. One of them was a friend of Ben Hitchcock: she weeps as she tells me about the events of the night he died. None of them belong to gangs; they are just normal kids living in the suburbs. All of them describe the way that as young people in London, they are affected on a daily basis by gang mentality. Young people are not listened to; were they given more of a voice, perhaps the full extent of the problem would be revealed.

One girl said: 'It affects my whole life. I had to choose my sixth-form college on the basis of where I come from. Only last week I was on a bus and a bunch of boys got on. They asked me where I went to school: I said Kelsey Park. They asked if that meant I was blue or Penge Block, because we have both at our school. I said I lived in Thornton Heath, so neither. They started spitting at me and telling me they were going to rob me. I've had boys asking me for my number, and then starting to get violent when I don't give them it, because I'm not affiliated to their crew. It's really hard for a young person living here. And adults don't listen to us: as far as they're concerned, all young people are a menace – but it's us who are suffering.'

Another girl said: 'I've been chased by about twenty-odd girls, all blue borough. There are a couple of boys in our school who have older siblings who've been in prison, and they start influencing everyone's culture, because they know people in crews – Gypset and all the rest. A few months ago, everyone was turning Muslim, like the PDC thing, yeah? And then they start talking about the whole Elders and Youngers thing. My family moved to Catford recently, and it didn't affect my mum or dad – but for me, well none of my friends from Bromley could come to see me. Every time we try to make a difference to young people we get beaten back down. There's only publicity when something bad happens.'

Another said: 'We went to an event in south London wearing our "RIP Ben [Hitchcock]" T-shirts, and these girls were like: "RIP Ben? Whatever." They didn't have it in them to say anything bad about him, but I thought it was going to kick off. What kind of mentality would make you act like that when someone dies? Everyone hates the police. We want to go to the shopping centre in a group. Why can't we? The police don't know stuff because we're scared to tell them. Even if you told them, would they be able to protect you?'

And another: 'The gang came into my college because they knew one of the boys was in P-Block. They waited outside the lesson – found where he was because the timetable was up on the wall. Some of them covered the exits, and they took him outside the college and beat him up. And another kid I know got kidnapped by them, and taken to Peckham. They made him rob stuff for them, and they pissed on him and caught it all on phone.'

Little by little, you realize that working-class children, even in the city's suburbs, feel as ostracized and vulnerable as those in the inner city.

The gang mentality plants its roots in areas that are distanced from the mainstream with a monotonous inevitability. Kingston-upon-Thames has something of the quiet provincial town about it, separated from the suburbs of London by Richmond Park and Wimbledon Common. The high street is reassuringly uniform, crowded as it is with every chain one might expect to find. The shopping malls are pristine and polished. Walk for half a mile out of the town centre down the Cambridge Road, past an array of luscious football pitches and tidy Victorian houses, and the one interstitial area in Kingston appears on the left. The Cambridge Road Estate is a colossal grey mass which has not yet been redeveloped into new flats; it's like a monstrous castle, jarring piercingly with the tranquillity of the rest of the town. In the inner city, the divisions within our society are covered up by redeveloped housing, and by the middle classes moving into areas that were once entirely poverty stricken. In an area like Kingston, the gaps in the fabric of our society are laid astoundingly bare.

The estate's youth dubbed themselves the ICE Crew (Invincible Cambridge Estate) about five years ago – the same time that the idea of the modern gang was popularized and so many of the adolescent crews were formed. In this small area in a small town, the graffiti is all over the walls of their fortress. Here, we have the large inner-city gangs' set-up in microcosm, with higher-level Elders controlling the drugs supply, and exploiting the fact that the Youngers will do anything to maintain their reputation. As everywhere else, the crew is ethnically representative of the estate – white, black, a few Asian. The Youngers do not create the fear in local residents in the way that they do in Gangland proper – but they are still all about hype, all about beating up alcoholics and vagrants, causing trouble and distracting from the Elders work, and at the same doing their jobs for them in hope of a leg-up the food chain. They do well for themselves.

There is another gang in New Malden – WK (Who Kares). Again, the same rules apply; formed in a small interstitial area, ICE and WK do business. Sometimes both gangs will travel up to Wandsworth and fight it out with the crews up there. Their violence is sporadic, but no less brutal when it does happen. One particularly violent stabbing in Kingston centre left a man with his entrails hanging out.

One of the best youth workers in the areas covered in suburban Gangland is an ex-underworld figure: he started his work after he finished serving a lengthy prison sentence. He is extremely good at winning people over. This is precisely why he is so good at his job, and why he was so good at what he did before the sentence. He is with some gang members in Wandsworth on the day the *Evening Standard* has published a list of what it says are all the gangs in London. The gang members' crew has not been named.

'Why weren't we in the *Standard*?'

'You ain't bad enough.'

'Not bad enough? What does man have to do? Do we have to merk someone?'

'Yeah. I reckon so. You think you can merk someone? You think you can walk up to a man and pull the trigger?'

'Yeah.'

'You don't have it in you. You don't have it in you for your conscience to haunt you your whole life, you don't have it in you to know that you've robbed wives, sisters, brothers of their loved one. You do not have it in you. Look at me: I know if a man has it in him. Do you have it in you?'

'No.'

And later:

'How much you made this week, playa?'

'Huh?'

'Your P's. I know you been shotting. How much?'

'Five-o-o.'

'Hoo. Not bad. So let me think now . . . five hundred a week, over a whole year that's, what, about twenty-five k? Lemme ask, what you gonna do with it?'

'I'm a buy a big-screen TV, and clothes, and I'm gonna save the rest.'

'Oh OK, where you gonna save it?'

'In a bank.'

A pause.

'You're sixteen. You're going to walk into a bank and give them that money, cash?'

Another pause.

'Yeah.'

'No you ain't.'

'Fuck you! It's my fucking money. They can't take it off me. No one can.'

'I'll tell you what'll happen if you do that. They'll tell the feds, and you'll do time. That's if you last that long. Because what'll probably happen is you'll get it nicked off you. And while they're at it, they'll probably drop you too.'

'Fuck you man, fuck you know?'

'What do you mean, what the fuck do I know? You know where I've come from. You know what I been. I don't have to put up with your shit either. Go on, you don't want to listen to me, fuck off you little prick. Go on. If you want to stay, then stay.'

The boy stays, and stays to hear about how, one day, he can make that sort of money legally – and no one will be able to take it off him. He talks about his dream – to be a professional footballer – and together they start to plan how he can achieve it. Soon the questions are flying. Has he approached the right training facilities to be spotted by scouts? How regularly is he practising? And all the while, he is teaching him to make the same demand to those whose help he needs: judge me by what I can be – not what I am. There will be knockbacks, he tells him – and they will only make you stronger.

This is the benefit of the voluntary sector: a statutory worker, constrained as they are by accountability, could never take that kind of risk in order to attract a gang member's attention. Later the youth worker says to me: 'I open their eyes to the harsh reality of what they're doing. I don't want to talk about my past too much, but I was a very naughty boy.

'However, I had rules. If someone owed us serious money, I'd wait outside his house. If the wife or kids are there, nothing doing. I'd just wait, till I got him alone. If someone needs to have a bullet put in them, then that's what happens. But never, ever, hurt an innocent. These tinies in the last few years, the Youngers, they have no such qualms. They will go to a man's girlfriend to get to him. They make good money. How do you get through to them? I bring myself, a man who was everything these kids aspire to be – a millionaire, a man every serious criminal in London knew and respected – and I tell them what will happen to them. Sitting inside a box all day, every day. No freedom, no power over your destiny. Yes, sir, no, sir, three bags full, sir. For day after day, week after week, year after year after year. People younger than you are with all the power in the world over you: the power to have you killed, no matter how bad you thought you were on the road. Wearing a set of clothes that have been worn by hundreds of other men, and rarely washed. I tell them it all.'

This man is very successful in his field. He has turned around the lives of countless children all over the city. He was approached by several charities while on day release – something he began in order to pass the time became an obsession. He is in the process of setting up his own trust to help offenders. There are others like him who, if trained and managed properly, might just change Gangland.

The title of this chapter is a phrase used by the gangs of inner London. It refers to committing crime out in the suburbs, a response to the saturation of their drug markets. There have been violent crimes in Essex committed by Hackney gangsters, in Kent by those from south London. Imagine the shock the police in Southwark had when they were told there were Peckham Boys in Cardiff attempting to recruit and set up business deals. Coupled with the phenomenon of youth gangs that are influenced by their inner-city counterparts, it may see the concentration of crime change in the next few years. We may begin to see far higher rates across the country; not just in the small areas that make up Gangland.

I spoke to a former police officer about this phenomenon. He said: 'When I joined the force thirty years ago, policing was brutal. If we wanted a statement, we did what it took to get it. Middle England knew how we operated, and it didn't care, because it was never on the receiving end. It's all changed now, not that it matters to most of the country. It's the same thing with crime, at the moment. Out of sight, out of mind. But given how these gangs are spreading their operations, I reckon they're going to see more and more of it. They can shut their ears to this problem, but wait till it lands on their doorstep. Then you'll hear them scream. Then you'll hear them scream alright.'

FIVE

Birmingham

When a general regards his troops as young children, they will
advance into the deepest valleys with him.

Sun Tzu, *Art of War*

The story runs that Birmingham's two main gangs, the Johnsons and
the Burgers, were formed out of the problems affecting black people
in that city in the 1980s. Under a climate of vicious race riots,
sparked by heavy presence of the far-right National Front, coupled
with an overzealous police force, young men banded together for
protection. They met in a fast-food restaurant in Lozells, planning
to run vigilante patrols to protect the community and fight its injus-
tices. As unemployment grew, they moved into the drugs market
and nightclub security: by the end of the decade, the Johnson Crew
were making a great deal of money. A rival firm was born out of a
disagreement within the crew. Some say it was over video games.
Some say it was over how to spend their money. Others say it was
over the rape of a gang member's sister. Whatever the reason, in a
small cafe on the Villa Road the Burger Bar Boys were born; bitter
rivals of the Johnsons, and ready to fight them for control of the burgeoning crack market. Soon, their war would envelop the city.

So the story goes. Like all urban stories it has some basis in truth and some in rumour. How many members were involved in the early years, and the level of crime they were committing, is hard to tell. You hear of other gangs from the same period, such as the Inch-High, the Black Rose Posse, that have not been immortalized in the unofficial underworld history. It's true that the Burgers and the Johnsons numbered some powerful criminals, who had criminal connections across the country in their ranks. There were a small number of men at the top of these gangs calling the shots. The Burgers and Johnsons were ethnically representative of their areas; the latter had a number of white members. People certainly know about them, but it's likely their name was more powerful than they were in the early years.

As one ex-gang member described them: 'There was really one head man at the top of both crews, with a couple of people working for him. That man had immense power: he could stop violence happening, and he could also gather a team together to initiate it. There was also an aspect of self-policing – if you knew a certain sub-group of one of the gangs had robbed stuff from you, you could phone him up and he'd find it. There were about a hundred hard-core mans – any shootings, stabbings or whatever was down to them. If you were a Burger or Johnny, where you lived didn't matter so much as now. People started to get flushed out of their houses – the number of houses shot up in this city must run into the thousands – and it got more territorial. White men were – still are – running the gun importation. If a black man wants a gun, he ain't gonna go to another black guy. Asians deal brown, black guys crack and skunk, white men deal guns – it's how it's always been.

'There was a lot more unity in the ghetto in those days. Individuals would certainly have violent battles, but still, you could go to a dance and see guys from X, Y and Z there. Now you can't even go on the same road as those groups. The kids have grown up in this culture where all they know and see is the presence of gang territories.'

What we do know is that the gangs' violence and their reputations began to gather momentum in the late 1990s. In 1997 several high-ranking members of the Johnson Crew were jailed at Leicester Crown Court after a man named Jason Wharton was shot dead in Handsworth. Witnesses gave evidence behind bullet-proof screens and in disguise, leading to several gangsters being jailed for terms ranging from life to five years. It was reported that they continued from inside their cells and the gang gained momentum during this period as it became more organized. Another seminal point in the gun wars came in 1999 with the shooting of Corey Wayne Allen. The press claimed that he had been shot by his own gang after double-crossing them. But his alleged murderer never faced trial, mainly because witnesses had refused to testify. One man claimed he had suffered sudden amnesia.

The violence between the two gangs was felt to have reached a peak in 2003 with the shooting of Letisha Shakespeare, seventeen, and Charlene Ellis, eighteen. The story behind the event had begun three years earlier when Yohanne Martin (street name '13') had been accused of murdering 22-year-old Christopher Clarke, who was beaten to death by a gang of twenty men in March 2000. The murder charge, along with counts of wounding with intent and violent disorder, was dropped in April 2001. However, Martin was sent to prison after admitting possessing a pistol and ammunition. On the evening of 6 December 2002, he took a hire car to see friends in West Bromwich. As he parked by the side of the road, a car pulled up alongside. Two bullets were fired from it and hit him in the head, killing him instantly.

Newspaper reports described him as a key member of the Burger Bar Boys, a gang whose territory was said to be nearby Smethwick and Handsworth. The reports said that their rivals, the Johnson

Crew, were based in Aston and Lozells, and were white, Asian and black. Yohanne's brother Nathan, whose street name was '23', believed the Johnson Crew – and one member in particular – were behind the killing. He began to plot his revenge.

He had found a recruit in Michael Gregory, whose sister Leona had been Yohanne's girlfriend and had a child with him. He also recruited Marcus Ellis, who was coincidentally the half-brother of Charlene Ellis. Gregory was given the job of co-ordinating the hit. He bought a pay-as-you-go mobile phone and used it to negotiate the purchase of the getaway car, a red Ford Mondeo, from a dealer in Northampton. On the afternoon of New Year's Eve 2002 the car was brought back to Birmingham and a window tinter hired to darken the windows. On 2 January 2003, another member of the Burger Bar gang, Rodrigo 'Sonny' Simms, was at a party at the Uniseven salon in Aston, which his cousin Selina owned. The prosecution claimed that Simms spotted several members of the Johnson Crew at the party and guided the killers into position just after 4 a.m. Earlier that night a man named Jermaine Carty had been taunting the Burger Bar Boys. Carty was named in court by witnesses as being in the rival Johnson Crew, although he denied being a member.

The Mondeo pulled up at the back of the salon and the attackers fired from a Mac-10 at partygoers. Ellis focussed on hitting a Johnson member – it was said that Carty was a principal target. Martin did not care who he hit. Within a second 23 shots had been fired. After making their attack they drove off to burn the getaway car. A bullet hit Charlene's left arm, the second her shoulder, and the third fractured her skull and killed her instantly. Letisha was shot four times. The fatal bullet pierced her heart and lungs; all four bullets travelled right through her body.

A few minutes later Michael Ellis, brother to twins Sophie and Charlene, was woken by a telephone call from Jermaine Carty, who told him 'the Burgers' had shot his sister. Michael followed his surviving sister, Sophie, to hospital, where she was rushed into theatre for surgery. As the doctors began to operate, He picked up a phone and called his half-brother, Marcus.

'Your lot shot my sister,' said Michael.

'What do you mean your lot?' answered Marcus.

'Your friends shot my sister.'

'Is she dead?'

'I don't know.'

The line went dead.

Michael called Marcus again later that morning to report that Charlene was dead. Marcus said nothing; he simply hung up. He went on the run immediately afterwards and would remain out of touch with family and friends for weeks.

It was some time before Martin, Ellis, Gregory and Simms were arrested and charged with the murders. All men were convicted by majority verdicts at Leicester Crown Court in March 2005 with the exception of Ellis, who was convicted unanimously.

The huge public interest in the trial meant that the logistics of the shootings were reported in depth, along with a number of interesting details regarding the trial itself. The main prosecution witness was a man named 'Mark Brown'. Due to his questionable background, he was allowed to give evidence without the defence knowing who he was. During the trial the defence made a number of allegations about his criminal connections, along with arguing the fact that he was paid £5,000 in various privileges for giving evidence discredited him. Yet he was the star prosecution witness: the only one who put all the murderers together in the same place.

Shots were fired at members of the Johnsons at a cafe called Ruthie's during the case; it was said it happened because they were friends of Mark Brown. There was an underworld investigation going on; everyone was trying to find out his identity. Another man named Tafarwa Beckford was tried, but midway through the case it became clear that the only evidence against him came from Mark Brown. When it became clear that Brown's evidence wouldn't be enough to convict Beckford, he was acquitted. The *Birmingham Post* had named him as a suspect prior to the trial, and a few days later he was shot in the head – he survived. Mark Brown also admitted in his evidence that he'd been told exactly what it was alleged the defendants had done – so while he gave a solid performance in the witness box, it might not have been the case that he was recounting what he saw. Another point is that the only evidence against Rodrigo Simms was the fact that he had received mobile-phone calls from the defendants. They could have been calling to ask where the Johnsons were, but it could have been for any number of other reasons. Simms was convicted of being a spotter. Were the right men sentenced? Most experts in the city will tell you they were, whether by fair means or not. Regardless, some heavily involved gangsters were sent down: the media upped and left the city, and the public was reassured that the gangs had been destroyed. In one way the trial was the beginning of the end for the city's gangs. In another way, the gang problem was just beginning.

The murders were the first time that the national press began to write about the Johnson Crew and the Burger Bar gang's rivalry. The names began to carry weight. In March 2005 the *Daily Telegraph* reported that the two gangs had 'fought relentlessly for two decades'. According to the report, after police breakthroughs in 1997, 'The A34, for so long the unofficial boundary separating the gangs' bases in Aston and Lozells, was ignored and the groups went all-out in their attempts to control the city's cocaine trade, leaving the police as virtual bystanders . . .'[1] The same piece described the two gangs: 'They are run by fear, intimidating members, potential witnesses and members of the public.' It added that 'despite being numerically inferior, the Burger Bar Boys have taken advantage of their small, tight-knit community and are seen as the more ruthless . . . They are led by a shadowy figure calling himself S1, who has developed links with black gangs in London and Manchester, often exchanging arms and drugs. None of the members are known by their real names, preferring – revelling, indeed – in nicknames such as Reaper.'

Let's return to the New Year's murders. The first thing that stands out is that these murders were not about the drug trade. They were about two men's furious response to a bereavement, which had in turn been brought about by previous killings. They were targeting an individual they felt was connected to the murderers of Yohanne Martin, but to them, anyone at that party was a legitimate target. As it happens, two girls had been implicated in Martin's murder; many journalists suggested this was why the killers felt no compunction about shooting whoever was outside the party. According to one paper, the Burger Bar Boys had coined a new term for the gun: 'a unisex weapon'.

They were horribly misguided in coming to this conclusion; something Ellis would certainly have felt after he discovered he had murdered his own half-sister. However, there clearly was a connection being made at the party by some of those there with the Johnsons, hence the DJ giving shouts out to them. What this shows is that the events of 2003 prove some of the points made in earlier chapters. It is perhaps better that an ex-policeman from the city explains:

'The 2003 murders were huge in a number of ways. Firstly, they were high-profile killings. The murder of young, innocent, teenage girls is obviously going to have a huge emotional impact. The police were under a huge amount of pressure from the media and public to catch those responsible. It was a crazy time for us. But the other reason the killings were so important was that it was the first time this sort of crime went truly public. Prior to 2003 people in those areas had known about the Johnsons and the Burgers. There were a couple of hundred people who would consider themselves members of each gang. Since the late 90s there had been killings, whereby the bereaved would target someone they thought was a member of the other gang in order to get revenge. That escalation went on up until the New Year's murders; this much is true. The gangs did feel affiliated to their areas, but 2003 was one of the few times that this connection was deemed reason enough for innocents to die.

'So the picture that was put forward when the trial was covered, of two huge gangs fighting for control of drugs markets on either side of Birchfield Road, was news to us. The trouble was that the coverage made people in those areas believe in the gangs' celebrity. So if you asked me about the core of the serious crews today, I'd say there were probably about the same numbers who were properly involved. But how many kids today, if you asked them, would say they were Burgers or Johnnies or, more so now, affiliated to one of the offshoots? It would probably run into the thousands. Part of the problem is that the media in this city dwells overwhelmingly on the negative. I would hear parents saying that they refuse to let their child go to the city centre because there was a report that the people running all the doors of nightclubs are Burgers. There's no doubt there's a connection: control the doors, you control a safe little drug market. But they don't run every club. And soon that myth perpetuates among the community so now there's suddenly a belief in Aston that the Burgers are running the whole town.'

One only needs to look at the area to understand what he's talking about, and how it contradicts newspaper reports. The area to the north of the city centre which stretches from Handsworth to Nechells is at least ten square miles and densely populated. For any gang to truly control the drugs markets in the areas they inhabit – let alone have any further influence – would take a supreme amount of organization. Furthermore, these are populous and culturally diverse areas. To reduce them to the level of mere untapped drug markets, such as a single inner-city estate, is impossible.

These areas are roughly separated from the city centre by a series of motorways or main roads, which must be crossed in order to enter them. Walk through the city's Jewellery Quarter, a small area of charming boutiques, cross the roaring Hockley flyover, and you enter Lozells. Huge blocks of council flats are visible to the south, but most of it is a hotch-potch of scruffy terraced houses. Soho Road runs for about a mile into neighbouring Handsworth. The dominant influence felt upon it is Asian – there are dozens of little shops selling food and other goods. At about 4 p.m. it's crowded with children leaving school, and then the rich smell of families preparing their evening meals seems to overcome the terraced streets that run either side of it. You can see the influence of gang culture on this area. Some of the street signs have tags like 'Bang Bang 21 territory' written on them in marker pen – 'Bang Bang' being a way for youths to buy into the gangster ideal, a rephrasing of Burger Bar, and '21' referring to the postcode.

A 2006 report into the area by Black Radley, a private consultancy, said:

'The Lozells and East Handsworth ward is the most populous and the most overcrowded of all the Birmingham wards. It has the highest ethnic-minority population (82.6 per cent). It has high levels of unemployment; high levels of teenage pregnancy; high levels of crime, youth crime, hate crime and drug crime; high levels of anti-social behaviour; the third highest asylum and refugee population in Birmingham; and significant health inequalities . . . It is overcrowded and suffers from poor housing . . . The number of high levels of young men with insufficient to occupy their time – is an incendiary mix.'[2]

It is an interstitial area; it is Gangland. North of this area lies Handsworth Park and the streets around it slowly become more affluent until they are full of larger, middle-class households. It takes a good couple of hours to walk the circumference of this area, a walk in which most races and classes of British society exist. If one keeps walking west from here then the A34 appears, the alleged dividing line between the two Ganglands. On the other side of this flyover lies Aston in the B6 postcode. It is a great deal scruffier, but again there is a mix of culture and class.

The main road that runs through Aston is a fast route for cars called Trinity Road, which leads to Aston Villa's ground – a huge structure that straddles the road in order to support itself. Beside it lies the picturesque Aston Park. It is only when you continue west that you encounter a more familiar Gangland in the mix of social housing and industrial land that comprises the south of Aston and Nechells. In the dark, these areas are threatening – they are too maze-like, with too much distance between the estates and the safety of the main road back to Birmingham. Much of Gangland has to be experienced at night in order to understand the fear that Youngers put into an area. Suddenly, it becomes terrifying; not because the buildings are dilapidated and there is obvious squalor, but for simple reasons of geography. There are few hiding places, few escape routes back to busier streets.

There is no doubt that there are large pockets of deprivation in all these areas – but they are huge, and varied. To walk through all of them would take the best part of the day; they encompass most of the land to the north of one of Britain's largest cities.

The city authorities' response to gangs after 2003 has not been perfect, but Birmingham has moved in the right direction. The authorities had two problems: the two gangs themselves, and the wall of silence that greeted them whenever they carried out enquiries. Of the latter, a local policeman told *The Times* in 2005: 'The people we were dealing with, the gangsters, the way in which they live their lives, makes any such investigation extremely difficult. They try and rule with fear and intimidation. It is a culture, as we have heard in the trial, in which no one talks to the police come what may. Anybody who does is considered an informant or a grass.'[3] It is a commonly cited problem when dealing with gangs. In London, Operation Trident has traditionally grappled with the same problem; there are dozens of stories involving the entire turn-out at a nightclub saying they were in the toilet when a shooting occurred.

However, the police explanation leaves out another significant reason for the lack of witnesses: the very nature of the zones in which the gangs operate. As previously mentioned, they are distanced from run-of-the-mill society. For the most part, their interaction with the authorities is a negative one. As well as the fear they have of the gang members, they also do not trust the authorities to keep them safe, or to act responsibly with information they might give them. It is all a part of living in Gangland: in many other cases anyone who gives evidence against a gang member risks upsetting not only them, but their family and friends. It's not that these areas are always gang dominated – more that the connection between gang and area run far beyond a mere intimidatory relationship; a point the authorities are not prone to making for fear of demonizing an entire area.

Time and again while writing the book I have heard disparaging voices with regard to the police; time and again those voices have come from non-gang-involved community figures. It is why the statutory sector in most of these areas has begun to work with voluntary agencies, which have a great deal more respect: as we shall see, this process needs to be developed. This needs to happen because the bottom line is that trials against gang members fail time and again due to the prosecution's case collapsing when people fail to give evidence. And this can lead to a feeling of helplessness within some parts of the community and a feeling of invincibility for those who are gang involved.

One also has to be careful when accepting the police's version of the gang situation and remember that it too has an agenda. As one criminologist put it to me during an interview: 'When there is a problem for which the police might receive funding, we always hear that the problem has suddenly got worse. Back in the 1990s I remember a meeting I had with some police officers about organized crime. The Chief Superintendent burst in and said: "Is this the academic? Look you: there is no organized crime in this country." And he stormed out. Then a few years later SOCA [the Serious Organised Crime Agency] was set up, and the police were all too keen to tell the media about organized criminals. It's the same with gangs – there have always been gangs, and now they are happy to talk about them – sometimes too freely for the communities' good.'

In 2004, Dominic White from Southampton Institute was already suggesting: 'It seems that the "journey into the spectacle and carnival of crime" in relation to street gangs in the UK has begun in earnest, with the media and the police arguably leading in the race of description.'[4] Such descriptions do not show how complex the gangs' relationship with their community can be. The relationships vary wildly, from fear to complicity, and it follows that the best placed people to deal with them are not always the police.

To return to 2003: staff at Birmingham's City Hospital became so adept at treating gunshot wounds that when several doctors were seconded for front-line medical duty during the Iraq war, they found they already possessed all the battlefield skills they needed. West Midlands Police had the highest number of armed call-outs in the UK; one detective referred to Birmingham as being 'like the Wild West', as firearms incidents rose to at least one a week.

As a city council officer put it: 'A few years ago the situation in Birmingham was out of hand. The city threw a lot of money into the gang problem. We realized that the way in which it was being tackled was completely disorganized, and we realized that the public authorities didn't understand the problem. There were 250 organizations purporting to deal with the gang problem; they were all scrapping for the same money. I did not feel that many of them were fit for purpose – how many of the organizations would last beyond a year's funding? There was another problem with the fact that the funders were all sitting at the same table as the people they were funding. Many of the same people judging contracts were writing the proposals: there was very little direction in what the city was trying to achieve.'

Nothing had been achieved by throwing money at the problem. One enterprising set of gang members had set up a community centre into which council money was being poured. Unsurprisingly, this cash was being used to build villas in the West Indies. The city realized it needed to accomplish two things. The first was to reduce high-risk offenders and manage them; the second was to build community resilience.

In terms of the first aspect, they knew they were dealing with around 500 individuals who were involved in gang violence in some shape or form. The first step was punitive. Around 80 senior gang members were arrested in the months following the New Year's trial. Yet this was the tip of the iceberg. As we have seen, the gang is not a single organism which can be killed by decapitation. And the police and other authorities came up with a creative way of dealing with it. They realized that their most potent tools had been there all along: they simply had not ever been applied to the gangs.

There had been public protection tools in the city for years. One of these is a Shared Priority Forum (SPF). It deals with what are known as Persistent Priority Offenders (PPOs). Any agency which will have a legal relationship with these criminals sits on it: youth offending teams, probation, prison services, child protection agencies, job centres and learning skills bodies. Certain individuals are targeted and a unilateral strategy for dealing with them is laid out between the various bodies. Most of these criminals are robbers or other minor crooks. The authorities realized that the same process could be used to target the gangs at a lower level.

How to identify and keep track of the gang members? Again, it needed imagination. The traditional view of ASBOs and injunctions is that they are a controlling measure, but in Birmingham the authorities view them as a means of risk management. Once a gang member has an ASBO, control measures can be put around him. As one policeman put it: 'There is no burden of proof beyond reasonable doubt. We can stand up in court and show the fear these people put into the community. It sends a message out to it: that the system is there to protect it. It is not always easy.

'The left is right when it says the Government has given us some pretty draconian powers: we can evict people from their houses, order them to attend things with the risk of being criminalized if they don't attend – and what we have to do is balance the gang members' human rights with the rights of the community. People don't realize how many families are left terrified by what street culture has done to their children. They don't see how they can control them. If we can exert a degree of control through civil law, then you can start to work with them.'

The SPF did not have a broad enough scope to deal with the most involved members. Once more, the authorities looked at existing processes and saw how they could be applied. It already had a forum in place for dealing with serious offenders. Most cities have what is known as a MAPPA (Multi Agency Public Protection Arrangements) for dealing with offenders who pose the highest level of harm to the public. The agencies that sit on it are similar to those in the SPF, but are operating at a higher level and have a different set of priorities. In around 90 per cent of cases across Britain, it is used to deal with sex offenders. The authorities realized that the SPF could simply refer the most serious gang leaders to the MAPPA.

This was half the battle; the enforcement side of what became Birmingham Reducing Gang Violence (BRGV). The other half of the programme involved making the communities more resilient. The voluntary authorities that worked there had to be more accountable, and had to work in partnership with the statutory authorities that dealt with the offenders. A line was drawn under the mistakes of the past, and the dubious charities such as those we mentioned earlier were slowly ostracized. As one council worker put it: 'We realized that it was less about battling criminal organizations from the top down or indeed the bottom up, and more about targeting specific offenders within the area before they offend. What the city understood was that when you get an incident like the New Year's murders all these authorities collaborate at the same time – why couldn't that be an ongoing process?'

One of the bodies that sits on the forums is the West Midlands Mediation and Transformation Service (WMMTS). The WMMTS was set up by ex-policemen, born of ideas from overseas. As one of its workers says: 'We were inspired by the gang mediators in Newark, New Jersey. They had accidentally learned the way that dialogue can slow conflict. The gangs do not have the control of geographical areas that the Americans have. However, if you are gang involved and you do enter a rival's territory it is likely to cause antagonism and that can then escalate.

'We live in a society where people are not trained to deal with conflict. When you are dealing with this kind of crime, it's very easy to be controlled by emotions rather than by rational thought. When you're dealing with conflict you have to get up close and personal. We have plenty of caring Christians in the voluntary sector [street pastors and the like] who teach us about love and forgiveness, but we lack skilled mediators who are able to tell gang members how it is in a diplomatic way: someone who can knock on a door and say: "You know what? You can allow this situation to escalate – you can go over there and shoot that guy and it'll be 2–1 to them; one for the guy they killed and another for the guy in your lot who went to jail." The first role of a copper is preservation of life. All the church stuff is very worthwhile, but it doesn't do the job that the police do.'

The implementation of these positive measures has not been flaw-less. Youth workers in some areas remain sceptical about the impact of BRGV and its mediation service. They say that 'underground' mediation services are the ones that do the real work due to a lack of exit strategies for those working with the youths. They regard the statutory service as merely a subtle way for the authorities to gather intelligence, and say that the youths in the area only give them lim-ited information, such is the lack of trust. As one volunteer said: 'How long will they keep banging the drum about the dodgy vol-untary agencies that received money in the past? They're still using it, years down the line, as a stick with which to beat the voluntary bodies, all the while dangling carrots to make them operate to their agenda.' Another group of voluntary workers say that the police have given a negative perception of their institution to the community, telling other bodies that they are gang members, and even raiding their premises for guns on one occasion, which led to an official apology.

One ex-gang member had an extremely negative perception of the authorities: 'There is no wall of silence. For years I've seen the police in this city do nothing, because ultimately if gangsters are wiping each other out it can only be a good thing. Then the 2003 murders came. Even now, you have to ask about which people are still oper-ating, and why. Why seize a man, however hardcore, if he's bringing in thirty mans a year, and a load of guns and drugs that you can impound? There is no real support to change the lives of people who've become involved in the lifestyle. I work with youths in this area now. What am I really supposed to say to a seriously involved gang member, with no qualifications? That he should give up the lifestyle and live like a tramp? Because if I refer him to the authorities he's most likely going to be arrested, not helped.'

The Johnsons and the Burgers make few headlines today, but the city's gang problem is far from eradicated. One youth worker described it thus: 'After the arrests there were few real leaders, so everyone is now doing their own thing in sub-groups. They're all in their own comfort zones, selling drugs and what have you – they don't go to different areas like they used to. Serious players still have a big influence on those kids, however. It's winter now, and so it's quiet. In summer it'll all kick off again – there are hot spots where people just congregate.' And quite apart from this, there have been changes to the city's gang culture that are a great deal more fundamental.

Leon walks into a coffee shop by the Bullring and asks what I fancy. He walks up to the counter and orders, pulling out a wad of twenties from his jacket pocket and selecting one for the cashier. Smiles, and sits down. He is a black man in his late twenties, short and podgy.

'OK, so the first thing I want to say is that I don't want you to describe me as a crew member. I'm not. I'm freelance. I'm cleverer than them. I've been told who you are and what you want to know. So don't say anything – just let me do the talking.

'First thing is, I was never a criminal. I wanted to be an engineer. Then I did time when I was eighteen, just because I was there when something happened. And I realized two things – the first is that I wouldn't be the person I thought I'd be, and the second is that my time in prison gave me more power than I could imagine. I had the contacts to make money without any trouble. For a time I chose to use it. Now you hear I'm out of it. Well, in as much as you can be, I am.

'The next thing to know is this. I live in Handsworth. I know a lot of Burgers. But I don't go in for that bullshit. I am not a Burger. The thing is, however clever some of these boys are, they're stuck in the same dumb bullshit. Fucking yada yada tried to do that to blah blah's brother? Well, we'd better get a crew together and teach them a lesson. We gotta be the ones with the respect. No, you don't, you fucking idiot. But that's how they are, and always will be. That's not me. I keep clear where I can.

'The ones to be scared of in this city are the ones you don't hear about. If you've got beef, why make a noise when you can just get in a Yardie? The guy will be in the country one day, smoke someone, and out he goes. No fucking around. You can see the signs in Villa Road – has anyone in the community had any contact with this man, believed to be in Jamaica and related to a killing? Makes me laugh.

'What did I do? It was mostly drugs. I ain't going into the ins and outs of it, but I had a man at the Parcelforce depot in Coventry picking them up, and I'd take them to London for the sale. Sometimes it was crack, sometimes brown, the same way. One time it was guns. There ain't no trade except the trade that's there. I don't give a fuck if you Burger, Johnny, black, white, Asian, fucking yellow . . . if we can roll, we're rolling. And this is the difference between being a crew member and being a criminal. And it's criminals who are successful. When people talk about crew members setting up shop in Derby, Leicester – they're not usually crew members. They're criminals. They might well be involved with crews, but they don't go in for bullshit, like me. Mostly the line between the two is age. It's also just intelligence.

'I avoid beef at all times. Because the thing about beef is – you can't shut it down quickly. You can't shut it down ever. You can be cold and take out a hit, or you can give hype, but it won't stop it. You know when you're fucking scared about something, and the butterflies in your stomach are going. Imagine that 24/7. That's a crew member's life. Never knows what's going to pop round the corner for him. It's not mine.

'Don't judge me. Those drugs would have got there with or without me. I don't draw a line between those transactions and the legit ones I've made since I'm out, 'cept the illegal ones were often a lot fairer. For me, money is money. For you, there's good and bad money. I respect that, but I don't get it. But the key thing is – I did not go in for violent bullshit. Clever man sits in the background, doesn't flap his gums, and waits.

'Now you want to know about tinies. It's like this. Some of those guys that I know – guys I guess you'd still call crew members – have good business heads. And what they've realized is that they don't need to do much to make paper these days. Because it's getting so if they have a supplier, they can sit back and use the kids: all of a sudden, they want to be like them. Now this to me is strange, because I never felt that I wanted to be a gangster when I grew up, nor anyone I know. It just happened. Is what they're doing good, or fair? I don't know. How else would they make paper? I guess it would be robbing. And robbing means violence, and robbing means recriminations. Stupid, when there are more and more kids around that they can use.'

Contrary to what he says, when he was active Leon was a gang member. In the drugs structure outlined in the first chapter, he is what I termed a Face. This definition still holds weight for the people who are trying to fight the gangs. But this is not how he sees himself: he sees himself as a drug dealer. He is prepared to work with anyone, anywhere.

And this is a vitally important point about how crime everywhere works: even at the highest levels, it is spontaneous and opportunistic far more than it is organized. For example, even the term 'Cosa Nostra' only came out during dubious evidence submitted by a criminal at a trial. The Mafia had degrees of organization, but it was not a corporation. It was a collective term for the criminal activities of small groups of immigrants. As mentioned earlier, so it is with the crime which we are investigating: it cannot be simply tackled from the top down. When there is announcement of a truce between gang leaders, or indeed mediation between them and the authorities, it is unlikely that this will hold. In a few big-city American gangs, there is more organization and certain individuals hold sway over large groups of people: in recent years in Birmingham, the potential for this model to take hold has grown.

Benjamin, sixteen, had built up a little enterprise for himself dealing crack in Nechells. One of the teenage cliques in his area decided that he should be taxed. They wanted £3,000, and he paid them. Then they decided they wanted more, and asked him for another £2,000. He wouldn't pay them; and he knew there would be trouble. He ran away to his grandmother's house, but one of his friends told them where he would be hiding. They broke in, and beat him up, before asking him which leg he wanted to be shot in. He asked if he could go to the upstairs bathroom to wash the blood off his face. Revelling in the moment, they allowed him to go. He was presented with a choice: jump from the window, or take a bullet. He chose to jump, and shattered both legs. He crawled away from the back garden. Thinking he had escaped, the gang didn't check the surrounding area.

Birmingham is perhaps the most organized city in the country in how it deals with the gang situation. However, the legacy of the New Year's murders has changed the nature of the problem. The arrests following the murders were part of a concerted effort by the police to wipe out the top tier of the gangs. A number of youths in their areas saw only a power vacuum: not safer streets. At the same time, with all of the talk surrounding the city's gang life, an increasing number of wannabes were stepping into the breach. It is the same process we saw in previous chapters: young boys who would normally hang around in groups suddenly seeing themselves as a gang.

With sad inevitability, a postcode war based on the received perceptions of the original criminal gangs has sprung up in the last few years. The B21, 20, 18 and 16 postcodes of Handsworth and Lozells, from which the Burger Bar Boys were drawn, has seen its youngsters redefining it as the BB area – it could be Bang Bang, or Blood Brothers – as well as those that name themselves after particular areas; Centenary Drive (a harmless-looking little close off Soho Road) and Raleigh Close too. In B6, the Johnson territory, there are now a number of little crews with variations on the SLASH theme: Stay Loyal and Stay Humble. Other names are mentioned in the local press and disappear – the Raiders, Champagne Crew, Badder Bar Boys. Both sets of gangs have their colours: red and blue. As in London's Ganglands, territorial rivalries make life hard for youth workers: 'You try taking five boys from each area on a bus,' says one. 'They'll be fighting in seconds.'

This is a long way from the Johnsons and Burgers when they began; two relatively durable criminal enterprises. By the time you read this these names and numbers will have changed any number of times. The problem is that there is a divide along territory: BB (Handsworth, Lozells) and Slash (Aston, Nechells). But these are children who base their territorialism on what they perceive is the province of older gang members. One notorious south London gang member who has, in recent times, begun to turn his life around, is greeted like a visiting dignitary by them when he visits the city. Experienced criminals with strong gang reputations have already seen the potential to exploit these rivalries. In a city where their areas are not dispersed in the way they are in London, there is no reason why large, American-style gangs could not emerge in the future.

For now these gangs are youthful, fluid and violent towards their territorial rivals. It is exactly the same phenomenon as the postcode wars of previous chapters – youths fighting old territorial battles which they believe echoes the criminal behaviour of the established gangs. What this seems to mean – as the will to establish reputation takes precedence over traditional feuds or drug-related violence – is that gang violence in the city is becoming a great deal more arbitrary, if less lethal. Violence against the person has increased in Birmingham since 2003, while the number of people presented to hospital with firearms injuries has dipped – after it shot up from 20 people in 2001–2 to 78 in 2002–3.[5]

It does not mean that the most dangerous gangsters have been eradicated. In 2005 Kairo Beckford, Josiah Faure, David Perry and Brett Anslow shot an innocent man, Daniel Bogle, three times in the head at point-blank range. They thought he was a member of another Johnson offshoot (the Raiders, who had previously robbed Anslow), but it later transpired he was nothing to do with him. In court it was alleged the murder was carried out 'to send a message to the street'. The killers went to a nearby pub to celebrate fifteen minutes later, where they were caught on CCTV.

One of the most prominent victims of the Youngers' more capricious battles was Odwayne Barnes, who was stabbed through the heart in 2007. Barnes was a Bang Bang member who had an argument with three Slash for Money teenagers – Damian Belle, Michael Hayles and Nathanial Darby – in the city centre. They chased him and he managed to get away, but as they were driving away from the city they spotted him again. Barnes was stabbed twice, suffering catastrophic injuries to the heart.

The mediation strategies, designed to deal with the core of small gangs, can only go so far in combating a mindset that is diffusing through the area's youth. In a youth centre, a fourteen-year-old girl mentions that she is part of SLASH. The youth worker immediately takes her aside:

'I don't want that talk around here, Beverley. There are other kids here, and I don't want them hearing that word.'

'But I am! We all are. It's just a part of living here, innit?'

'Why, Beverley? Why does it have to be that way? Don't you have a choice? Is that all you are?'

She says nothing. It is not an easy battle to win. Later in the day I speak to him. He feels that Birmingham's gang situation is worse than it has ever been. The tit-for-tat killings of the Burgers and the Johnsons have been replaced by an increasing number of Youngers who wish to impose themselves. He describes how the Youngers he has worked with begin to learn their trade, shoplifting at first, then shoplifting to order for the Elders. He has seen the Elders plant their drugs on ten or eleven-year-olds, knowing that when the police come to call they are unlikely to ask children of that age where they might be. He traces the changes back to the period around the New Year's shootings: 'It made the idea of a gang carry so much more weight. How could a little organization be so powerful that it could make a brother kill his half-sister? There was a vacuum there, and people wanted to step into it. We are still feeling the backlash within this community.

'There were always gangs of youngsters fighting in Birmingham. I grew up in Edgbaston; we called the place Bitter Creek. Borstal Heath was Sodom, and Handsworth was Texas. We'd meet up at a patch near Birmingham Prison and fight. But we never saw ourselves as any sort of a gang. It's the high-profile cases that have given the kids some sort of identity.'

*

Given that the areas to the north of Birmingham's city centre hold the same interstitial qualities defined in Chapter 3, we should not be surprised that other symptoms of the disorganised society besides gang culture reveal themselves. This is a crowded area in which everyone is competing for resources, be they access to jobs or public funds. The fault-lines between the different ethnicities and ages will always show under this pressure. In October 2005 Lozells exploded in two nights of carnage. The spark was a series of rumours involving a black fourteen-year-old girl who was apparently caught attempting to shoplift from a branch of Beauty Queen Cosmetics. Pirate-radio stations alleged that she was caught by the shopkeeper and gang raped by a group of Asian men. Afraid of being deported due to her illegal immigrant status, the girl apparently refused to provide a statement to the police. This incident has never been proved, despite extensive police investigation. These rumours circulated through the black community.

A picket was set up outside the store: Ajaib Hussein, 33, the shop owner, denied the event ever occurred and blamed business rivals for starting the rumour. A public meeting was held on Saturday 22 October at the New Testament Church of God. In the late evening the meeting ended and violence erupted outside. Gangs of men fought running battles and Isiah Young-Sam, who later died, and another person were stabbed. Three men were later convicted of Young-Sam's murder. A man named Aaron James was accidentally shot by his friend as they ran away from police. Rioting also occurred to a lesser extent during the night of 23 October. Between thirty and fifty individuals were thought to be involved in the most serious incidents; 347 crimes were recorded, including twelve firearms discharged, and five attempted murders.

Some community workers blame the riots on the way the authorities handled the situation. One said: 'It was the end of Eid. The Asian youths had started making their way to the church, and we said to the police that they should not bring the opposing group that way. We were out in the hot spots and knew who the main people involved were.'

As we have seen, gangs do not have the structure implied by media coverage, but they are still an expression of the desire for order in a place that has none – that order might translate to financial success in the drug market, or it might merely make one feel safe, or perhaps more threatening. A riot is also about individuals who live disorganized lives finding a common purpose within a group. All it takes is for a few elements to take control and a herd mentality sets in. The riots were reported as being the result of a festering resentment between blacks and Asians. Some newspapers said the blacks were jealous of the Asians' entrepreneurial success in the area, while others reported how the Asians looked down on the blacks as subhuman. In a few cases this might be true, but a riot, so spontaneous and unpredictable, can happen with many fewer conditions behind it.

This model also leaves out a component of the resentment, perhaps for fear of painting a picture that could be portrayed as racist. Many of the rioters that were arrested for attempted murders and other serious offences after the riots were gang members. It is said that the black gangs put aside their differences for the riots, in order to get on with attacking the Asian community. Certainly, gang-involved youths were at the forefront of certain violent incidents. This was because the resentment towards the Asians' success in Birmingham extended into the criminals within the community.

One policeman said: 'In a way, the Lozells riots were born of the success we had in dealing with the Johnsons and Burgers. We had done a huge amount of work and had masses of intelligence on black gangs in the city. The fact that we were so successful probably made them feel like the Asian criminals were getting away with it. And if I'm honest, they were.'

SIX

From Brick Lane to Bradford

Now I know you've got some sort of romantic notion about
crime . . . I bet you wish I was a bank robber, something
glamorous like that. At the heavy like some sort of modern-day
Robin Hood. But it wasn't like that. You see, crime, well what
I did, it was just business with the gloves off.

Jake Arnott, *The Long Firm*

The area around Brick Lane is the very epitome of an interstitial
zone: for centuries successive races of immigrants have made it their
home. The area saw anti-Irish riots in the eighteenth century, fuelled
by builders who believed the Irish immigrants were undercutting
them. In the late nineteenth century, East European Jews began to
arrive in the area after large-scale anti-Jewish pogroms across
Imperial Russia. Some only passed through the area on their way to
America; many stayed.

It has a vibrant culture – many different traders, artisans, entrepreneurs and criminals have passed through it. Prior to the 1960s,
this was the dockers' area, overrun with racketeers from across the
globe, and the subsequent crime they brought with them; the
all-night clubs were full of prostitutes, pimps and other ne'er-do-
wells.

This was still a tightly knit community, whose decline commenced with the decade-long demise of the timber and furniture industries during the 1960s, which resulted in the loss of over 26,000 jobs. In the same decade 40,000 jobs were lost in London's clothing and footwear industries, which were centred on the East End, while new handling measures reduced the need for manual labourers on the docks. By 1971 the Port of London's workforce had shrunk to 6,000.

As Professor Dick Hobbs has described the place: 'There was a real vibrancy in Spitalfields in the 1960s. Working-class neighbourhoods, social dereliction, upwardly mobile villainy and elite manual labour were wedged tight against the pervading power of the City of London . . . Some streets hung on to a semblance of proletarian respectability, as working-class families attempted to establish themselves in direct opposition . . . to the legal and illegal clubs and spielers that were long-established features of the area.'[1]

It is in this context that the growth of the immigrant population from Bangladesh must be seen. By the 1970s the streets around Brick Lane were full of Bengalis. There was an influx of curry houses, fabric stores and factories. However, while the ethnic culture changed, it remained a violent place. The National Front set up its headquarters on Great Eastern Street in an attempt to exacerbate the area's tensions following the murder of a Bengali man. This was a time of great tension – of children being allowed out of school early, of women arriving to work in groups for fear of being ambushed, of flaming rags being forced through letter boxes and regular clashes between the gangs of Bengali youths and the NF.

By 2002, in recognition of the Bengalis' preponderance in the area, it was dubbed 'Banglatown': its lampposts are the colour of Bangladesh's flag; the street signs are in Bengali. Already the signs are that the ever-increasing gap between rich and poor in the capital will eventually push away the last remaining interstitial zone in the centre of London. For several decades Brick Lane itself has been charmingly incongruous as the border between the immense wealth and shining, steely prestige of the City and the scruffy poverty of the Tower Hamlets estates beyond it. One day this border will no longer be required. The area has already become infamous for its trendiness – the media workers and artists have bought into the shabby urban chic of the place, while the transport links to Canary Wharf, its skeletal metal and glass shadows looming over the entire area, has meant that an influx of luxury flats is being filled with money men.

This is the Spitalfields of today. The area's history has been subsumed into redeveloped dockyard warehouse flats and the like; the streets around it are bustling with rich and poor. And it is this juxtaposition of immense wealth and the high levels of unemployment within the Bengali community that makes Brick Lane and its environs perhaps the strangest Gangland of all. Commentators such as Professor Hobbs see these gang members as being little different to the delinquent youths of the 1960s: '. . . the key to understanding East End delinquency has always been its ever fluctuating economic fortunes, and the impact that these changes have had [on the] population'. Hobbs sees deviant activity as an integral part of these local conditions, citing: 'thriving illegal gambling clubs fading with the introduction of the 1960 Gaming Act, and a booming local hijacking trade disappearing with the queues of lorries that no longer lined Commercial Street'.[2]

There are threats all around the area's youth. Good-looking American women are dispatched there as a lure to recruit them into militant evangelical Christianity: they claim that a dislike of Israel, which by extension must mean the Jewish race, is common ground. Various forms of racism still make occasional forays into the area: one night while I was there I saw a group of thugs striding down Brick Lane, attempting to start fights with the curry vendors. I waited to see what would happen: the police arrived just before a group of Bengali youths, who scuttled back into the surrounding estates when they saw them. Of all these threats, the road to criminality is just another one.

Thus far, the gang members in this book have been either a mixture of ethnicities (in Waltham Forest and the suburbs), or predominantly black (in the case of Hackney, south London and Birmingham). In this chapter, they are Asian. This is a crude division along ethnic lines, but it is made in order to show the homogeneity of the street-gang phenomenon.

The situation we find among Asian communities is in many ways similar to those we have observed in previous chapters. Contrary to popular perceptions, the violence is still very real. The *Evening Standard* reported on a terrifying gang battle in 2003, when the Drummond Street Boys (a Camden gang) were ambushed by the Brick Lane Massive. For weeks they had been kidnapping youths from Brick Lane and beating them up back in Camden. When they realized they had walked into a trap, they turned heel and fled. The chase, involving more than 50 youths, ranged up Brick Lane, along Bethnal Green Road and Shoreditch High Street and into Great Eastern Street, prompting more than twenty 999 calls to police. Once in Great Eastern Street, a full-scale street fight got under way after the Drummond Street Boys' vehicle was forced off the road.

When the police arrived there were arrests and several were taken to hospital. Those who remained dumped their weapons and scattered.[3] Another battle occurred in 2005 when three members of the Drummond Street Boys were handed over 400 hours of community punishment orders after a gang fight in Shoreditch with the East Boys of Bethnal Green. Over a dozen people were involved in a brawl in which samurai swords, metal bars and hockey sticks were used.

In the light of what we have learned so far, it is unsurprising that these are not battles between organized criminal groups. They are

born of territorial rivalries between groups of young men, of antagonisms between individuals that pull in others: the chances are that
the members of the gangs which fought each other in those reports
have fallen out themselves and that those collectives are no more. A
survey of the Bengali gangs around the Tower Hamlets area would
reveal a large number of different territories: Globe Town, Vallance
Road, Brick Lane, Cannon Street, Brady Street, Bow, Stepney Green
and Turin Street as the most well-defined.

Within this area, Brick Lane Massive, Cannon Street Posse and
other gang names are simply labels that young men call upon to
show the passionate relationship with place that is the hallmark of
the gang member. And in these territories there is the same fluidity
as we have seen everywhere else. As elsewhere it is the ideal of the
gang that is more solid than the gang itself – I met two young men
who claimed to be members of the Brick Lane Massive who came
from Hanwell. As always, the gangs are an articulation of the need
to help friends against their enemies and to scare one's foes.

Dr Claire Alexander's excellent sociological account of her time
as a youth worker with a group of Bengali youths, *The Asian Gang*,
talks about their relationship with other peer groups in great depth.[4]
Her subjects talk about the reputation of their estate, but the internal boundaries of this and the rules of engagement with other groups
are complex: 'Peer group identities became at once a source of
engagement and expulsion, often shifting status at a dizzying
pace . . . For the younger group this revolved primarily around
family members in other parts of London . . . whereas the older lot
had a more extensive network of friends and foes from all over
London and all Asian groups.'[5] As in the earlier chapters, allegiances
are mostly predicated around bloodlines and geographical territories.
Dr Alexander's book also covers a period in 1996 when the Bengalis
on the estate had a series of fierce battles against local black youths.
One of the catalysts was a falling out between two individuals – one

black, one Bengali – at the local school. The way the gangs that fought were formed is telling:

> Humzah: We started giving names, just as a joke . . . it was BBB, one was – that was the older ones gave that and we carried it though.
> Claire: What did it mean?
> Humzah: (laughing) Bengali Bad Boys! . . . I remember boys used to come and they're asking about the BBB and we're like, 'how do you know about the BBB, we were just talking about it ourselves.'[6]

As in places such as Hackney and Brixton, the broad picture fits the Hallsworth/Young model described in Chapter 1: there are peer groups, which feed into street gangs, which feed into organized criminal gangs, and a great many overlaps between these three distinctions.

I meet Rana and Mohammed near a park in Bethnal Green. In their appearance they are like so many of the young men who make up the street gangs in this area. Both of them have slicked-back hair, and designer labels different to those worn by other groups: their trousers are tight, their jackets not Nike or Fubu but Ted Baker or Calvin Klein. Their mobiles are constantly ringing, with loud R&B ringtones. They deal, usually in small amounts – usually 0.6 of a gram of heroin at a time. They are typical of the Bangladeshi boys in this area who would not dream of accepting the jobs their grandfathers took, who are angered every time they venture past Brick Lane into the cold wealth around Liverpool Street station.

Rana is the most talkative, touching his carefully crafted goatee as he speaks: 'I guess the main reason I spent so much time on the street when I was young is 'cos my home's so shit. It's like – I'm one of six, the second oldest, and we had two and a half rooms between us when we were growing up. I just used to roll round here because it meant my little brothers weren't in my face.'

The situation he describes is not uncommon – the problem of overcrowding due to the typically large size of many Bengali families is a very specific one in this community.

Mohammed speaks next: 'I got into it because of my brother . . . he was in BLM (Brick Lane Massive), but he's inside now. He knows the guy who I get my supply from. It's just a buzz most of the time, innit – making money, knowing your crew'll support you.'

The more time you spend with them, the fewer differences you see between them and the gang-involved youths in any other area. There is resentment at friends of theirs who have done well at school and moved on. Their talk is mostly of beef, and the beef is always over very little – a boy from Globe Town was recently seen with a girl who they consider 'one of theirs' and it nearly kicked off, but for the fact that the police were coming around the corner. The amount of money they make is dubious. Rana says that he only need sell five bags of heroin a day to make a good monthly salary. However, the more we chat, the more a picture emerges of it being difficult to make this money consistently – there is a fear of drawing too much attention to yourself, of getting caught. Criminal enterprise, here, seems to be just something else to do, along with hanging around and wolf-whistling at any girls that pass by, and fighting anyone who wants to fight.

They inhabit the same cognitive landscape described in previous chapters, seeing very little beyond this lifestyle and this area. Neither of them has any qualifications, and they see little point in attempting to find work. They talk with the same contempt as any other gang members of the police, who they see as racist, unfair and ineffectual. They talk of overzealous, violent arrests, and about how there was a huge increase in stop and searches a couple of years ago because a senior officer had visited the area and some youths had abused him. Whether or not all this is true is perhaps not the point: it is the perception that matters. They detest the local council, who

JOHN HEALE

they feel have not done enough to address the issue of housing provision, or to provide any kind of meaningful youth service: they have
both passed through probation teams and youth workers, and little
change has been effected.

There is the same ghettoization of the mind that we see in other
areas: at one point Rana says to me: 'They do nothing around here,
and spend billions on a war – I could become a terrorist, that would
fucking show them. I see those cunts come to Brick Lane from Essex
on a Friday night and give the waiters shit, the guys who are on fuck
all despite all that hard work. I'd fucking stab them all if I could.'
The statement about terrorism is not meant seriously: it is a
common line that these youths fire out to me, mindful that it carries a specific charge; that it serves to underline their detachment
from the mainstream.

When I ask them how their lives have changed in recent years,
there is an instant answer: drugs. They are finding it easier to get
hold of drugs than before, and were recently involved in a battle with
some youths in Stepney – not because of petty territorialism, but
because they were taking their customers. They are moving up a
familiar ladder of criminality.

One day, they will become like Aftab. He is the equivalent of a Face
or Elder in previous chapters. His lifestyle has no hanging around on
street corners, no pointless fights. He is a businessman. And he is not
impressed with my project.

'The thing you fail to understand, my friend, is that 90 per cent
of these boys are just lazy. You can talk about poverty and all the
rest of it, but ultimately they make their choices, like I made
mine.'

'Do you think the boys round here are more lazy than most
middle-class boys?'

'No.'

'So how come they're the ones beating each other up and dealing drugs?'

'Because . . . I dunno, there's something in them . . . they don't dare to dream.'

Earlier, Aftab told me his story.

'The funny thing was – and this isn't unusual – is that my dad was fucking strict. That was why I spent so much time out on the street. I never got on at school, and I don't think he knew what I was doing. For a few years he actually thought I had a job. By the time he knew what was going on – my first arrest – he was too old, and too sad, to do anything. In my day it was all dealing, but low level. I'd do most of it on the bus – it's easy to get away and you can see everything that's coming. These days it's all on the street, in safe houses, in hired cars. There were fights, but mostly it was just knives. A gun was two grand back in the day. It's changed. More of the boys are carrying straps. I was one of the first to get a gun, and I remember the buzz. I used to watch a lot of *Rambo* films. I just felt so much more powerful with it. Used to keep it in my trousers when we went out to bars and restaurants . . . looking back I'm amazed I didn't blow my dick off.

'The fights back then were the same as now – one person angering another one, and then everyone gets involved. I guess there's a slight difference in this community compared to say, the black one – and that's the family structure. Most of the kids have family units, and that can have all sorts of different effects. In many cases, it keeps the kids out of it. You'd be surprised at the trials a lot of the kids go through to keep things secret from the parents. They'll go and do shit in other parts of town – head all the way to Hendon or wherever. There are several families around – in Brick Lane, Cannon Street, Stepney – and everyone in the family is involved. Daddy might import, older brother manages, you see the drill? The thing is that blood ties mean a lot here.

'A guy will always support his brother, so if he's in a crew, the chances are you are too. These days, I have nothing to do with that silliness. I'm too old, and I don't need that support. I'm a business-man. It's just that sometimes the business I carry out isn't always legal. I don't see a problem with it . . . it happens everywhere: there are more than enough rich white guys dodging taxes and costing the country a lot more than I do.

'That thing about the families – it's important. I mean, every bit of progress I've made in my life has been down to my older brother. He was the one who I joined the gang for. He was the one who always had my back, and I always had his. But he's got a very keen business mind, my bro. He was the one introduced me to the bent surveyor who undervalued the house I bought a few years ago. He's very good at finding people in the community who'll play the game. There's a restaurant nearby that my bro invested drugs money in. Let me put it this way – it wasn't worth shit when he gave them the money, and now it looks fucking swanky, and it's doing very well for itself. Not only do we clean our money, but we'll make a return. What we've picked up on is the business skills of our fathers and just shifted them a bit.

'Some crews are organized – there might be up to four tiers within these gangs, usually generational levels. Sometimes you find that the older brothers and cousins are in one tier and they have got their younger siblings working for them. That is where a lot of the loyalty within Bengali gangs stems from. If the brothers are in the same tier, i.e. around the same age, they will branch out, so nobody is stepping on anyone's toes. The older guys will keep a careful count of how many wraps they're giving to the younger ones: they'll keep a care-ful count of exactly how much they're making.

'Guess on the whole we've got more business sense than black dealers . . . with those guys, it's kind of like they watched *Scarface* but fell asleep before the end. And what's the ultimate lesson from that film? Don't get high off your supply. I reckon they do that too much for a start.

'I've been dealing for ten years. Now I deal in clubs in Mayfair more than anywhere else. I've sold to everyone – bankers, celebrities. I'll work with anyone now – there's some Eastern European guys I met who are dealing in jewellery, some white boys I know south who are selling flake cocaine. There was a prostitution racket going big time round here, but I don't get involved in that any more.

'I don't think anything's going to change round here. It's like *Blade Runner*. Just watch that film. Gang members can't change what they do. And you can't change them.'

The drugs trade in east London is thriving, perhaps more so than anywhere else. The import and export business provides a perfect front to bring drugs into the country. One of the most high-profile cases came in 2006, when the chairman of a company that supplied spices to curry houses in the UK was arrested in Bangladesh on suspicion of trafficking hundreds of kilos of heroin in the previous fifteen years. Customs were alerted after £10 million worth of the drug was found unclaimed at Southampton and Felixstowe. The High Commission requested that the Bangladeshi Government establish a committee to investigate. The arrest shocked the business community: the company employed 3,000 staff around the world. The case gives a clear indication of exactly how well crime can pay, even to those who are successful within more conventional enterprise.

In another case in 2001 police managed to break down an operation that was worth around £12 million. The head of the gang was Shamshad Ahmed, 28, who organized a network of twenty foot-soldiers to peddle drugs to addicts in several east London boroughs. Ahmed, a married father-of-one who lived at home with his father and mother, earned the loyalty of his dealers by paying them rewards and bonuses which could double their weekly salary of £300. They were also given the use of expensive hire cars, mobile phones and expense accounts which meant they were reimbursed for petrol, drinks and meals. Ahmed had at least two dealers working shifts to receive orders at all times. Those who made four purchases would receive a fifth free, and customers were given an extra £20 deal for bringing new business. Hundreds of cards advertising AKS Licensed Mini Cabs were printed which gave the dealers' mobile-phone numbers. These would then be offered to prostitutes and drugs users in the area. Dealers met customers via prior arrangement; they carried rocks of crack or wraps of heroin in their mouths which could be swallowed in case they were arrested. There was a complicated money-laundering side to the operation that involved the use of playing cards as code and which meant money could be transferred to Bangladesh without leaving the country.

Fascinating though they are, cases such as these do not give a true representation of Bengali street gangs in the area. For the most part the gangs are as chaotic as elsewhere, while Asian heroin dealers form only one part of the picture. Much of the heroin in the UK originates from Afghanistan, and could pass through any number of traders on its way here. A great deal of it travels through Russia and former Soviet states. Likewise, in 2000 the British Crime Survey found 26 per cent of white people in the 16 to 29 age group said they had used illegal drugs in the last year. The figure for Pakistanis and Bangladeshis of the same age was 8 per cent.

There are some differences between Asian gangs and those described in earlier chapters, however. On the whole, Aftab is right when he says a brother or older family relative who is involved in crime appears more likely to be supported by his siblings in these areas. Due to the fact that there are fewer tiers to the supply chain than in previous chapters, the relation between gangs and the drug trade is closer. It is easier for gang members to become involved in what is a more organized criminal venture. For the time being battles between youths with those from other areas is a separate phenomenon from the drugs trade (apart from the fact that those who fight may well be involved in both), but anecdotal evidence suggests that disagreements over drugs are becoming more common.

And at the same time, the organization of the community elders gives a degree of stability. Looking at the young gang members, it appears that while many feel estranged from their families, they often impose a brake on their behaviour. And Rana and Mohammed speak with warmth of their mosque, and of an imam there who listens to and understands their problems. Aftab tells me about a group of influential ex-criminals in the area who have gone straight. He has his pet name for them, a Bangladeshi word. If a youth is in trouble, he can approach them, and seek their protection. He must renounce his ways: if he turns back to crime, their protection is void. However, security they provide is absolute: any gang member who attempts to fight them would be resisted with force; these are men who have it in them to kill, but their names carry such weight that they are rarely, if ever, pressed into violent action.

There are more conventional initiatives within the area. Around ten years ago there was a marked increase in gang conflicts. At one incident there were three or four groups brawling with knives, primarily from Bethnal Green, Poplar and Cannon Street. Many of them were hospitalized. At this point the community initiated a meeting between the gang members. It was held in a mosque, which meant all of the members left their weapons behind. AASHA, a gang-mediation team, was formed out of that meeting. The main workers were leaders from those warring groups: they formed an informal network across Tower Hamlets. They were seen as individual, impartial, and had street credibility. They established an outreach team, keeping in touch with the main players. Soon Tower Hamlets Council copied the initiative, creating a Rapid Response Team along the same lines. This put AASHA under pressure as its funders wanted to know what value it could add, and so it began to concentrate on intervention, on stopping people becoming gang members in the first place.

Ultimately, the gangs may not be destroyed by any initiatives, but by the simple economics that imperil their habitat. As Professor Hobbs has demonstrated, the local youths are exposed to the extremes of the housing market in an area where just 28 per cent own their own homes; an area that has seen a property boom in the wake of London's successful bid for the 2012 Olympics. As he puts it: 'Despite the deluge of wealth that has flooded the area, opportunities to engage with the local economy are probably more restricted now than they were forty years ago.'[7]

Sukhdev Sandu made a similar point about the gang members in the *London Review of Books*:

These kid-warriors may not have much, but they have always had their estates. Nowadays, as they roam around, treating Brick Lane and its surrounding streets as military zones to be occupied and fortified, territories worth annexing, anxiety and resentment are in the air. Nobody is exactly trying to winch them out of these estates. But denied the resources that might allow them to work their way out, watching the area become a playground for a leisure-rich salariat, and seeing their own status as the newest immigrants supplanted by Somalis and the new wave of white settlers from Russia, Kosovo and Lithuania, these Bangladeshis are finding themselves slowly, subtly estranged from the ghetto they called home. Walk around and you will notice that the sari stores have become designer furniture shops, the dress factories art galleries. Bangladeshis may be wilting into history.[8]

The bad headlines about Asian gangs began to spring up in the 1990s, when a series of riots and high-profile gang battles across the country produced a number of reports about a traditionalist Muslim community's younger generation struggling to integrate under the weight of working-class life in modern Britain. However, in Southall, ten and a half miles to the west of London's centre, we find much the same phenomenon among a population that is mostly Punjabi and which contains a mixture of Sikhs and Muslims. Southall is a relatively small south Asian community that settled fifty years ago, when a British businessman hired large numbers of Punjabi Sikhs to work in his rubber factory. However, it is densely populated, and the atmosphere here is very much that of an Indian city: the smell of spices, the 'Welcome' signs in English and Punjabi when you leave the train station, the strings of lights along South Road that lead to the centre, where it joins the Broadway. There are sari stalls, chefs preparing food in the open air, and all sorts of other small businesses in every nook and cranny.

The original two gangs there, the Holy Smokes and the Tooti Nuns, were formed out of fights with the National Front. As in Brick Lane, these groups shifted into criminality as the Thatcher years began to bite. They began to get involved in protection, VAT scams, credit-card and passport fraud, and smuggling. Through family ties, they were able to bring heroin and cocaine into the country. There was plenty of friction and violence between the two – again, the battles did not serve any kind of economic purpose.

Most of the main players moved away, or became fully fledged drug dealers. As in Hackney and Tottenham, or Handsworth and Aston, these battles between a few dangerous characters started to take on a territorial aspect that had not been a crucial part of the original conflict: again, residence and affiliation became the same. The Tooti Nuns' territory was New Southall; the Holy Smokes were based in Old Southall. Again, the battle changed from one between two groups to individuals, sometimes from the same gangs. In the midst of this chaos, two new groups in particular rose to the top in terms of power and influence: the Bhatts, formerly Holy Smokes, and the Kanaks, formerly Tooti Nuns. Rivalry led to drive-by shootings, pub bombings and beatings.

The Bhatts were controlled by two brothers with a string of business interests and an opulent lifestyle including the ownership of a popular west London restaurant. They were called Sukhdev and Rajinder Bassi. Their street gang were called the Fiat Bravo Boys – named after the nondescript cars they drove to avoid police attention. This rivalry reached a high point when the Kanaks gave one of them a vicious beating. A few days later, an attempted drive-by shooting of a Kanak gang member was followed by the nail bombing of a local pub, The Lady Margaret. The following day a car dealer was executed in a local restaurant by one of the Bassi gang.

In 2003 the Bassi brothers were finally jailed. A member of their family, Jaspal Bassi, turned informant after police raided his home in November 2001 and found £89,000 worth of heroin in a rucksack. By the time the Bassis had been arrested, they had flooded the area with around £17 million worth of heroin. In total, the brothers and their two co-defendants were tried on sixteen different gun and drug-related charges.

It would, of course, be too simple to suggest that this left the Kanaks in control of the area; the opportunistic and untidy world of criminal endeavour is not simple enough for that. New tensions have emerged. In 2003 a 21-year-old Sikh was killed and several others injured in a brawl between two groups. Thirty officers and a dog unit had been called to quell the gang warfare. As soon as the police cars reached the spot, the warring crowd vanished. The officers found Balkaran Singh lying on the ground with several stab wounds. Two others, a 17-year-old and a 24-year-old, were also stabbed. The three were taken to the nearby Ealing Hospital, where Balkaran was pronounced dead.

A local who related the history of the area to me said: 'It's this simple. Half the kids here will become doctors and lawyers. The other half will become a part of the drugs distribution chain. They can make a wrong decision, early in life, and it's very hard to go back.' He himself had just finished serving time in jail for a crime that was actually committed by a friend who is a member of one of these gangs. Prior to his arrest he had held down a respectable job in the City; another little reminder of the problems of living in an interstitial area, and the difficult gap between gang and non-gang within it.

Another Asian community that has received a great deal of attention is in Bradford. There were reports that the riots there in 2001 were an excuse among the drug gangs to attack the police, and in 2002 Ann Cryer, MP for Keighley and Ilkley, allegedly said that Asian estates in the city were rife with drugs. There had been recent fights between groups of young Asians, which left four dead in the space of six months. The last to die, 24-year-old Qadir Ahmed, was beaten and stabbed to death in the street after his killers shunted his car off the road as he drove home from a football match.

National newspapers visited the city to report on a place that was being dubbed the country's 'heroin hub'. One paper interviewed a drug dealer who could make £200 a night, and described the organized tiers of the drugs gangs, which it called 'runners', 'street dealers' and 'the murky upper echelons of the gang world'. It described a 'conspiracy of silence' hanging over the city's Asian drug problem. It said: 'From within the community few are willing to speak out, while outsiders – such as outspoken Keighley MP Ann Cryer – are castigated as damaging race relations.'[9]

The first point which needs to be addressed is the conflation of gangs with the drugs trade. As we have seen, it is an oversimplification of a complex relationship, similar to that of black gangs and gun crime, and it is commonly made with regard to Asian gangs. People who are likely to offend are more likely to be in a gang, but it does not mean that the gangs exist solely because of the drugs trade. In fact, a tour around Manningham, to the north of the city centre, reveals yet another interstitial area – one of historical poverty and disorganization. Within it, as in previous chapters, there are youths that organize themselves into groups, some of whom are participants in an informal economy. But to trace the problems that the media described down to heroin alone is misleading. If ever there was evidence of the fact that the gangs are symptoms of wider social problems, it lies with the riots in 2001.

As in Birmingham, riots, like gangs, are born of one of the most common attributes of an interstitial area: young men hanging around them with little to do, in search of any sort of group direction and unification. Tensions rose after the far right attempted to organize a march in the city which was banned by Bradford Council. The Anti-Nazi League organized a counter-march which was allowed to proceed. During the course of the march, a rumour was spread by some of the marchers that National Front sympathizers were gathering at a pub in the centre of Bradford. A confrontation then occurred outside the pub during which a Pakistani man was stabbed, and the riot was initiated. Many of the individuals concerned voluntarily gave themselves up to the police, but were awarded harsh sentences. Again, street gangs and riots are a similar problem, a manifestation of a disordered youth attempting to organize itself.

The notion of Bradford as a heroin hub is not completely inaccurate. There have certainly been a number of large drugs busts made there in the last few years. Drugs that traditionally enter the north of Britain come by boat into Hull and by air into Manchester

Airport: they can then be transported from Bradford down the M1. But this does not make Bradford 'the' hub – it is 'a' hub, one of several. Another well-known focal point is Birmingham (via its airport), and this time the route the drugs often take is north, to Scotland, a path followed by so many different castes and creeds that one gang member described it to me as, 'like a UN operation'. Again, it is the opportunistic nature of crime which must be stressed; there is no doubt that large shipments of drugs pass through Bradford, but it is hardly the only city in the country in that regard.

When you spend time talking to people within the community, you realize the street gangs are nothing special either, nor do they have any special hold over it. It is, as always, a minority who are heavily involved in the core of the gangs, and as always they are a risk to other youths in the community, pulling them into their ways, which often – though not always – involve the sale of drugs. The concept of 'Asian Drugs Gangs' has been formulated the wrong way round: youths form gangs, which may then give coherency to the act of drug dealing. And as always, the 'conspiracy of silence' is the same problem as elsewhere: these individuals are still members of the community – someone's son or brother – and as such this is a problem that it would rather deal with itself. There seems little evidence that the dealers in Bradford are in any way more successful than those elsewhere, or that their violence is any less random than that elsewhere.

One community figure said: 'Drugs is nothing new. The heroin has been brought here for decades, primarily by individuals in the Pathan community. But it's about the choices made by individuals, which reflect back on the entire community. I know one man from here who lives in London – in Hanover Square – he's made millions in drugs. Yet his son works in a factory up the road, and refuses to have any part in it. You will find a gang of fifteen kids, of whom one might be into drugs. And if these kids were making the money the papers make out, they wouldn't be selling little bags of heroin on the street. There are large-scale heroin importers, but there are also many people involved in the trade in this city who are white. Most of the bad Asian money comes from VAT scams. The trouble is that there's been a conflation between the importers and the kids in the minds of the police that isn't really there.'

Other community figures had negative feelings about the way the authorities dealt with the riots. One claimed: 'I think you saw that in the police's behaviour during the riots. The white racists were in all the pubs, provoking the demonstrators, who were having a peaceful march. There were twenty or thirty police horses and a load of vans: I could tell something was going to happen, and told my sister to take my kids home. The police encircled the demonstrators and marched them through the streets like cattle, while the racists were jeering at them, inflaming things further. If that isn't provocation I don't know what is. Then there were the newspaper men, who were offering hundreds of pounds to kids if they'd pose throwing objects. It was a despicable day, and there has been no justice. A lot of the kids handed themselves in voluntarily, and received very harsh sentences indeed.'

As in Brick Lane, the street gangs and the organized criminals have been lumped together as one and the same. Furthermore, there is a developing myth of an insidious, secretive community that is afraid to reveal its problems to the wider world. Stories about the exploits of the most prolific Asian criminals and the ways in which they tap into the traditional Asian economy help to propagate the generalisation that Asian gangs are in some way more cunning and secretive than their black or white counterparts.

One might take the case of the Bradford Travel Agency, reported in 2007. Here Revenue & Customs officers uncovered a huge criminal operation that laundered at least £500 million of criminal assets between 1997 and 2001. Couriers collected hundreds of thousands of pounds each day from drug gangs in London, Manchester, Liverpool, West Yorkshire and Scotland, Leeds Crown Court was told. They delivered the cash to *hawala* brokers based at travel agents in Bradford, Birmingham and Halifax.

In Urdu *hawala* means 'reference': a *hawala* broker in Britain collects cash and instructs a counterpart in the recipient's home country to pay out the money in the local currency. Few records are kept of where the money comes from; rather there is a running total of debts between the brokers that is settled later with cash, gold or consumer goods. A case such as this can cast a bad light on practices within a community, when in fact the point should be that criminals from any area will find opportunities to exploit any system they can find. Now the *hawala* system has found itself called into question.

In the same way *mujra* performances (a traditional Indian dance put on by women that takes place in Asian communities after hours) have been presented as a tool for the purposes of sex trafficking, in stories which suggest an 'otherness' about how Asian criminals operate. One paper reported on it in 2003, under the headline 'Revealed: Bollywood craze that is fuelling London's vice rackets'.[10] It told of the murder of Tahir Butt, a man found beaten and strangled in a country lane in Hertfordshire. He was 'heavily involved in the mujra scene', but the story concluded: 'Ultimately his death turned out to be unconnected to mujra. The married father-of-two was murdered on the orders of his long-term lover who had grown tired of him and fallen for someone new. But the information gathered about mujra during the course of the investigation has been fed back to the Specialist Crime desk and is adding to concerns about the growth of Asian organized crime.'

Finally, it is worth mentioning one incident that had a huge part to play in enforcing all sorts of negative perceptions of Asian criminality, most importantly in terms of its estrangement from other ethnicities: the murder of Kriss Donald. On 16 March 2004, the fifteen-year-old was abducted from Pollokshields, in Glasgow. The gang who kidnapped him took him on a 200-mile journey to Dundee and back while they made phone calls looking for a house to which they could take him. Having no success at this, they returned to Glasgow and took him to the Clyde Walkway, near Celtic Football Club's training ground. There, they held his arms and stabbed him thirteen times. He sustained internal injuries to three arteries, one of his lungs, his liver and a kidney. He was then doused in petrol, set on fire and left to die. He attempted to roll around to douse the flames but was found dead the next morning. The killers fled to Pakistan and were only extradited thanks to the intervention of a local MP. Three men were convicted of his murder.

It is a barbaric and inhumane case that was certain to stir up all sorts of tensions – and it was made all the worse by the fact that it appeared to have been racially motivated. According to one version of events, one of the killers, Imran Shahid, had been hit with a bottle in a Glasgow nightclub the evening before, and had simply selected a white person from the area in order to exact his revenge. Right-wing extremists quickly jumped on the case, citing the lack of coverage it had received in comparison with that of Stephen Lawrence. At the same time, Shahid had stated that he wanted to find the 'white bastards' who injured his pride. The suggestion remains, however, that race was a subsidiary issue. Donald was in fact a friend of the person Shahid was seeking. Interestingly, Donald's mother had appealed for calm, saying: 'It doesn't matter to my family what colour these men are. Kriss is gone because of gangs, not just in Pollokshields but every area of our communities.' The gangs of Glasgow are too large and divergent a phenomenon to deal with in this book, but the fact remains that Kriss Donald's murder did more to the perception of Asian crime than a hundred drugs busts.

*

All of this brings us back to Birmingham. For it's not just within the media that a conception of Asian criminals as being in some way cleverer, more detached and more subtle than other gangs can take hold. While the causes of a riot are generally complex and the result of a multitude of factors, those who are to be found at the core of one deviant behavioural pattern are often to be found at the core of another. As mentioned previously, there were a number of black criminals in the area who felt their Asian counterparts were getting away with crime in comparison to them. In some cases they were, but the reasons were not down to any particular craftiness on their part or racial prejudice on that of the police. It was down to the fact that the scale of the investigation into the New Year's murders had produced an unprecedented amount of intelligence on them.

The riots left divisions within the community between Asian and black, and no more so than among those involved in criminal activity. One Handsworth gang member said: 'They do what we do at a much higher level. I've heard one of them talking to his mates, and saying that all he needs is ten customers a day to make £600. I guess we get into fights because there's a lot of hype . . . but the Asians . . . they're sneaky.'

This brief analysis of Asian gangs has shown that if they differ from other ethnicities, it is only noticeable in that there can be fewer tiers to the drugs chain, which puts a slightly greater emphasis on dealing drugs at a street level. In terms of territorialism, the structure of their gangs, the types of people who become gang members, their relationship to the community and the reasons for which violence happens, there is little difference. The only noticeable difference is in the lack of gun crime. One theory is that the low amount of gun crime among the gangs is down to a greater community *organization*, both positive and negative. This theory would argue that the protective structure offered by two-parent families imposes a ceiling on the young gang members' behaviour, while the fact that there is less point in robbing other gang members when there are more opportunities to deal drugs means that the Asian community suffers less than the black one in this regard. This theory may be true, but these protective factors are ebbing away across all communities, as we shall see in the next chapter.

SEVEN

Manchester

The police came, of course, but discovered nothing. Their
inquiries were met by stares. But the tale spread quickly from
mouth to mouth, was deliberately spread amongst us, was
given to everyone, man and child, that we might learn each
detail and hide it. The police left at last with the case unsolved:
but neither we nor they forgot it . . .

Laurie Lee, *Cider with Rosie*

A Home Office study of south Manchester revealed that in 150 separate shooting incidents between 1997 and 2000, only one witness
came forward to testify.[1] Manchester is little different to London or
Birmingham: it has its interstitial zones, within which we are dealing with both criminal enterprise and the way in which a large
section of the urban youth perceives itself. The gap between the two
phenomena has always been difficult to define, and if we are to
believe the voice of the community, it is becoming smaller. We
should begin with the received picture of the city's gangs.

The gangs first came to prominence in the 1980s. The first division was between the mixed gangs of Cheetham Hill in the north
and Moss Side in the south. Soon, another split took place.
Alexandra Road, which divided the small estate of Alexandra Park

in the south of the city between east and west, suddenly became a territorial line. The youths on the west side later became known as the Gooch Close Gang. They carried on dealing with Cheetham Hill, and began to war with the Pepperhill Mob on the other side of the road. After the Pepperhill pub (where the latter crew was formed) had closed down, they became known as the Doddington Gang.

It was alleged that in 1994 a truce was called between the warring gangs. In 1995 the murder of Raymond Pitt meant it broke down. Pitt's younger brother, Tommy Pitt, broke away from Doddington to create the Pitt Bull Crew, while Julian Bell created the Longsight Crew in the area of the same name, to the east of Moss Side. Conflicts arose between Longsight and Gooch, Longsight and Pitt Bull Crew, Pitt Bull and Doddington and the Doddington and Gooch. Tit-for-tat gang shootings increased dramatically towards the end of the 1990s.

A huge amount of gang activity at the time was centred on the burgeoning club scene within the city. 'Madchester' was based around the new institutions such as the Hacienda, 21 Piccadilly and Konspiracy. The growth of rave brought with it a market for ecstasy dealers. The key lay in controlling the doors: if a gang can take them over, the interior of the club suddenly becomes a safe and lucrative drugs market for its dealers. Many of the violent confrontations were between the rival gangs as they fought for control of these markets.

According to the *Observer* in 2004, today's gangs exist in

the city's 'gang triangle' between Longsight, Moss Side and Hulme [in which they have] fought a bloody battle for control of the city's multi-million-pound drug trade . . .

[A policeman says] Giving the gangs names makes them seem more organised than they actually are. We're not talking about slick criminal organisations – we're talking about kids with guns.

Others disagree. Many of the gangs are said to be highly sophisticated and some have access to private doctors who will treat
gunshot wounds without informing the police.[2]

One of the most prominent recent battles occurred when the
Gooch and Longsight crews clashed at Manchester Royal
Infirmary. According to the *Manchester Evening News*: 'As brave
medical staff tried to protect patients, the gangs hunted each other
through the corridors on foot or mountain bikes. Three members of
each gang threatened rivals with a gun and a hammer before dis-
persing when officers and security arrived. No shots were fired and
no members of the public or staff were hurt.'[3]

As in Birmingham and London, the reality is that this chronology
of the gangs has its basis in truth only if one gives credibility to the
mythologized hierarchies and groupings that are merely muddled
groups of people taking part in undisciplined battles. It is not a picture with which those involved in the events would be familiar; it's
instead an attempt by the media and authorities to impose a structure upon the city's chaotic interstitial areas. The *Observer*
misconceived the nature of the policeman's quote, which implies a
lack of order, not intent or criminal potential. There is no doubt that
the 1980s and 1990s saw the emergence of organized criminal
groups who had interests in the clubs, other drug markets, any illegal opportunities that presented themselves, and who had violent
rivalries with each other. However, as elsewhere, many of these
'gangland executions' were more often than not the result of personal
disputes. In this light the 'truce' and its subsequent breakdown into
what seems like all-out war between the various gangs could be seen
as illusory.

Again, it is hard to say who is 'at the top' of any of the gangs: only
that there are those who are more involved in gangsterism than

others: it is a model for how one chooses to live, and a willingness to support one's peers and fight their enemies. It means that in some cases gang members only come into existence once they have been arrested. In January 2007 *The Times* reported on how a giant billboard had been set up in Moss Side to tell potential witnesses that it was safe to come forward after four of the city's 'most notorious gang members' were jailed for armed robbery. According to the report, 'The poster, to be put up in the heart of a crime-ridden inner-city suburb, will carry photographs of four black "soldiers" for the infamous Gooch gang, blamed for much of the gun violence and drug rivalry in the city in recent years.' The board had pictures of four men: Errol Junior Reynolds, 20, Laine Williams, 22, Paul Dunn, 18, and Reece Ming, eighteen, along with the words: 'These men thought they were untouchable and above the law. They relied on people being too scared to stand up against them . . . they were wrong.'

The report went on to reveal that Reynolds had shot dead Ramone Cumberbatch, 18, 'a member of the rival Doddington mob' in 2005, a fact that could not be reported as it would have prejudiced the robbery trial in which Reynolds was a defendant. *The Times* went on to say: 'It appeared that Cumberbatch's only "offence" had been to stray into Gooch territory. Cumberbatch had only a short time earlier promised the mother of his newborn baby that he would renounce the gang life.'[4]

Many in the community would say that two of the four never claimed to be members of any gang, Gooch or otherwise. As one youth worker put it: 'It's simple: gang member equals top end of the sentence for that crime.' Rather more telling are the details that were not reported. For such 'notorious gang members', they were far from skilled criminals. They had continued to wear all of the clothes that they wore to the robberies afterwards, because they were worth too much to be thrown away. They had driven a Jaguar which they'd bought with cash, and had ended up stuck at a petrol station attempting to fill it up with diesel, such was their haste to get away from one robbery. They had even turned up with the car at a youth club before hanging around with their friends. They looked at a jeweller's shop for four minutes, and then returned with balaclavas on in the same clothes, all caught on CCTV.

Reynolds' story regarding the murder of Ramone Cumberbatch is very different to the notion that he had been killed for straying into opposing territory. Reynolds claimed that he and Cumberbatch had a series of disputes, which led to him threatening him with a gun. Cumberbatch ignored the threat, and walked back into the house. In a fit of rage, Reynolds fired at the house. Unfortunately, the bullet passed through the door and hit Cumberbatch. As a story, it makes a good deal more sense than trying – and succeeding – to assassinate a man by shooting through his front door because he wandered into your territory. This is not to excuse the crimes perpetrated by these individuals. It is merely to show once again that the facts behind the headlines are more complex than the relentless polarization of good and evil that is usually reported.

As elsewhere, the gang image in south Manchester has been sensationalized beyond the point of parody: a September 2007 *Manchester Evening News* story about a 'gang armourer' who 'stockpiled handguns and bullets to supply to members of the Longsight Crew' named Leon Searle-Edwards is illustrated with a picture of him covered in gold jewellery and looking not unlike Mr T.[5] A police raid recovered only two guns in his house, which were in such a bad state that even the prosecutor admitted they were to be used only to cause fear. Due to a gunshot wound he had suffered, at the time of his conviction he was fitted with a colostomy bag and struggling to breathe.

Just as we need to be careful in accepting the media portrayal of gangs, so we should take the authorities' claims of triumph in 'fighting' them with a pinch of salt. For instance, a series of police raids around Moss Side in March 2007 was hailed as a great success, because it resulted in the recovery of two firearms from 300 search warrants. As one youth worker put it: 'I had friends from other parts of Manchester phoning me laughing and saying if they had randomly raided houses in the streets where they live they would have found many more firearms and weapons.' After another attempt at raiding houses without success the police claimed that the gang members were becoming more successful at hiding their weapons, a claim that does not hold a great deal of weight given the success rate of previous attempts.

Moss Side has developed an abysmal reputation over the last twenty years. The area is only a mile from the city centre, just to the west of the busy Oxford Road and the University of Manchester's gleaming halls of residence. There is, like the Ganglands of London, little that is threatening about it. The infamous areas – Gooch Close and Doddington Close – are no more. In their place are newly built red-brick housing. Alexandra Park, just to the south, is surrounded with evergreens and boasts a beautiful pond.

The city's reputation as 'Gunchester' should be kept in perspective. The reported gun-crime figures run thus: in 2003/4 there were 129 discharges, 11 fatalities and 40 injuries. The next year saw 114 discharges, 8 fatalities and 38 injuries. The year after saw 109 discharges, 5 fatalities and 37 injuries. Only 0.03 per cent of reported crimes involve a gun being discharged. However, of these, 40 per cent were in the Metropolitan division, with a concentration in Old Trafford, Hulme and Moss Side.[6]

In fact, the city's real gun-crime hot spot in terms of deaths is not Moss Side, but the more ethnically diverse area of Longsight. The area can be reached by walking down the fast Stockport Road, which heads to the southeast out of the city. Again, the properties off this road are either brand new terraced houses, or are in the process of being built. On one side of the road is Langport Avenue, a tranquil cul-de-sac of red terraced houses where in 2002 Aeon Shirley was shot four times in the back as he ran to a friend's house – described as the Longsight Crew's headquarters in the local press.

Shirley was said to be someone 'not known to the police as a gang member'; the press added he was 'a promising student who fell into bad company'. Across the road there are a number of brand new properties, all arranged in smart little closes and squares, with building going on all around them: this is the Plymouth Grove Estate. A look at the killings in this area shows just how entwined and dangerous the lives of those involved in the core of gangster life can be.

In Frobisher Close, one of these small roads, Tyrone Gilbert, 23, was shot dead on 27 July 2007. He was attending a friend's wake and at around midnight gunmen opened fire on the mourners. Gilbert had moved away from the area in an attempt to leave gang life behind, hoping to spend more time with his children. His death is at the centre of a tragic web of murders in this area. Gilbert had been one of the gang members convicted of affray after the incident at Manchester Royal Infirmary. The wake that he was attending was for Ucal Chin, who had been killed in a drive-by shooting a month before. Just a couple of blocks away, and several years previously, Marcus Greenidge, 21, died after he was shot in the head at close range in Bletchley Close while riding his mountain bike around the estate: he tried to reach for a pistol, but did not manage it in time. Greenidge was heavily involved in the gang life. He was also Tyrone Gilbert's half-brother.

He had been shot by the gangster Thomas Pitt, who had marched into Longsight intent on carrying out a killing spree. That night, Pitt ordered a sixteen-year-old called Thomas Ramsey to move a gun that was hidden in a flat in Longsight. Ramsey forgot. When police searched the flat and found the weapon with Pitt's DNA on it, Pitt was furious, and apparently summoned Ramsey to a meeting behind Levenshulme Baths. Ramsey arrived wearing his black balaclava and a black glove, part of the Pitt Bull uniform. He was shot twice and died within seconds. Pitt was cleared of his murder, but not that of Greenidge. Ramsey had himself been a suspect in a trial a year earlier, after Judah Dewar, 35, had been shot dead at the wheel of his BMW. He was shot in the same road where Marcus Greenidge died.

In Ganglands across the country the same tragic patterns and symmetries between the most highly involved members emerge. While the names of the gangs involved carry huge weight, the core of people involved in the most violent incidents is far smaller and interrelated. As we have seen, the bulk of these take place because of issues of respect. Sometimes they are over women. Again, it is the very disorganization of their criminal endeavours that causes the problem. Many gang members, lacking the acumen or organization to make the kind of money available to those who commit sophisticated crimes such as fraud or high-level drug dealing, resort to mugging and robbery. These crimes, because both perpetrator and victim are known to all, can lead to an escalation of recriminatory violence.

Manchester's gangs, like those of London and Birmingham, are about hype and reputation more than they are about the dealing of drugs. There is no doubt that the Moss Side shopping precinct had seen a great deal of drugs selling in the early 1990s, and that the original Gooch and Pepperhill mobs had been relatively well organized in their distribution, along with their involvement in the lucrative club drugs trade. However, this is not today's situation. It seems that many of the surviving gang members from those days have mostly moved out of town, to places like Bolton, Sheffield and Preston. They still have an involvement, but like Leon in Birmingham, they take opportunities that present themselves: again, it would be more accurate to see them as criminals, irrespective of the gang to which they claim allegiance. The gangs do not have complete control over any territory for open drug markets; if they did, it would be relatively easy for the police to make arrests. England's interstitial areas simply do not suffer from the lawlessness and neglect of their American counterparts. Today's Gooch, Doddington and Longsight gangs are far less organized and membership ranges from the experienced criminal to the disaffected urban youth.

Mark, sixteen, is not a gang member, but he soon could be. One month the police called at his school and told the teachers that they suspected he was a gang member, but they didn't know which gang. He was studying for his GCSEs at the time, and due to the pressure he felt at school after the visit he headed away on holiday to family in the West Indies. While he was away the police raided his house.

Mark claims he has been stopped and searched at least once a week for the past few months. The aforementioned 2007 Home Affairs Select Committee report into black people and the criminal-justice system concluded that they were six times more likely to be stopped-and-searched than white people.[7] Mark has been out with his girlfriend when it happened to him. He found it utterly humiliating, and as he said: 'If they stopped half the students outside the university they'd have a higher arrest rate.'

The Government recently published a response to the Home Affairs Select Committee report. The report said:

'Our witnesses made clear that in some cases, the benefits of stop and search might be outweighed by the negative consequences in terms of the willingness of young people to communicate with and trust the police. Stop and search is not a notably productive means of tackling crime, particularly if done on an uninformed basis. Alternatives to stop and search that might help the police engage better with young people should be considered.'

The Government's response ran: 'We disagree. This Government is committed to the appropriate and proportionate use of this power. While we recognise that the proportion of Stop and Searches leading to arrest may be relatively low, we consider it important that the police continue to have the ability to use Stop and Search powers to enable officers to allay or confirm suspicions about individuals without exercising their powers of arrest.'[8]

It would not be fair to portray the city's police in a wholly negative light. I spoke to a former policeman who had recently retired after working in London and Manchester. He said: 'I don't want to downplay gun crime at all, but the bulk of murders I covered during my time in the city were people [drunken white men] being violently assaulted on a Friday night and sustaining head injuries. When gang violence occurs it's very dramatic, but the high-level stuff where people are shot is relatively sporadic. It is the case that there's an added public interest pressure on us when a gang killing occurs, and it makes witness protection very hard. People within the community will often know who's talking when they read about it, even if that person isn't named.

'I see few differences between any of the forces. There are a lot of good policemen in Manchester, who understand the limits of what they can achieve. Certainly there's a very keen awareness that any kind of zero-tolerance policy has to be followed up with something that's led by the community. I don't think the police goes out of its way to portray a gang situation that isn't there; it's more that the media will ask leading questions which you can't avoid. For instance, I remember giving a statement about the murder of a guy who was a gang member, and the very first question the reporters asked was not anything about the details of the killing, but whether or not he was a drug dealer. And victimhood takes a strange shape in these areas: on a couple of occasions I remember the Crown Prosecution Service asking me whether the victims in cases on which I was working were "good" enough.

'I would say that London differs slightly in that there are a larger number of individuals within the black community who provide a reliable bridge to the authorities when incidents happen. Manchester's black community is relatively small, and there are fewer of these people. It can be frustrating, because it can sometimes feel like the community wants us to provide protection, but it simply doesn't have the trust in us to give us the evidence that we require.. We'll regularly be given information, but not enough on which we can act – anonymous tip-offs can only go so far. Paradoxically, I'd say that some black communities in London have far less trust in the police – it's just that there are more people to provide bridges between us and them when required.'

And on the subject of stop and search, he had this to say: 'The problem is maintaining the balance. Our primary role is protection of life – so if we were to search a kid in the street and find a gun, isn't a hundred searches with no arrests worth it? At the same time, it's obviously an issue for the communities, so we have to tread carefully. If it means they detest us it's always going to be counterproductive. And inevitably, some policemen will get the balance right better than others. I think with this issue you have to understand there's frustration on both sides. However, we are starting to see new recruits going into the area and engaging with the community. I just hope we can keep that up.'

Few people noticed the gang member at the meeting. He looked little different to anyone else. It was only when he stood up to speak that people realized who he was. The forum had been hastily arranged in an African church in Moss Side. There were a number of community figures there – voluntary workers, teachers, youth workers. There were no police or council officers. A teacher had just finished talking. He had lived in Moss Side for thirty years, and said he felt that his role had changed: that teaching at his school was only concerned with academic achievements now; that if he could offer one reason why so many of its boys were involved in gangs, it was because he wasn't able to do his job any more. Another youth worker pointed out that witness protection never worked, because everyone knew who the perpetrators and potential witnesses were long before a case came to court.

Now the unremarkable-looking young black man, his glasses perched on the end of his nose, his clothes a conventional black jacket, white shirt and jeans, took to the stage: 'I wasn't going to talk, but I thought I should. I've been in and out of prison my whole life. What I know is that rehabilitation is a myth. There is no rehabilitation. Prison brutalizes people. Guys go in there and come out a hundred times worse.

'The other thing I know is this. There are dozens of people like me. We can help: because we know who all the people involved are. And we want to help. But time and again, whenever we try to help, it gets thrown back in our faces. Who knows the gang members? Who are the gang members going to listen to – other gang members, or some guy with his suit and tie on?'

He began to shout.

'We can help, and we want to help, and no one's letting us. If you want young boys to stop killing each other, we're the ones who can make it stop. No one here trusts the authorities. I say give us the power to do something, give us the encouragement, and we will. They know who we are. It's not that difficult.'

He stormed back to his seat. After the meeting it became clear that a number of the young men there had been, or still were, involved in the gangs. As in London, the talk among those present was of the Youngers. They spoke of how they were scared of twelve-year-olds who had access to guns, and how they needed to engage with the Elders who were provoking them. One incident that took place in 2006 gave an ominous sign of how the stakes have been raised.

Jessie James was fifteen when he was shot dead in Broadfield Park, Moss Side. He had been hit three times by a semi-automatic pistol as he rode his bike. There is a little tree standing in the park where he was hit, with a poem on a plaque beside it. The spot where he was hit is by Moss Lane, a relatively busy road, with houses around it. He was shot at approximately 1 a.m. on Saturday 9 September 2006. An officer, who was off-duty and suffering from a chest infection, was awoken at 1:19 a.m. by a telephone call from a witness with whom he had been working on a police operation. This witness reported seeing a disturbance in Broadfield Park in which there had been flashes and an individual had been seen to fall to the ground. The officer chose not to act on the information received until 8:30 a.m. The first 999 call about the shooting was made at 2:38 a.m. – approximately 100 minutes after it took place. Greater Manchester Police were on the scene within six minutes following this call.

The Independent Police Complaints Commission (IPCC)'s independent investigation determined that the officer's decision not to act immediately on the information received was a failure of duty. As a result of the findings a recommendation has been made that Officer 'A' receive a Superintendent's written warning. For James's parents and their lawyer, this is an insult. The question being asked around the Moss Side community is why an incident such as this was not deemed worthy of immediate response. Are the police so anaesthetized to violence within the community? The fact that little action was taken against the officer has been a cause for frustration within the community.

Part of the IPCC statement ran: 'It is deeply saddening that this investigation has highlighted that police officers were dealing with another incident within yards of the scene of the shooting shortly after it had occurred – but nobody reported anything. I must question whether people had actually seen the shooting but were too fearful to act.

'It is equally saddening that a young boy lay dead for more than an hour before the first emergency call was made.'[9]

Admittedly, one wonders how many potential witnesses there might have been. The shooting occurred in the early hours of the morning in a park where, on one side, the houses are over a hundred yards away, and on the other the majority of properties do not have a clear view of the spot where Jessie was shot. By the time the residents would have woken up and got to the window, it's likely the killers would have fled.

Two men, already in prison, were arrested in August 2007, yet no trial resulted. CCTV footage showing people cycling away from the murder scene was released in a bid to help catch Jessie's killer along with a £20,000 reward for information. Still no one has been brought to justice. The word on the street differs, however. The same name is mentioned around the community. The killer was a young man himself.

There are several gang factions around the city that contain a number of young teenagers. In Moss Side there are the likes of the Young Gooch, the Old Trafford Crips and the Fallowfield Man Dem, all of whom fall under the original Gooch Close umbrella. Likewise, the Doddington faction is the Moss Side Bloods, and Longsight's is the Longsight Street Soldiers. To the north of the city are the little Cheetham Hill gang. In many cases, in the arbitrariness of their violence and their determination to secure a reputation, their members scare the community more than any of the established gangsters.

The strange thing about Manchester is that when we look around the rest of the city, the gang picture appears quite different.

The Brass Handles pub in Salford on a rowdy Sunday afternoon. Manchester United are playing, and the pub is packed. Among the crowd is a blonde woman sending texts on her mobile phone.

Suddenly, two black men walk in. As they do so, she calmly walks into the women's toilet.

The two men are Carlton Alveranga, 20, and Richard Austin, 19. Alveranga pulls out his pistol and fires six shots at two men sitting at a table, David Totton and Aaron Travers, both 27, injuring them. Austin's handgun jams. The pub's patrons overpower them, a known gangster in the area shoots them with their own guns, and the mob beat them as they lie dying outside.

Alveranga and Austin had been hired to kill Totton by Ian McLeod, 42. McLeod had been portrayed in the press as the 'leader' of the Doddington gang. As we know, this is not an accurate description because of the way gangs work; but he was an experienced and well-connected criminal. He, in turn, had been contacted by the blonde woman who retreated to the toilet – Constance Howarth, 38. She was directing the two men to their target with her mobile phone.

Howarth worked as a secretary at a Salford security firm, PMS. Her boss, Bobby Spiers, was a well-known gangster who had ordered the hit after a petty dispute with Totton at a nightclub. She had an interesting past. In May 1997 she was arrested in north London with notorious criminals Paul Ferris and Henry Suttee by the National Crime Squad. She was attempting to transport Mac-10 machine guns and explosives north in the boot of her Vauxhall Nova when officers swooped at traffic lights in Colindale. At the time she told the court: 'I am just a girl – I don't know anything about guns. I was just running an errand for a boyfriend.'

Bobby Spiers fled the country after the hit. The company of which he was a director, PMS Security, had an even more interesting past. In 2003 a Manchester councillor raised questions after it won a contract to provide security on the site of a new police station that was being built. He complained that the company had links to Salford's original 'Mr Big', Paul Massey.

In July 1998 Massey took a film crew on a tour of the city's night spots. During the night an exchange of opinion occurred with a group of men from Leeds, and a Leeds man was stabbed. Paul Massey went missing, and Greater Manchester Police tried to get hold of the footage. This included getting a court order against the BBC at the Old Bailey. When the police did eventually get hold of the footage, it had been altered. Paul Massey's eventual trial was a huge event: he was the police's public enemy number one. Journalists were vetted and given special passes under the Official Secrets Act and the court was surrounded by armed police. Despite this, the case was not followed in detail by any of the national media.

Massey's Salford crew had been one of the pre-eminent forces in nightclub security throughout the 1990s. At the time PMS denied any links to Massey. Its owner told the *Manchester Evening News*:

'The company was originally called JS Security and ran into financial difficulties. A consortium of people including Mr Massey bailed the company out with a loan on the condition that he was put on the books as a director and the name was changed to PMS. I agreed to that. When the loan was paid back Mr Massey had nothing else to do with the company. We are a good company. We don't owe anybody anything. Everything is done above board.'[10]

The company does regular work for Manchester Council. Its managing director stressed that the company's name stood for Professionally Manned Security. Massey himself cut what seems a contradictory figure within the area. In his determination to keep heroin off the Salford estates, Massey once had stickers put on lampposts warning smack dealers that they risked being 'smacked'.

Constance Howarth is Paul Massey's cousin.

*

In 1997 the satirical ITV show *In Bed With MeDinner* turned its gaze to a documentary that had been recorded in Salford that year.[11] The format of the show took edited highlights of other television programmes and allowed the host, Bob Mills, to make jokes about them. This particular episode featured the story of Ken Keating.

The first excerpt showed footage of Ken at home with a family photograph: 'That's my son, Sean. If I'd known what he was going to do to his family, I'd have smothered the little bastard.'

It transpired that Sean had turned police informant, and that in response Ken had put a £10,000 reward on his head. The preposterous story, all told straight-faced by Ken, with Mills' humorous comments in between, was greeted with rousing laughter in the studio. Perhaps the biggest laugh came when Ken revealed that his wife had persuaded him not to destroy the photographs of Sean around the house. 'I think he reached a fantastic compromise,' said Mills. The show cut back to Ken, who showed how he'd kept the photographs but had attached Post-It notes saying 'Fucking Grass' to them.

Mills joked about the absurdity of the show, imagining the police coming round Keating's house:

'Excuse me, Mr Keating.'

'What do you want, coppa?'

'We're arresting you for putting a reward on your son's head. That's incitement to murder.'

''Oo informed on me?'

'Well, you did, on that TV show.'

'Oh . . . I'm a fucking grass. Kill me!'

Of course his humour was based on just how extraordinary this attitude is. No doubt Keating was an extreme case: heavily linked to the criminal fraternity in Salford, he would drive around the Ordsall Estate in a white van which said: 'Do you know? You can still deal in DRUGS and still beat the law, be the DRUGS good or bad only if your JACK STRAW'S LAD. A law for them and a law for YOU and ME. Let's have zero tolerance for the Police. CAUTIONED!'

The Keatings were well known: every element of the documentary was true. A *Manchester Evening News* report at the time indicated that Sean had already survived two assassination attempts. Neighbours in Bolton were asking for him to be moved for the safety of other residents. In the light of the previous areas at which we have looked, it is perhaps unsurprising that Keating, like any resident of Gangland, would be able to hold these views and not feel out of place. Salford is in every way an interstitial zone. As Peter Walsh wrote in *Gang War*, his history of the Manchester gangs:

> The opening of the ship canal in 1894 to bypass Liverpool turned Salford into a vital port – and ports are unruly places. Some of the worst Scuttler mobs came from Salford and the gang culture never really died out there . . . As they grew older, the young Salford lads looked up to some of the Scots, people like the McPhees, a family involved in armed robbery, counterfeiting and burglaries. They envied the wealth that crime could bring, at a time when legitimate work was drying up. Salford was an ailing city. The Quays was once the world's third busiest port, but in the seventies it was declared no longer viable. The docks were obliterated and families began to disperse from the area. The population fell as people left to look for jobs and Salford became one of the ten most deprived of the 366 urban districts in England and Wales.[12]

This is now a dual city. The city is separated from Manchester by the River Irwell. The area around the Quays and adjacent to Manchester has seen modern living spaces, offices and shops springing up due to a huge amount of investment. However, you only need walk for fifteen minutes to find the deprived areas in the centre such as Ordsall – run-down red-brick estates, with the bright lights of the new buildings visible just to the west. As far as the visible gap between prosperity and poverty in Britain goes, it rivals anywhere in London.

Says one source: 'Sure, I knew Dessie Noonan. He used to play football with me. There'd be dozens of people there, and quite often there'd be a fight. But whenever he was there, you never saw any trouble at all, just because of who he was. He was a lovely guy, was Dessie.'

Noonan emerged from poverty and into the criminal scene with his brothers Damian and Dominic. His criminal career began as a doorman in the early 1980s: he had a fearful reputation. Noonan then started to put his own men on the doors and by the late 1980s 80 per cent of the Manchester nightlife security was said to be controlled by his family. Around this time Dominic Noonan was jailed for fifteen years for his part in an armed robbery at a bank in Cheetham Hill, Manchester. During his imprisonment his brothers were forging links with other Manchester gangs.

The Noonan family tended to have nothing to do with the Moss Side gangs, although Desmond was part of a group of men who provided the black gangs with guns and other weapons. After involving himself in Manchester's nightlife, Desmond started to get involved with other criminal circles outside of Manchester. By the end of the 1990s the Noonan family had been linked to 25 gangland murders, dozens of robberies and had a stranglehold on most of the nightclub security in many of the major cities across the UK; they had also made over eight million pounds from bank robberies and security alone.

Yet, bizarrely, Noonan was also the head of Anti-Fascist Action in Manchester, a militant organization that were involved in serious clashes with the far right in the city. He used a gun to threaten a BNP member. While the extent to which he can take the credit for stopping the BNP making headway in Salford is debateable, there is no doubt that the far right see him as a hate figure. His picture can be seen on any number of far-right websites, where they condemn him as a criminal and murderer.

Desmond developed a crack addiction and was eventually stabbed to death by his drug dealer. The killer had to be placed in solitary confinement in jail for his own safety. His brother, Dominic, took over. Donal MacIntyre's 2006 film *A Very British Gangster* portrayed him as a complex figure. Dominic, a devout Catholic, a homosexual, and a man who couldn't give MacIntyre a straight answer about the number of killings for which he was responsible, was also portrayed as the area's primary deal-maker and fixer. In the film he comes across as the man to whom residents in trouble turn. In a world where his mother burned down their home in an effort to move up the housing list, and a relative in debt ineptly robs a post office because he can't conceive of any other way to pay his loans, Noonan is portrayed as a more efficient justice system than the police force.

After Desmond Noonan was killed, Dominic gave an interview to the *Manchester Evening News* about the fact that the schools were closing early as the city did not want the children coming out into Desmond's funeral: 'St Thomas Aquinas was Dessie's old school and he would have been devastated if he knew it had shut for the day. Education is so important for kids, especially for those from deprived backgrounds. A lot of them are in the middle of exams.'[13]

Most of the facts about these characters have already been reported. They are included because, on the surface, analysis of criminals such as Massey, Keating and Noonan could lead to a simple, flawed formulation about ethnicity, similar to the one mentioned in the previous chapter: that white interstitial areas are more organized than their black counterparts. The leading criminals in their areas have respect and as such there is a form of community policing, which takes its shape in such things as Massey's campaign against heroin,

Keating's exhortations to the community, and Noonan's general fixing and anti-fascist activities. Moreover, these are criminals with links to the legal economy through their business enterprises. This allows for the easy laundering of money which opens up the possibilities for criminal endeavour.

We assume there is a structure to their crimes, and a natural criminal order which keeps potentially violent competitors in their place. The black community, lacking these controlling figures and without this organisation, is more prone to random acts of crime – and with them come escalating conflicts. It's not that there are more guns within the black community, but that the type of crimes in which they are used are 'expressive', rather than 'instrumental'; the latter serving an economic purpose (robberies, to facilitate drugs payments), rather than the complex reasons of brinkmanship seen in earlier cases. The great irony is that the increased violence that comes with this disorganization has led to the word 'gang' being used more frequently in its areas, when in actual fact it is the anarchic nature of the criminal enterprise that creates most of the violence. If one is looking for organized criminal groups, the people involved with the likes of Massey and Noonan are far closer to that definition.

There is, or was, an element of truth in this reading, but we must be careful about how myths are made and stories are told. Massey, Noonan and Keating influenced the public's perception by perpetuating the image of the 'noble gangster'. This is a widely received portrait of traditional white British villains that stretches back over half a century, but it has now started to be adopted by gangsters in black communities. How far these gangsters mean what they say – that they're somehow noble or helping their communities – is open to debate. Most importantly, a racial reading of the situation ascribes a degree of control to white urban youth which is not always there, as we will see below.

*

I meet June, a middle-aged lady, in a cafe in the district's shopping precinct. 'I was out with my daughter, when I saw five or six teenagers ganging up on one boy. They slammed a bottle over his head, and while he was on the floor, they started kicking him again and again. He was unconscious. They grabbed his head and held it up, then they took the broken bottle and ran it down his face. Then they ran off, whooping and hollering, like animals.'

Eight miles south of Manchester city centre lies the district of Wythenshawe. It has been described as one of the largest housing estates in Europe. The district comprises nine areas: each one of them has its own gang. One of them, Benchill, is the most deprived ward in the UK. Wythenshawe is Manchester's largest district, created in the 1920s as a so-called 'Garden City' where an overspill population was resettled from the slums of industrial Manchester, without any social cohesion taken into account. By the late twentieth century Wythenshawe suffered many social problems. It was an area ripe to suffer under the economic changes described in the second chapter of this book, with traditional industries in decline.

The area began to come to media attention in 2007, when David Cameron visited it. A photo that made the front pages of all the national newspapers featured a boy in a tracksuit behind him making a gun gesture with his fingers, as if to shoot him. The boy, Ryan Florence, later appeared on the BBC's *North West Tonight*, with members of his gang, the Benchill Mad Dogs. The reporter asked him what he thought he would be doing in five years: 'I'll be dead, innit. There's bare people trying to shoot me.' What did he think of David Cameron? 'Nothing, he doesn't do fuck all round here, does he?' Later in the report, the Mad Dogs pulled machetes out of their tracksuit bottoms and waved them around.

A visit to Wythenshawe reveals the full extent of the problem. Youths hang around the municipal precinct, the smell of marijuana heavy in the air around them. They are all teenagers, all white, and they are all menacing. I speak to them, and they say little more than you'd expect: 'There's fuck all to do around here, there's no chance of getting a job.' One of them offers me drugs. Not only does he have a selection of marijuana on offer, but he can get me 'flake' cocaine, and anything stronger if you want it'. These are youths involved in serious crime. I heard a number of stories that have not been reported and which are hard to verify: one boy was apparently tortured with a metal chair leg for two hours by a Wythenshawe gang before he was killed.

I spoke to a University of Manchester researcher before heading there: he told me Wythenshawe was the most violent place he'd worked, and he had covered the entire city: 'Girls who've been slashed with Stanley knives . . . every boy seems to have a scar on them – it's got serious problems with its young.' As with most areas covered in this book, these problems can be revealed by a quick search of YouTube – videos of boys speeding through the estate on motorbikes and showing off their weapons do not take long to find. The youth gangs in Wythenshawe are as territorial as those described in London's suburbs. The biggest divide is between Newall Green and Benchill, with the youths of each area protecting their territory fiercely.

On the surface it appears to be very much a generational problem. It is the area's youth and not its adults that are committing the bulk of the street violence. The *New York Times* also visited the area in 2007, and said: 'The problems here – a breakdown in families, an absence of respect for authority, the prevalence of drugs, drunkenness, truancy, vandalism and petty criminality – are common across Britain.' It later cited a Unicef report that placed Britain second from bottom in a report that measured various social and economic factors to reveal the well-being of children in 21 industrialized countries. It also cited a paper by the Institute for Public Policy Research, a progressive study group, which concluded that Britain's young people were the worst behaved in Europe, spending less time with their parents, drinking and fighting more, and trying drugs and sex earlier than their counterparts across the Continent.[14]

The article cited three main reasons for the youths' behaviour. The first was drinking, which can be overlooked for now as a subsidiary issue; a symptom which becomes a cause. However, the second two reasons carry weight. The first, as discussed previously, was the gap between rich and poor in Britain. The piece argued that although Britain has the world's fifth-largest economy, it also has one of the worst rates of child poverty in the industrialized world, with 3.4 million children, more than one in four, living in poverty, and about a million, or nearly 10 per cent, living in severe poverty. This squares with the points made in previous chapters: in fact the poverty in Wythenshawe is more pronounced than in other places covered previously, where it only forms the background to behaviour. The final reason cited in the report is young Britons' tendency to spend time with their peers rather than with adults which, it argued, robbed them of even basic social skills. It claimed that in Britain, 45 per cent of 15-year-old boys spend most of their evenings out with friends; in France, the figure is 17 per cent. This suggests that the arguments advanced earlier regarding absent father figures within the black community are too simplistic.

The true extent of the problem in Wythenshawe has been overlooked for years. The Gooch and the Doddington made all the headlines throughout the 1990s: the gang names became sexy stories, with gun crime an exciting angle. Yet gun crime is not uncommon in this area: some residents claim there are discharges every week. It is of course hard to tell the extent of the problem, because of the huge number of unreported incidents.

In 2004 Ashley Bowman was on his way to a party when he was blasted in the back of the head with a sawn-off shotgun. The story received few headlines, although it did become the subject of a BBC documentary on police procedure. Bowman had been shot because the leader of a local gang, the Greenwood Boys, had ordered the killing of someone else who was due to be attending the party, having argued with him earlier in the day. He was a victim of mistaken identity. The documentary revealed that anonymous sources phoned the police with a number of names (mostly correct) from day one, but that it was a struggle to secure enough evidence to mount a case. The same problems of trust in the police and a simultaneous culture of fear and/or loyalty are present in Wythenshawe as elsewhere. Eventually two witnesses were prepared to come forward, explaining that they did so in order to prevent anyone else getting shot. However, there are signs that senior figures within the community are beginning to fight back.

'I've seen another lad getting hit around the head with a spanner, horrible noise it makes. The thing the community is most afraid of is twelve-year-old boys. Let's say a kid throws a brick at your car. And you get out and try to teach him a lesson. All of a sudden you're the one who's likely to face jail. And the worst thing is that the kid knows that too. When I grew up the traditional authority figures were the police and parents. That's gone.' I am talking with these figures in a gym in Wythenshawe, having been escorted to the gym by one such small child on a mountain bike, who told me how the place had turned his life around.

The gym, the United Estates of Wythenshawe (UEW), has a remarkable story behind it. It was set up by Greg Davis, a former nightclub doorman who had grown up in the area. He is a mountain of a man, who despite growing up in care homes had established the largest door-security firm in the northwest of England. He owned a farmhouse in Cheshire, and drove a Porsche and a Range Rover. But drugs were beginning to take over the club scene. Greg was in the middle of a very dangerous business, and he was a family man. He had his epiphany staring down the barrel of a sawn-off shotgun. Something had to change, but he did not know what, or how.

During his infrequent visits to Wythenshawe, he felt there was a 'toxicity' flooding through the area. A chapel at the centre of it was being utterly vandalized by the local children, who were tearing holes in the roof and defecating in the corridors. He paid £4,000 a year himself in rent and rates to take over the building, and began to fix the roof. Out of his 140 doormen, he had builders, roofers, plasterers, plumbers and joiners. They borrowed scaffolding and fixed the roof themselves. Then he got in touch with the area's 'leaders'.

These are the people he describes as the ones whose houses don't get burgled, whose cars don't get broken into. He had either fought or knew every kind of problematic, powerful, persuasive family in the area at one time or another. He summoned one representative from each to a meeting. Some were hostile to him, others to the other families that would be coming. Eventually the meeting happened, and the management team for the UEW was born. It now has a gym, a hairdresser's, a fitness suite and therapy rooms. It is also the one building on the estate that does not require an alarm.

At the time I visited it there were a bunch of children from a local school in there. They had been put into the gym because their school had reached their quota for exclusions. Instead, they had to be placed in special provision. Down on the gym floor were also convicted muggers, violent people and thieves, all of whom were beginning to turn their lives around with the support of the UEW. It fills a social space too. Due to the drugs problems, there are no local discos, and the police stopped 'garage' nights after a number of violent incidents.

Davis now wants to take the idea out to other communities: to gather together the 'baddies', and 'squeeze the goodness out of them'.

There are two main points to take from this story, beyond the fact that it is simply positive. The first is that it stands up to the theory of the interstitial area finding ways to organize itself. As one of the leaders told me: 'Replace "black" and "ethnic" with "white" and "working class" and it's pretty much the same story.' And this leads to the second point, about the issue of neglect. There's no doubt that the people of Wythenshawe feel displaced from the economic mainstream, to the extent where an ex-doorman and various shadowy figures have taken it upon themselves to deal with the problem of youth crime. But has the council actually neglected Wythenshawe? On the surface, it appears not. For example, it has invested in a kids' 'lifestyle centre' in the area. Yet this was a bone of contention for those I met.

One said: 'They have a few kids in there any given night, tops. Yet once a kid goes there he's a member, so the target's met for how it's getting on. They never consulted with the people about that place – it doesn't serve anyone's needs. We asked the kids what they wanted, and that's why this place is what it is. A lot of the kids wouldn't be seen dead in there, and those are the kids that matter. But they'll come here [the gym], and that means they all come here.'

Another said: 'They'll just get consultants to tell them what they want to hear, rather than admit they're not making a difference.'

Another added: 'A bike was taken from a kid on the estate and we could see the little fuckers riding around outside on it. When we called the police they simply said, "Why are you riding an expensive bike in Wythenshawe?" So we made another phone call to . . . someone, and the bike was returned. The police react to crime – but they don't stop it: law and order has to be provided by someone. How much use is a police force that pisses off at 5 p.m.?'

It is not for this book to prove whether or not those at the UEW are right in their disparaging comments about the police and the authorities. But there are several simple points about them which should be taken into account. They have all lived in the community for years. They are more likely than any outsiders to know who the most at-risk youths are. They have respect – a respect which in some cases might border on fear, but which has been turned into a positive force. As we begin to look for solutions to the gang problem, it might just be that the UEW can point us towards some of the ways in which a community that is economically and socially distanced from those surrounding it can be healed, and bridges back to normal behaviour established.

But it's not a battle it can win alone. Indeed, for all the good it does there is a feeling among the community that elements of its youth are moving beyond its control. The situation in Wythenshawe would seem to make a point that traditional white working-class communities are good at uniting to combat adversities in their midst, but an escalation of violent behaviour by some of its youth appears to disprove it. Is it that the white working class are starting to experience the kind of neglect and deprivation that has up until fairly recently been suffered only by other ethnic groups? There is enough empirical evidence to suggest that, with the growing influx of guns into it, this is a community heading for a tragedy like that which befell our next city.

EIGHT

Liverpool

Mankind are an incorrigible race. Give them but bugbears and idols – it is all that they ask; the distinctions of right and wrong, of truth and falsehood, of good and evil, are worse than indifferent to them.

William Hazlitt, *Common Places*

On 22 August 2007, a gang situation that I had been monitoring while writing this book exploded on to front pages and television screens around the country. At 7.30 p.m., Rhys Jones, an eleven-year-old boy who played for the Fir Tree Boys football club in Croxteth, Liverpool, was on his way home from football practice with two friends. It was broad daylight. He was walking across a pub car park on Fir Tree Drive South when he was shot in the back of the neck. Rhys's mother rushed to the scene and held him in her arms. He was unconscious, and although paramedics attempted to resuscitate him, he was pronounced dead later that evening in hospital.

The murder dominated the news agenda: 2007 was the year that violent youth crime became a major story, and the shooting of an innocent eleven-year-old was bound to be of huge public interest. There were dozens of reports on the gang warfare that was raging in the area where Jones was killed. They centred on the youth gangs

185

in two communities, both within the Liverpool 11 postcode. One was Norris Green, whose crew was variously known as the Nogga Dogz, The Strand Crew, or other names. The other was Croxteth, a mile or so away, whose gang was known as the Crocky Crew. Googling the names led to a series of YouTube videos which had been posted by the gang members, which showed them posing with guns and knives and driving at high speed in stolen cars. These two areas, it appeared, were anarchic.

What was interesting about the coverage of the situation was the way in which the gangs seemed to have appeared from nowhere. There was little discussion of the circumstances that had lead to their creation. From the coverage it appeared that one youth's death had created the gangs. The murder took place a year to the day before Rhys Jones was killed, and a jury had been deliberating the verdict only hours before the latter's killing. Many commentators wondered if this had marked a heightening of 'gang tensions'. The youth was called Liam Smith.

This was a story about which I was already aware and had been starting to investigate further. On 23 August 2006, Smith, nineteen, had been visiting Altcourse Prison, where he had argued with a man named Ryan Lloyd, also nineteen. As he stormed out of the visiting hall, Lloyd is reported to have demanded a phone from his cellmate with the words: 'Quick, quick, give me the phone. I'll get the boys up here to pop them.' Forty minutes later, outside the prison, Smith was blasted in the head at close range with a sawn-off shotgun.

The reports stated that Smith was a member of the Norris Green Crew, and Lloyd was a member of Croxteth. Lloyd, Thomas Forshaw, eighteen, and a sixteen-year-old boy, all from Croxteth, were convicted of Smith's murder. During their ten-week trial, estimated to have cost £5 million, the court heard a violent rivalry had existed between the Croxteth Crew and the Strand Crew since 2004, and there were at least seventeen occasions when members fired guns at each other. A picture emerged of youths wandering around housing estates dressed in body armour, and guns being shot at houses and shops.

The gangs seemed somewhat different to those with whom I'd dealt previously. The first thing that struck me was the mugshots: Smith, in particular, looked like a young boy, and Lloyd little older. There seemed to be the same chaotic structure to them as those I had researched in London and Birmingham: another man named Liam Duffy, 26, was sent down for manslaughter, but he still claimed to have been Smith's friend, and to have socialized with him. The final thing which struck me had been the remarkable story of Smith's funeral, which I had read about on local Internet message boards.

One poster wrote: 'I watched the funeral today. Not from the line of people in the street, but from a window. It was nothing short of an episode from the Soprano's [sic]. The yobs must be feeling pretty special. Police helicopter in the air, hearse with flowers spelling out "Legend", coffin in a glass casket pulled by horses and nothing short of 13 limousines. Not one of these scallies has probably ever worked a day in their lives. Drug money certainly pays.'

Smith, known locally as 'Smigger', received an illustrious send-off. Graffiti appeared around the Norris Green Estate, reading 'RIP The Don'. The *Liverpool Echo* was told by shopkeepers that the removal of a 50-yard memorial to Smith reading 'SMIGGER – SOLDIER' would have 'brought about World War III'. The police urged the council to leave it there until after the funeral. Members of Smith's gang were said to have visited the local shops and told them they had to close for the day of the funeral procession. After the wake, sixteen people were arrested as mourners turned on the police, hurling abuse and threats.

There was a reason that the situation in Liverpool was of interest to me. I was familiar with gangs that regularly committed gun crime that was expressive, rather than instrumental. I was familiar with this gun crime occurring between disorganized groups of youths, many of whom had connections to the drugs trade and who fought others for respect, on a territorial basis and under the name of a gang. These youths, as in their YouTube videos (in which they were stomping on police-car windscreens and swearing at officers, all accompanied by congratulatory comments), tended to define themselves by their opposition to the authorities. But in my experience all of this was happening in areas of the country that were more heavily urbanized, where there was a far more longstanding history of poverty and disorganization, and within which the majority of residents were drawn from ethnic minorities.

Now, one year on, Rhys Jones had been shot. The key question remained unasked: exactly what had happened to this area of the city?

I arrived in Liverpool with a notepad, pen and a few mobile-phone numbers. The city was preparing for its year as European Capital of Culture. Posters around the town were publicizing the effect it would have. It was all set to begin with an open-air event in St George's Plateau, followed by a concert at the Echo Arena. There was a buzz in the air. This was an optimistic time for the city; a time when its heritage, people and achievements would be celebrated. Events are scheduled to run all-year long in the city's art galleries, theatres and museums. I told the taxi driver what I was writing about. He didn't want to know; he wanted to concentrate on the city's positives: its two prime ministers, the comedians and musicians to have come out of it, the success on the football field.

Less glitz and glamour three miles or so to the west in Norris Green, however. There is a huge amount of social housing in the area, but much of it is respectable-looking. No tall high-rises, just row upon row upon row of terraced housing; some elaborately gentrified, many more simply plain. And that, for the most part, is all there is. It has its shopping centre, a small row of shops called the Broadway, and there are a few more newsagents a few blocks further down in Scargreen Avenue. One can follow the main road, Utting Avenue, to the northwest for half a mile, before reaching a crossroads and seeing the 'Welcome to Croxteth' sign familiar from the gang members' YouTube videos.

Croxteth itself is shabbier and run down; here there are blocks of flats, some not so well maintained, and some shrubland. On the whole it seems a poor place, but not utterly deprived. After all, it only takes a few minutes' walk from here to the grandiose gates that form the entrance to Croxteth Hall Country Park. Beside them is Fir Tree Drive, the long circular road that follows the high fences around the circumference of the Croxteth Park Estate, the overall impression being of a moat around a castle. Through the small lanes that lead off it are the estate's well-tended drives and houses. It is a picture of self-contained suburbia. The Fir Tree pub, scene of Rhys Jones's shooting, is on the south side of this circle.

You have to look a little closer at the area for signs of deprivation. You see it in the sign that was in the newsagent's in Scargreen Avenue: 'No smoking spliffs outside the shop.' You see it in another newsagent's that has plastic shields over the chocolate bars so that only the vendor can access them. In the roads a little further away from the centre of Norris Green; in Braithwaite Close, for example, where the doors and windows of one of the many long rows of ter-raced houses are entirely boarded up with steel panels, and have been for a long time. Indeed, it is underinvestment that leaps out: where once there was a purpose-built gym on Long Lane, now there will be more houses. Houses and houses all around, and not a thing for the children to do. It is a common plea among working-class com-munities, the importance of which does not always register among the rest of society, who are able to transport their children to activities like swimming pools and holiday camps. And now, as one resident put it to me: 'As if house prices weren't low enough round here, all we hear about Croxteth and Norris Green is the gangs.'

And what of these gangs? What to make of the news that I wouldn't be able to talk to any of the Strand Gang, not because they didn't want to talk or were too hard to reach, but because it simply didn't exist any more? A criminal empire, whose nineteen-year-old boss's death closed the area's streets, completely disbanded? What to make of these words, from a man who knew Liam Smith well: 'Smigger got his reputation for one reason. He was the one out of that group who'd go further than anyone else. There's a fight? Smigger's the one who'd jump on someone's head. Guys from Crocky are terrorizing the group? Smigger's the one who wasn't scared.

'Now don't get me wrong, Smigger had a lot of respect among the kids, and a lot of people were scared of him; but to describe him as a crime boss is crazy. Have you seen the lad? I couldn't imagine him getting served in a pub. No – I don't think the money from that funeral came from Smigger's exploits. Someone else paid for that. If he ran a huge crime empire, like the press said, I don't think he'd have been hanging around the Broadway smoking gear all the time.'

Likewise: what to make of one of the shopkeepers in Norris Green's take on Smith: 'Don't get me wrong. Him and those boys were a real nuisance, and very intimidating sometimes. Once one of them set a dog on one of the shopkeepers round here. They were always just hanging round, smoking weed and what have you. So no, I didn't like them. But you know what? At the same time, when he died, I, and a lot of other people round here, just thought: what a waste of youth. Yes, his group made people's lives miserable. Yes, a lot of people get out of these shops at 4 p.m. because we don't feel safe from them kids. But ultimately, it's just sad, is what it is.'

There is no doubt that Smith's funeral was a huge event; no doubt that there were older, middle-aged adults wearing their 'Nogzy Soldier' T-shirts, a sign of the mentality of those who brought up the young gangsters. But it would be wrong to see the event as a ceremony to mark the passing of a criminal empire's leader. It was a funeral for a boy who – though negatively in many cases – was well known by most of the community in a city that has a tradition of passionate and uninhibited commemoration of death. It does not hide the fact that many of the people in the community were upset to see the negative aspects of this character's life celebrated so brazenly: but this was no Mafia-style funeral.

Moreover, while I may have been speaking to the wrong people or may have been lied to by store owners who did not want to put themselves in danger, I could find little evidence to support the story about the shopkeepers being threatened into closing by Smith's gang. They may well have asked this of some of the stores in Broadway, but it seems none of the stores in Scargreen Avenue, where Smith was wont to spend most of his time, were threatened. An arrangement was made with the police to take down the floral tribute to Smith on the anniversary of his death, and there seems to have been a row between local youths and *Liverpool Echo* reporters at the scene over what the youths felt were lies that had been printed in the local press.

In the light of previous chapters, none of this should surprise us. The overwhelming majority of the population is white, but economic changes in previous decades have given these areas the characteristics of the interstitial zones visited in previous chapters. It should not be news to us that the gangs are fluid and disorganized, nor that there is a historical and territorial pattern above this: Croxteth, Norris Green and Sparrow Green, a neighbouring area, have seen their youths fight each other for decades. The T-shirts with their 'Nogzy Soldier' slogans are symbolic not of any organized criminality, but are a statement of the paradoxically strong feelings that deviant individuals have for the very place they terrorize – a set of feelings defined more by hostility to other areas than anything else. We should not be surprised that the gang crime committed by these youths is a fatal re-imagining of an older territorial battle; nor that gun incidents are usually expressive: it is about proving oneself; the same way that youths from Norris Green stole the former Everton footballer Andy Van de Meyde's car and paraded the theft on YouTube.

And so it was not hard to find gang-involved youths. It was a simple case of waiting around on the Broadway and engaging them in conversation. After a few hours, I had met Paul and his friend Andy. Both were about fourteen or fifteen years old, and wearing black tracksuits and trainers. It has been said that the youths all wear these clothes so that the police can't tell them apart. However, it is also a general fashion among young people in the city. Paul was pedalling his bike slowly down the road, and was quite happy to talk to me. At first he thought I wanted drugs:

'What do you want, mate? I can get you beak – thirty quid for a gram, and it's good stuff.'

We talked more. I asked Paul about Croxteth: 'They're the ones that start the trouble. Most of Nogzy is about grafting. I'll deal and some of the boys do cars, but we're not violent unless we're provoked. And anyway the Matrix [the city's gun-crime police task force] are all over our backs the whole time these days. I've got an injunction which says I can't hang out in a group.'

A mile or so away in Croxteth, I had met another youth, Gary, in a black tracksuit, again by simply hanging around. The striking similarities between his words and Paul's were telling. Again, he cast the other area as the aggressors.

'It's Nogzy are the violent ones. It all comes from them. We graft. Crocky eds aren't even a gang – it's just, you're Crocky if you live here, d'you know what I mean?

'I was really sad when Rhys died. I mean, what happened to Rhys . . . if you read the papers you'd think it was the only thing that had happened here. But it's been going on for years. Like, not long before him, there was a lad shot in the face with some cheap shotgun they'd filled with bits of metal. And they all stuck in his face, like. And now he can't talk properly any more.'

Back to Paul. I began to ask him about his home life. At first he was guarded, but he began to open up: 'It's like, me mum and dad, they don't actually like dealing; but some of the other parents are fine about it; they're proud to be Nogzy. And you see they don't like me doing it, but they don't stop me. They've got debts after Christmas. The bailiffs keep coming round for the TV and stuff. You know how it is. I'll give back to them, if I can.'

Gary tells me about drugs: 'Everyone round here smokes puff, and most do beak. But there're quite a few people on crack and brown. They're scum. I know plenty of people who sell that stuff, and they hate them too. Fuck them. You know what – we don't give a fuck at the end of the day. Look at what happened after Liam Culshaw got stabbed to death – they were phoning the lad's friends and taunting them. There's no fear here: everyone can get a gun.'

Liam Culshaw was killed in Walton, in March 2006. A gang had been spinning the wheels of their bikes on the grass outside his house, and spraying it with mud. He had walked out to confront them, and was stabbed eight times. I ask Gary where the drugs come from.

'People . . . there's one guy in particular. He's a very big librarian [criminal who loans out guns].'

Liam Smith was not, in fact, the first high-profile member of the gangs to have been killed. On New Year's Day 2004, a leading member of the Crocky Crew, Danny McDonald, nineteen, was shot dead in the Royal Oak pub in Norris Green. The youths began to wear 'Danny

MC' tattoos. The murder suggests a link from the Croxteth street gangs to higher levels of crime. McDonald was apparently killed in revenge for a failed attack he had carried out on the Dickie Lewis pub in Kirkdale, north Liverpool; he had a packed a bomb with razor-sharp pieces of metal, and thrown it inside. It failed to detonate. It appeared that the attack was part of a feud between drugs families from the Grizedale area of Everton and those of Kirkdale.

In 2007 Liverpool was revealed as Britain's centre for organized crime outside of London: there were 24 prosecutions in the city in the first year of Britain's Serious Organised Crime Agency (SOCA), out of 283 nationwide. Newcastle, Manchester and Birmingham saw half as many. Liverpool is a port, and as such it has a history of large-scale criminality, at least since the 1980s when heroin began to sweep the city. And the crime which takes place at this level does undoubtedly have a knock-on effect on the street gangs. Some commentators have seen the arrest of Curtis Warren in 1996 as having had a huge impact. Worth an estimated £125 million, Warren built his massive criminal empire by importing vast quantities of drugs. After his incarceration, criminal families muscled in on his old distribution. The route from Ireland to Liverpool became full of guns and drugs, helped by the fact that the IRA had kept the drug culture in Northern Ireland under control. At the same time, there was a surfeit of guns entering the black market from Eastern Europe; since the Cold War, prices had dropped.

In 2007, the *Observer* reported:

Much of the drugs money went into Liverpool's regeneration, buying up apartments around the docks. Today police sources believe the big drug barons are paying inflated prices on new developments so that they can fix the property market and keep prices artificially high. Amid the rush to build, officials were bribed to turn a blind eye if bureaucracy got in the way of profits. Several of the city's plethora of tanning salons and hand car washes became prized money-laundering operations.

According to the same report, battles between the new crime families began to intensify. It describes how former *Brookside* actress Jennifer Ellison found herself caught in the crossfire after her then boyfriend, Tony Richardson, became a target of the rogue security firms. Their house was sprayed with bullets in a drive-by shooting. Richardson's younger brother was shot in the back by two gunmen in 2004. A man named Darren Gee who was in the car with him vowed revenge – and later that year David Regan was shot dead on the forecourt of his car wash by hit men working for Gee. The report continues: 'The battle to own the drug distribution networks filtered down from the security firms dominated by the likes of Gee to their loose network of lieutenants, the teenage gangs such as the Norris Green Strand gang, also known as the Nogzy soldiers, and the Croxteth 'Crocky' Crew, both from north Liverpool.'[1]

It would, of course, be incorrect to see the youth gangs of Croxteth and Norris Green as working under the orders of these characters. Rather we should remember the careful definition between the gang members and organized criminals – and in using the term 'organized criminals', we are referring more to their individual actions than their relationships with each other. It seems, in Liverpool, that the older criminals tend not to claim allegiance to the gangs as often as they do in London or Manchester, where the gang names that they might have operated under in the 1990s still carry weight. However, they are opportunistic and currently well aware of the prospects opened up to them by youth gangs.

It might seem logical for the police to concentrate their efforts on apprehending these characters; but as in every other interstitial area, there is a perception that their efforts are being concentrated on the wrong people. As always, this injustice is in part perceived, and partly justified. The words of various interviewees provide a picture.

A sixteen-year-old, not gang involved: 'Everyone says death to the Matrix. Everyone hates the cops. They move us on everywhere; even use Section 30s in parts of the city centre so we can't hang out together. It's not fair; why can't they just leave us alone? They should be catching serious criminals, not attacking us.'

A youth worker: 'The Matrix demonizes the young ones. The problem is that the area receives a lot of hype because of recent events, so extra officers are drafted in. And so you see things like the lads who are hanging around getting picked up and bundled in the back of a police van, then dumped somewhere else thirty minutes later; sometimes in another gang's territory. You see a group of three girls told they can't walk home together, and so one of them has to walk home alone, a teenage girl. There's no connection between the police and community. If someone dies, the Matrix will allocate a liaison officer. But if it's just a shooting, then there'll just be a preliminary interview.

'The truth is it's not the gang members, per se, that are the problem: it's the older people giving them guns and drugs. Even the worst ones are still just kids. I'll have them in here for a session, and they'll be really well behaved. Then I go out a few hours later, and see them smashing something up. So I tell them to pack it in. And they do. They like me. I guess I give them something they don't get at home, a lot of them anyway – attention, and care.'

And finally a former criminal now working as a manual labourer: 'I live here. My dad grafted – he blew safes – and I dealt drugs. So I know how wrong the police are getting it. If they caught someone like Liam Smith, they'd have said they'd caught a big fish. But they're not: the scary ones – the Gees, the Wrights – that's who they should be concentrating on.'

Against all this, we should lay the police's side of the story – the success of SOCA; the feeling of safety their obvious presence in the community gives to many of the residents. The problem is that for some people the targeting of youths has become symptomatic of a wider social problem. As the former criminal put it: 'The problem is that society in general is so keen to see the difference between right and wrong these days; it's black and white. I help a lad out who's been involved in all sorts; but for most of his life he had been a straight A student. Never been in a bit of trouble. Then he found the bodies of two women who'd been killed by a madman in an alley near his house, and he went straight off the rails. Is he a bad lad? What about my mate who served in the army for years, who was traumatized, and who would drink and get violent when he came back from service overseas. Is he a bad man? No, but his CRB says he's violent, so he's not allowed to work with society – no job as a bus driver, or in Asda, or wherever; he's completely limited. It's not the reality the police and papers portray.'

In October 2007 the Rhys Jones case took an unexpected twist. The name of his killer apparently became public knowledge. There were reports that it had been plastered in mocking graffiti around the area in which Rhys had died; some of it read: '—— is a bad shot'. A comment on a YouTube gang video was soon picked up on by the media: One commenter wrote: 'Who da fuck is no one? It was —— who killed Rhys and everybody knows.'

And so it appeared that everybody in Croxteth and Norris Green did know, but it seemed they did not want to tell the police. There had been a number of reports in the national press which quoted police sources and made insinuations about the community's complicity in protecting his killer. One *Independent on Sunday* story said: 'A vow of silence – a Scouse version of the Sicilian mafia's *omerta* – means that no one is prepared to "grass up" the gunman.'[2]

Yet, as with Jessie James in Manchester, this is a far from clear-cut truth. The community figures to whom I spoke were certainly dismissive of such reports. One said: 'There is no wall of silence. Who, actually, would have seen Rhys Jones's killing? There were a lot of phone calls after the event, giving them the names – what else can the community do?

'It's not that there's no fear of reprisals at times – it's just that it's more complicated than that. One child recently was kidnapped by another gang: the family wanted to go to court, but the house was firebombed. They were put under police protection, and eventually ended up in a hostel, which puts a bad message out to the community. If you want to make a complaint about something to housing associations, it's not going to be anonymous. Your name will be read out in court. The point is that there isn't a fear of the gangs, so much as certain individuals. We've known who the dodgy families are in this area since the 1980s, and nothing's been done about them. So the community just gives up.'

Again, against this we might put the police's side. Emotive as Rhys Jones's killing was, the huge public interest takes no account of the fact that it was no easier to solve than any other case; it arguably made it more difficult. Yet despite this pressure, on 16 December 2008 Sean Mercer, the youth who killed Rhys Jones, was sentenced to a minimum of 22 years in prison for murder. The prosecution at Liverpool Crown Court revealed that Mercer received a call at 6.40 p.m. on 17 August 2007 from Melvin Coy, 25, to alert him to the presence of three Norris Green gang members in the area. Eighteen minutes later, he received a call from Gary Kays, 26, who told him their precise location. Mercer was at the home of a friend, seventeen-year-old Dean Kelly, at the time. He left the house and went to pick up a gun, a 1915 .455 Smith and Wesson revolver, from twenty-year-old James Yates.

Outside the Fir Tree pub, there were people on benches, drinking in preparation for the England vs. Germany football game to be played that evening. Rhys Jones was crossing the car park in his football kit. At approximately 7.30 p.m., Mercer rode out from behind the pub and stopped. Still astride his bike, he took careful aim with both hands on the gun and fired three bullets across the car park at his targets, one of whom was twenty-year-old Wayne Brady. The first bullet shattered the rear light of a car twenty yards away. Rhys turned at the sound of this shot and was struck in the neck by the second. Sharon Lynch, 48, had seen Mercer take aim. She ran over to Rhys: 'I ran to help him,' she later said. 'I put him in the recovery position and opened his mouth to feel for obstructions. I saw a wound to his neck. It was a teardrop shape.'[3]

Mercer immediately rode to the house of a boy who was known in court as 'Boy M'. He knew what he'd done: 'I saw a kid go down,' he told Boy M.[4] His bike was left there, and later dumped on waste ground in Kirkby. James Yates and Nathan Quinn, 18, arrived at the house. Mercer used Boy M's mobile to ring a seventeen-year-old known as 'Boy X'. Boy X took the weapon from Mercer, and hid it under blankets in a dog kennel at his home (ten days later, Dean Kelly would arrive at Boy X's house and move the weapon from the dog kennel to the loft). Melvin Coy and Gary Kays arrived in a people carrier: they picked up Mercer and Quinn and drove to Coy's lock-up in Kirkby, where Mercer was doused in petrol to remove the gunshot residue, while his clothes were burned.

The police responded swiftly. On 24 August, bugging devices were placed in the homes of James Yates and Boy M. The next day several people were arrested in connection with the inquiry, one of whom was Sean Mercer. On 30 September the murder weapon was found. On 16 April 2008, Sean Mercer, then seventeen, was charged with murdering Rhys. Kays, Coy, Yates, Quinn, Kelly and Boy M were all charged with assisting an offender. The Director of Public Prosecutions decided that Boy X should be offered immunity from prosecution, an identity change and a move away from Croxteth in return for his testimony. It was only the second time that police had used the appropriate powers under the Serious Organised Crime Act 2005, and the first involving a youth.[5] Boy X gave police a description of Mercer's Hardrock Mountain bike, his most prized possession. An insurance claim revealed its serial number matched that of a bike found near Coy's workshop in the days after Rhys's death. Coy, Kays and Yates were each later sentenced to seven years in prison. Quinn received two years, Kelly four years and Boy M was given a two-year supervision order and a four month curfew from 7.00 p.m. to 7.00 a.m. Another man, James Hughes, 22, was jailed for six months for lying to police about Boy M's whereabouts when Rhys was killed.

Many of the lessons we have learned about gangs were repeated during the trial and its aftermath. Liverpool police were keen to make it clear that the 'gangs' of Norris Green and Croxteth were not organised bodies. Detective Superintendent Dave Kelly, the officer in charge of the investigation, said: 'We are not talking about the mafia here, we are talking about kids, teenagers, who lived on a housing estate. I do not want to overstate the sophistication of these groups. In essence they are very often a collection of dysfunctional and feckless youngsters who associate purely on the geographical basis of where they live.'[6] None of these people were particularly skilled or successful criminals. They could have removed the gunshot residue just as easily with water as with the petrol that would later provide a clue for the police to follow. Much was made in the press of Kays's £45,000 Audi Q7, but it turned out to have been leased.

The court heard how Mercer and his intended target had been at school together and how theirs was a longstanding and personal antagonism. Boy M, to whose house Mercer went straight after the killing, said: '[It] wasn't like a big gang, just a bunch of lads who sit by the shops. We didn't see ourselves as the Croxteth Crew . . . I've been beaten up by the Strand but that is a completely different thing because I live in Crocky.'[7] This was a boy who had not left his house in two years after a beating he received for naming Croxteth gang members to the police. As he told the court, he would 'just sit in my room, and I have got an X-Box and Sky and a Playstation 2 so I've got three things to choose from. I play that all day, then I go to bed and I get up the next morning and that's another day of my life gone.' Yet in the witness box he still said: 'I hope all Norris Green people die.'[8]

This territorialism does not exist in a bubble. It may be the preserve of a youthful, violent minority, but it is a problem the whole community must deal with, for it drags everyone in – the innocent along with the guilty. The girlfriend of Wayne Brady, the intended victim, had to move house along with her family after their home was shot at because of her relationship with him. Boy M's grandmother had pressure put on her to change her story, while his mother told the court that since telling the police about the three defendants' presence in her house, she had become known in the area as a 'grass'.[9] Despite this the problem for the police was finding proof, not dealing with a community gripped by fear: 190 witnesses came forward.[10] The families and loved ones of some of the accused subsequently also found themselves facing charges for their involvement. Janette Mercer, the 49-year-old mother of the killer, who worked in the city centre as a prostitute, was jailed for three years after admitting lying to the police about the colour of the bike her son owned. Francis Yates, 49, and his wife Marie, 51, the parents of James Yates, received sentences for perverting the course of justice. Marie, who was heard on surveillance praising Mercer for his 'bottle', destroyed an incriminating SIM card, while Francis suggested an alibi to Mercer.

We were reminded that those involved in this sort of criminality are not necessarily living in absolute poverty. Boy X, accused of harbouring the murder weapon, was on a family holiday in Florida when the police raided his house. Mercer frantically phoned and texted him 13 times in 15 minutes to alert him of the raid. His sister described her horror when, shaking, he came into their villa and told her a gun had been found at her home. She told him not to say any more, because she'd repeat it to the police.[11]

One development which received mostly positive coverage was that Operation Matrix, set up by the police early in 2008 to combat youth gangs, resulted in 5,800 stop-and-searches in its first twelve months.[12] Few commentators asked whether this was the only, or even the best, way of dealing with the problem. While there was plenty of interest in the gangs of the area, the fact that they were just one manifestation of high overall crime rates was ignored. Only the local press reported that the pub outside which the shooting had taken place was shut down in February 2008. The police found £2000 in cash, nine ounces of cannabis and empty drugs wrappers under the pool table.[13] Surveillance showed that drugs were being sold in the same car park where Rhys had been shot only six months earlier.

The gangs of Norris Green and Croxteth need to be seen in the context of the entire city. Crime in these areas is actually lower than the rest of Liverpool – 159 crimes per 1,000 population, compared to 175 in Liverpool as a whole.[14] They are far from being the only gangs, and the individuals within them are not all violent. The nature of the gangs' violence in these areas draw a great deal of attention; but it is hard to gauge whether they are more brutal than other gangs in the city. We could find gangs in Bootle, or Kirkdale, or many other areas. In Kensington, the L7 postcode which lies just to the west of the city centre, the main youth gang is the Kensington Riot Squad (KRS), which is occasionally backed up by the Wavertree Riot Squad. They are predominantly white, and are involved in street robbery and drugs dealing. Children within primary school claim to be members.

I found out about them from a non-gang-involved girl who attended a local state school:

'You can always see the KRS coming; they have caps which they pull up and over their ears. I'd say about seventy-five per cent of the kids in my school are involved in the KRS in some shape or form. They threaten anyone at school who isn't a part of the crew. They'll pull their hood down and give you a quick punch in the stomach in the corridor as they walk past. You'll never know who's doing it, but they'll just let you know they've got a problem with you. One of them told me he was going to get the Ungis on to me; said he knew them all – they're a crime family. It's all mouth – well, most of the time it is.

'There's kind of a race issue going on there, because they usually have fights with the Young Offenders Crew [YOC], which is mostly a black gang. It happened because the black guys were dating white girls within the school, so they went after them. There were stabbings in school and then the YOC started going after white people. They shot one, knifed another. The Young Offenders Crew is everywhere – there are people in Crocky, Toxteth. If you want to be in that crew, you have to have done time for assault. I know one of them because he was at an anger-management class with me; we get on well. The day he got out of prison there was a girl waiting outside with a baby saying it was his, which kind of gives you the idea of the kind of life he leads.

'The KRS will sometimes go to Crocky to fight with the gangs up there, but since all the headlines everyone thinks they're more serious than the other crews; some people are terrified of them. The kids I know who come from there say it's not really the case, there're just a few more guns about. I don't really know, but kids from Norris Green will always get a lot more respect. But I sometimes wonder, what happens if one of those crews had, say, managed to kill some-one in the school? Then all you'd hear about would be them.'

I asked the girl why she wasn't involved in gangs. She replied: 'It's just not my thing. I have my own friends and places I'm hanging out because I'm heavily involved in politics.'

It is politics, ultimately, which gives us a good picture of how this area has changed. Of the youth gangs and of the influence of 'organ-ized' criminals upon them, there is little difference to what we see elsewhere. They are problems that could, in theory, hit any area – but what makes a community like this less resilient?

The most obvious factor is the issue of poverty, and with it unemployment. The damage was done in Liverpool, as elsewhere, by a series of large-scale industrial closures in the latter half of the twentieth century: Plessey and GEC closed down, as did car plants and industrial estates around Bootle, and there was a decline in dockyard labour. Forty-one per cent of Norris Green is unem-ployed, compared with a citywide average of 34 per cent. It is not a surprising figure, given that 45 per cent of the youth have no educational qualifications. There are a few building sites around the area; I spoke to the builders about the area, but discovered little: not one of the builders was local. Those who do have jobs earn an average of £17,000, compared to a national median of £23,244.[15]

The bulk of Norris Green is formed of social housing – only 42 per cent own their own houses, in comparison with 70 per cent in the rest of the city. There has been a lack of investment in the area. One must sympathize with a council that in recent history has been faced by a declining population as its residents headed south to find work – with fewer tax revenues, it still had to provide the same infra-structure. But the city centre has had large-scale reinvestment, while poorer areas have been left untouched. An indication of the quality of housing is the council tax band – 0.3 per cent of Norris Green houses are in the C band or above, compared to 21 per cent in Liverpool as a whole.[16]

The council has invested in certain areas, but it creates jealousy elsewhere: the residents of Norris Green and Croxteth can look with envy down the road to Kensington, where there has been money poured into a new project around Edge Lane; the population of this area comprises more people from ethnic minorities. Locals say it was a big factor in the BNP fielding a candidate in Norris Green in the May 2006 elections, who finished second to Labour.

This returns us to the issue of politics. In 1983 a new Labour-Militant council was elected. It was, in the words of Tony Byrne, an important figure in policy formation, a cry for help on behalf of the city:

> The interplay of economic decline and social dislocation acted as a foundation . . . Militant were able to convince the Labour Party and working class Liverpudlians that there was no alternative to their 'plan' . . . People did not vote for it because they were Marxist. They voted for the popularity of its Labourist shout for 'no cuts in jobs and services' . . . There was a sense that Liverpool had been left to rot in a policy of 'managed decline'.[17]

This council's conflict with the Thatcher Government was a fascinating period. The council threatened to set an illegal budget in order to provide a £100 million housing scheme, threatening to bankrupt itself if the Government did not provide the £30 million shortfall. It received £20 million. It tried the same trick in 1985, pressuring the Government over grant cuts by sacking 31,000 council workers, infamously delivering their redundancy notices in a fleet of black cabs. By November 1985 Labour had purged leading local figures from the party, including maverick left-winger Derek

Hatton. The legacy of this council is controversial; certainly, power was over-centralized on just a few individuals. While there were many new houses built, there were also a number of clashes with local authorities in north Liverpool over its bullying stance to housing, and with the black community in Liverpool 8.

The local attitudes which formed the background to Militant's arrival are telling. It was a politicized time within the city. The more sensational stories of violent clashes between far left and right groups received most of the headlines, but the effect was felt at a much deeper level, in local areas. In 1980 the city's Liberal Council announced plans to close Croxteth Comprehensive School. The Liberals, who had no overall majority in the council, relied on the Tories to push closure plans through. Parents and staff were angry at not being consulted: their children were to be sent to Ellergreen School, two miles away. They began a campaign of letters and petitions.

However, by November 1981 Keith Joseph, Secretary of State for Education, had approved the closure plan. And so the campaign took to the streets; acts of 'civil disobedience', such as the blocking of the East Lancashire Road and the occupation of the *Liverpool Echo* offices created publicity and generated interest. However, there was no withdrawal of the closure notice. And so on 13 July 1982, the day before closure, the community occupied the school. Parents, teachers and pupils all sat there in unison. There were about 200 people inside. The pupils set up a school council, while parents cooked and cleaned. It took £500 a week to keep the occupation running. It became a beacon of political resistance to school closures across the country, as similar campaigns sprang up in other cities. By 1983 the Labour council had come in and vowed to save the school.

One local resident who lived in the area at the time described it to me thus: 'You'd never see anything like that happen in the area today. It gave the kids a chance to fight the mainstream, but in a legitimate way. We've lost that sense of community we had at the time. And the sense of hope. There's still that spirit there somewhere, but we need something to bring it out. At this moment, there's too much mutual distrust. Why should people need the police around 24/7? Shouldn't their friends and neighbours protect them? Now they're talking about bringing in a new school for kids from Crocky and Norris Green. A great move but twenty years late.'

One local wrote a piece for a left-wing magazine which contained a telling passage regarding how he felt times have changed since the occupation of Croxteth Comprehensive:

> How can the problems of drugs and crime be solved in an area like Norris Green? The government has one answer – the Criminal Justice Centre, a fast-track court dealing with offenders in the area, pioneered in the area of Liverpool covering Norris Green. I was part of a group that met with David Fletcher, appointed as the Judge of the CJC just before it opened. He outlined the social poverty and deprivation that lay behind crime in Norris Green. 'And so' he said, 'the government has decided to grant unlimited funds to' . . . wait for it . . . 'the Criminal Justice Centre'. Not to housing, jobs, education, social centres or sports centres, but to one of the plushest courts in the country with oak panelling and marble flooring . . .[18]

The growing radical Labour movement within the council and the actions of a local community were specific to a time and a frame of mind within the city. Radical politics certainly left a negative impact on the image of Liverpool, and many feel it set back the economic re-inflation and job creation that the city badly needed.[19] But at the same time, this was a period in which communities felt they could tackle their hardships in unison, and radical politics at a local authority level undoubtedly encouraged this. In the end, we are left with

Margaret Thatcher's famous dictum: 'There is no such thing as society.' It has been interpreted in many ways; from a tribute to the joys of unbridled capitalism to a nod towards early postmodernist thinking. For many places, Croxteth and Norris Green included, it was simply a prediction.

NINE

The End of the Line

... no law-and-order initiative is going to touch the social chemistry which produces . . . drug dealing or any other major crime pattern. It's like asking doctors to prevent car crashes. What is less obvious is that when the law-and-order machine goes to work on those things which it can touch, it also tends to fail . . . this is because it still relies on the equivalent of leeches and bleeding.

Nick Davies, *Guardian*, 10 July 2003

A long train ride, and finally there is no more track. The line ends at a coastal town in the south of Britain. To name the town would do it no favours, but its problems are far from unusual.

It's a winter's evening. The place has seen better days. Once, city dwellers would flock here to take sunshine and sea air. Now, the seafront is bleak, haunted by echoes of the life that once buzzed around it. An arcade's neon lights bleed into the cold mist, their clarity underlining its emptiness. Beside it there's a foul-looking chippy and a few desultory tourist shops, all closed.

A hill leads away from the seafront. Up here, past rows of huge Victorian houses, most of them with peeling plaster and rotting doors, there is a small row of shops. Here a group of children smokes and drinks outside an off-licence. The tattered pub is closed. There's not much else. And just off this street, a huge house, bigger than the others. It costs £40 a week to stay here, and around 200 people do. They have one communal kitchen, which is open for just an hour. A family walks in, mother, father, two small children. They have come from abroad and are seeking asylum. They prepare pasta for the evening, then leave. Next, an ex-convict, released after eight years. And after him, a street drinker, a paedophile, a heroin addict, and many more come and go.

The boy smokes his roll-up. He is about sixteen, tall, and wiry. His pale skin is covered in sores. His fingers are nicotine brown. He's on a come-down from heroin. He cannot sleep. He doesn't know why he took it. He can't even remember how it felt. 'I just need some sleep . . . I just can't sleep,' he mutters. It's a long journey to get to this point, to reach the end of the line. But these people are not alone. They have company. The gangs have come here too.

The people in the huge hotel are far from being the only vulnerable ones in this town. It's a desolate place. Like many seaside towns, there are a number of reasons for its decline in a generation – the demise of fishing and mineral extraction industries and of the tourist trade. These were only the start of the community's problems.

In October 1996 the High Court ruled that local authorities had a duty under the National Assistance Act (1948) to provide care and accommodation to adult asylum seekers and appellants who were without any other means of support and who could also, therefore, be considered to be at risk. On 6 December 1999 the Asylum Support (Interim Provisions) Regulations made provision requiring local authorities in England and Wales to provide support to asylum seekers and their dependants who appear or are likely to be destitute.

This presented a problem: how could a local authority in, say, London, provide housing for these people in B&Bs and elsewhere?

It would cost a huge amount. The answer was to farm them out to places such as this town. It could offer to fill every room in a hotel for a lengthy period at a vastly reduced rate, and at the same time could legitimately claim that it had reduced the number of people staying in temporary accommodation. These people would use facilities such as doctors and libraries within the area, guaranteeing even more savings. This influx of needy people from the inner city created a huge chain of supply and demand that fed social problems. There are at least 100 foster homes in the area, and in one road there are 29 children's homes – and 19 registered sex offenders. Children are sent around to foster parents, then aged eighteen they are abandoned, as the parents need a new child in order to receive their weekly payments.

It's a damaged area, full of helpless people. At a nearby hostel, I met a group of heroin addicts and street drinkers. Some are young; some old. They are like wraiths, their faces distorted as they glide around the centre, murmuring and muttering as they come down. There are mental-health issues with many of them: depression, schizophrenia, the legacy of child abuse; any number of others. Crime, as we have learned, is opportunistic more than anything else. Where the chance to deal drugs presents itself, it will be taken. And so members of some of the gangs mentioned in this book have come here and set up shop in microcosm. They will recruit a couple of Youngers working for them in order to push the drugs. They will head into a homeless hostel, register themselves as homeless and start to give out rocks of crack in order to build a market. The workers can do nothing to stop them.

Within this market, with its steady demand and lack of competitors, the gang members make huge profits. They sell their drugs at treble what they would have paid for them at home. The people who buy their drugs can only fund their addiction for so long, and in so many ways. In order to sustain an addiction to crack, you have to spend around £300 a day. There is a finite amount of shoplifting, burglary and prostitution that anyone can do: sooner or later, they will enter the criminal justice system. This is the reality behind Britain's failure to battle crime. Crime knows no boundaries, has no scruples. It will hunt out every vulnerable person, wherever they may be, in order to exploit them. It does it in all the cities this book has not covered: in Leeds, in Sheffield, in Nottingham, all of which have attendant gang problems similar to those we have already described. And it has even found its way to the vulnerable people in this small town, hundreds of miles from the cities within which the gangs are based. It will go right to the end of the line.

The experiences of this seaside town reinforce an earlier point: the fact that today's gangs, disordered though they are, still provide the notion of order that is required for the purposes of effective drug dealing. One need only return to London and look at the exploits of one gang – the MDP (Murder Dem Pussies) – for an illustration. This gang hit the headlines in March 2007, after the murder of Kodjo Yenga, sixteen. Yenga had been walking his girl-friend's dog with her in Hammersmith Grove when a boy had approached him and asked for a fight. Kodjo had initially refused, then said: 'Let's do this.' At this, a group of youths appeared with knives and baseball bats. Witnesses claimed that there were girls chanting 'Kill him', as Yenga was stabbed twice in the heart. His girlfriend told the court: 'I ran straight up to Kodjo. He was hold-ing his heart. He was lying and I turned him over. I put his head in my lap and I was crying and I said: "Please don't die, please don't die." There was blood coming out of his mouth. I rocked him. I put my hand on his heart and said: "Please don't die." He was just moaning, making noises.' She said she had pleaded with Kodjo not to go into the area.

Two youths aged 14 and 17 were found guilty of murder, while three others, aged 17, 14 and 15, were found guilty of manslaughter.

After the verdicts, it emerged that the 17-year-old found guilty of manslaughter was in court hours before Kodjo's death. He had been arrested for the theft of a bicycle and for intimidating a witness. He was remanded on bail before a West London Magistrates' Court juvenile panel. Police had objected to bail.

This would be a brutal enough case of youth violence, but the gang element adds a disturbing dimension. The prosecution told the court that Yenga's murder was a typical MDP assault, and that it was typical to suggest a fight with youths who are not part of the gang outside of their local area and then to attack them. The gang appears to have little geographical base besides being in west London; the White City Estate and council flats around Hammersmith are the most likely places from which the gangsters will hail, but they have been found to be active across Ealing, Acton and other areas. There are signs, as with other gangs, that it is becoming more organized. MDP members now wear their gang colours at different heights on their bodies in order to signify their position – Elder or Younger. The way the gang template is able to infiltrate the interstitial zones in a large and predominantly affluent area through the power of its name is astounding: it roots out the risk individuals within it, programming them into its way of life. The fact that the gang presents this sort of danger means that it is hard to deal with it through conventional methods. Bold initiatives are required in order to target those individuals at risk and turn them away from gangsterism before they commit crimes that would not otherwise happen.

This chapter will look at traditional approaches to tackling crime in general, and show what they teach us about gangs and vice versa. Gangs are a ladder to a criminal lifestyle, and it is this lifestyle that traditional policing – detection and arrests – fails to stop. A civil servant who had worked for years in the criminal-justice system was quoted in the *Guardian* in 2003. He said:

The old Benthamite theory of a rational system producing results has collapsed. We are left with a different set of objectives which are really to do with pleasing people – the electorate, the civil servants, the prison officers ... The public and the press sing a constant mantra about putting more police back on the streets. It doesn't work. Same with long prison sentences in unpleasant conditions – they don't work. But they do work as ways of making people happy. So that's what we do.[1]

What he says is borne out by the reconviction rates of prisoners – around 80 per cent for those aged between 18 and 21. Perpetual criminals are not deterred by the threat of imprisonment; indeed within gangs it is often a badge of honour.

Are there any answers to the problem? One of the most basic facts we know about crime is that it is opportunistic: and this is where problem-oriented policing comes in. For a simple definition; let us suppose that the police have a problem with crowds gathering outside a nightclub at closing time, making a row or fighting. Traditional policing would see officers stationed there attempting to arrest members of the crowd who broke the law. What if the problem were analysed, and it was revealed that the nightclub could open another exit so as to disperse the people inside onto separate streets? On a much wider level, this policy means addressing the personal and social factors that make criminals, removing the opportunities for crime, while still making full use of traditional police powers.

Gangsterism – being a lifestyle choice, a template which can be prevented from spreading – is suited to this style of policing. But the question here is by whom the policing should be carried out. On one level, for example, it is a question of child welfare – surely not the police's job; it requires partnerships. The more time you spend with people who work in the sectors that deal with gang members, the more you understand that there is an official and an unofficial discourse. The official discourse is for the public: relentlessly author-itarian, it speaks of more police, more patrols, more arrests. But behind it, the Labour Party has made attempts to implement other ways of dealing with the situation. The struggles that it has had in doing so are fascinating and show the difficulties with manipulating large statutory bodies.

The most obvious effort in the early years of the Labour Govern-ment was the Crime Reduction Programme. By 1998 the party had implemented hundreds of Crime and Disorder Reduction Partnerships (CDRPs) across the country. In each area, the police were to work with community bodies such as social workers and housing officials to set their priorities and come up with tactics required for them. However, the whole enterprise was poorly implemented at both the top and bottom levels; a lack of funding (then, later, overly centralized funding) and lethargy among the local partners was exacerbated by the fact that there was neither the time nor the training to record and evaluate data, and produce the tactics required. By March 2002 the Crime Reduction Programme had closed. A Home Office review of it found it to be a failure: it bluntly asserts, 'The focus on innovation all but disappeared from the programme within 12 months of it beginning' and 'The level of crime reduction activity was well below the original expectations and projections for the CRP'.[2]

However, the legacy it has left has not been entirely negative. The Youth Justice Board now has Young Offending Teams and Youth Offender Panels in every area. Many of the local schemes that were born of the programme are still running, albeit without - central funding. The law still requires police and local authorities to work together. Perhaps the biggest damage that has been done is not at any practical level, but at a sentimental one. The appetite for radical initiatives has been dampened; there is no more guidance from researchers nor funding for evidence-based innovation.

The problem is that if there is one thing the gang problem as covered in this book requires, it is radical solutions. No other problem is as entrenched within youth of certain communities, and what appears to be happening in some areas – the clear conjoining of the youth and the organized criminal group under a single cultural umbrella – sets a dangerous precedent. At the moment, it appears that traditional law enforcement is taking priority; and with it comes targets, which lie at the centre of an extraordinary story on which the *Guardian* reported in 2003.

In July that year, the journalist Nick Davies covered the case of Steve Pilkington.[3] Pilkington was the Chief Constable of Avon and Somerset Police at the time. His approach was radical – as Davies reported:

> 'Believing that there is more to policing than simply arresting and convicting offenders, Mr Pilkington has championed "geographic policing", using beat managers to build links with communities so that finally and genuinely, his officers can claim to be policing by consent; and he has trained all his officers in problem-solving so that they can try to cut crime before it reaches the criminal justice system, by working with other agencies to unravel the problems that lie behind offences.'

Under Pilkington the police in Bristol had been able to win the trust of the black community there, even after a black man had been shot by armed officers, by telling it all the facts about the case and by allowing it to communicate directly with the police.

However, as Davies reported, Pilkington's job was suddenly put under threat by the Home Secretary. In July 2001 a team from HM Inspectorate of Constabulary arrived in Bristol to review the work of the central district Basic Command Unit (BCU). Before it arrived, it asked for the force's figures. Policing figures are a much debated point among chief constables. It is only right that forces are held to account, but like the disturbance that Pilkington prevented, much police work is not quantifiable. Davies quoted an officer who says that certain targets give an incentive to ignore serious criminals in favour of 'hunting down the young . . . and the mentally frail'. Likewise, the Home Office defines a Persistent Offender as one who has been convicted of six offences in twelve months – as Davies retorts, not so much a persistent offender as a stupid one.

Davies reported that Pilkington's number-one priority at the time was an ongoing battle between Yardies and the city's original drugs gang, the Aggis. He claims that the year the Yardies had arrived in the city, 2001, had seen a rise of 72 per cent in terms of serious crime. They could not be simply arrested away – instead there had to be cooperation between the police, the immigration and customs authorities, and the community. As Davies puts it:

> Fundamentally, the operation against the Yardies was part of a wider effort to work outside the frame of conventional law enforcement by taking a 'problem-solving approach', recognising that most persistent offenders were drug addicts and/or illiterate and/or homeless and/or mentally ill and/or jobless, and that there was simply no benefit to the community in arresting them yet again and sending them off on a tragic roundabout of ineffective consequences . . .
>
> The report into the force took little notice of this: the inspectors went on to say that central Bristol was underperforming compared with the other 17 BCUs in its family, even though none of the others contained a city centre (15 of them were suburbs, two of them provincial towns); and none had been invaded by several hundred armed Jamaican gangsters with a ready supply of crack cocaine.

The report suggested that the new police standards board would take over the BCU, forcing Pilkington out of his job, and destroying the years of groundwork that had been put in place. The Association of Police Officers intervened in the matter. It was reported that the then-president, Sir David Philips, was appalled at the report. He is believed to have visited the HM Inspectors at the Home Office, where he warned they were making a mistake. The standards unit eventually agreed to collaborate with the central Bristol BCU, and allow it to continue with its original methods.

As an aside, while the story behind Davies's article is important, we should be cautious in accepting the idea of a sudden battle between the Aggis and the Yardies for control of the drugs trade. Gangs in the city are no different to anywhere else. There have been Jamaicans living in Bristol since the seventeenth century. The violence between the two groups was, according to community figures, more to do with individual antagonisms and issues of respect than control of any drug market. While we have not analysed the influence of the Yardies' arrival in the 1990s on black British communities (it is covered in other books at length)[4] there is a general belief that their influence upped the stakes for gang members in those communities, in a way which was not experienced by others. The Yardies are just one criminal group among many, but their legacy is still felt today.

As elsewhere, bloodlines are a crucial factor. One community figure put it to me: 'There are certainly organized and dangerous drug dealers, but the whole gangs thing is really about hype among the kids. You tend to find the most likely reasons a kid will get involved is because they want to live up to the reputations of their brothers or their cousins. Most of the major battles are between large groups of people who are related in some way, all trying to protect each other.

'If you look at the Aggis now, a lot of the major players have been arrested. There's constant pressure to prove themselves from the streets. It's not a gang that people will say they're a part of if they don't want heat on them. But the name of a gang can carry weight. I was in one secondary school recently and the kids were wearing hoodies over their uniforms with a gang tag embossed on the back.'

Bristol works a little differently to some of the areas we have visited, in that there are a relatively high number of areas that incorporate different ethnicities. The low-rise flats and terraced houses of St Paul's comprise far from the only interstitial area in the city, and certainly not the only area where crime is committed. In Barton Hill and Hillfields' council flats there is a mixture of white working class and Somali, and both groups have class-A drug dealers in their midst. Surprisingly, upmarket Clifton is the easiest place to buy guns, from the predominantly white or Asian criminals who have made the big time. In Easton there is a mixture of white, black, Asian and African, and all groups have their various criminals.

One community worker showed me a square in one of the parks: 'On that bench we have Somalis, on that one we have Asians, on that one we have Jamaicans, and all of them have their own client base. So much of the violence in Bristol is unreported. I mean recently you've had a Somali guy getting his throat slashed, a couple of shootings – and you never hear a word about it, until something happens to make it a story: usually if they can find a gangs angle. Sometimes the different cultures can bring negative things, but it doesn't always work like that. I showed a bunch of kids a video about a killing – the Brits were laughing, but Somali kids – well, one of them started vomiting. Some of them have seen war, so they know what violence is about. Some of them might be disturbed from it, but others can tell the kids how it's not a game. There was a shooting at a club recently that was reported as a gang incident, but it was nothing to do with that; it was groups of relatives who had issues. Violence is just an everyday topic for the kids in these communities to talk about.'

Crime does not differ dramatically along ethnic lines, though the different groups do tend to specialize in types of drugs. In terms of gangs, this chemistry makes life difficult for youth workers: they need to unpick layers of loyalty. Are the gangs loyal to their ethnicity or their area, or both? There have been sporadic outbursts of violence between the different groups, but it is often too simplistic to ascribe it to racial tension. Antagonism between individuals will draw in friends and family members, who are likely to be of the same ethnicity. The territorialism of postcode rivalries, primarily between BS5 and BS6, had created a situation which has, as elsewhere, allowed senior criminals to carry out their activities under less scrutiny.

Beyond the difficulties with how problem-oriented policing has been implemented, there have also been theoretical mistakes made by Labour. There has been a de facto acceptance of the 'broken windows' thesis. This idea, pioneered in America, runs thus: evidence of decay (accumulated trash, broken windows, deteriorated building exteriors) remains in the neighbourhood for a reasonably long period of time. People who live and work in the area feel more vulnerable and begin to withdraw. They become less willing to maintain public order or to address physical signs of deterioration. Sensing this, teens and other possible offenders become bolder and intensify their harassment and vandalism. Residents become yet more fearful and withdraw further from community involvement and upkeep. This atmosphere then attracts offenders from outside the area, who sense that it has become a vulnerable and less risky site for crime. Its influence is seen in a number of Home Office publications, through phrases such as 'physical and social disorder are distressing in their own right, but they are also important because they can lead to more serious crime'.[5]

As mayor of New York, Rudolph Giuliani (with his police chief, Bill Bratton) famously adopted the broken-windows approach. During his reign the number of police officers was increased, and all manner of minor criminals were targeted. The city's crime rate plummeted. Overall violent crime was cut in half and the murder rate went down a stunning 70 per cent between 1990 and 2001, silencing all but the most stubborn critics. However, retrospective research by academics has begun to question whether it was the result of Giuliani's policy at all. Some have claimed it was down to a drop in crack prices,[6] others due to unrelated growth in the prison population due to Rockefeller drug laws,[7] others that the number of males born into broken families was dropping due to changes in abortion law,[8] and still others that there were simply more jobs at the time.

The broken-windows theory might hold truth in some areas, especially with relation to vandalism, but as a general theory of crime it is dubious. Much of the time I spent writing this book involved walking around housing estates and blocks of flats that were in better shape than the areas in which most of Middle England live. It is indicative of an earlier criticism; that much Government thought on crime looks at it pathologically, rather than structurally. The danger is that this style of thought can (indeed, already has, in the minds of some police leaders)[9] translate itself into what has been known as 'zero tolerance' policing, whereby there is an attempt to chase down every minor offence possible, under the misapprehension that this is tackling the roots of crime. Rather than badly implemented, this manifestation of problem-oriented polic ing is misconceived. The dangers of this style of policing in the areas already covered in this book should be obvious, serving to further damage a relationship between community and authority that is often under pressure.

We can show the dangers of this style of policing by looking back in time. What if we were to broaden our definition of the word 'gang' for a while, beyond those with a name and territory (very much a modern phenomenon), to incorporate all violent youth groups? One of the best ways to reconsider this is through a reappraisal of Beatrix Campbell's 1993 book, *Goliath*. Campbell, a journalist and broadcaster, investigated a series of riots that took place across housing estates in Cardiff, Oxford and Tyneside in 1991. Many of her conclusions are relevant to this book. As we have stated previously, the riot and the gang have much in common, in whatever shape the latter may take. As with the riots mentioned earlier in this book, those investigated by Campbell differ from the legal definition of a riot in the Public Order Act: 'a collective disturbance for a common purpose'. As Campbell puts it:

> The riots of 1991 were something else: they were a cacophony of dissenting voices – dissenting from each other. What they showed was what divided the communities, not what bonded them. The protagonists were young men whose response to the world they lived in was pestering and predatory. The *places* they firebombed were not icons of public pain and punishment – there were no Bastilles; they were mainly public service buildings or small shops.[10]

Furthermore, the riots were about gangs – in this case without name or territory, but still groups of young men for whom criminality was commonplace, and who tormented their neighbourhoods while simultaneously being a part of it. Campbell's take on the communities is unapologetically feminist: she defines the different ways that the women and men react to poverty; the latter with chaotic violence, the former providing 'survival and solidarity'. She describes

> . . . a young man who is a glue sniffer and petrol bomber, a burglar and joyrider who takes tea with his mother and tidies his room. He costs his community a fortune. But he has lived his life in an era which disinvested in the social skills he might otherwise have acquired – literacy, work and cooperation. Nothing made a difference,

except now and again his mother and his girlfriend. They were the ones who made him get up in the morning and keep appointments and think about something else other than having hallucinations, cars, and breaking and entering.[11]

Campbell's argument demonstrates that criticism of the single-parent family, as applied by Jack Straw to the black community, is nothing new in terms of official rhetoric. It has been directed at the white working class for decades. She argues that as this class became known as the *underclass* throughout the 1980s, mothers (especially single mothers), rather than masculinity, were scapegoated: 'The effect of economic crisis was, of course, *gendered* but mothers were culpable for the lads' culture of predation that tyrannized the places of the poor.'[12] Yet as Campbell proves throughout the book, the mothers were all that stood between the boys and outright anarchy. She describes the problems of parenting teenage boys when the 'things which other classes can call upon to calm the maelstrom . . . playgroups, cars, tutors, swimming baths, videos, cubs and brownies, music classes . . . all cost money'.[13]

As she correctly points out, the problem within these communities is not a lack of male role models, but rather the female impotence in the face of the masculinity within these areas:

'As that child entered his adolescence, what alternative way of being could attract him? . . . his *mother* . . . she could not be his role model, it seems. Anyway, he was already at war with her. What she did was take care of people. What all the other men in his life – his father, his uncle, the brotherhood who threw bricks at the buses, the police, the court – promoted was what he himself now perpetrated, simple force.'[14]

However, I cannot agree with every aspect of her argument. Just as she is quick to criticize the columnist Tony Parsons for writing about the 'tattooed jungle' and in doing so conflating 'the working class with the lads he meets on the terraces', so she presents the women she meets who commit crime with an economic purpose (such as fraud) in direct contrast to the male vandals and joyriders of their estates. There are plenty of men who 'graft' in the way that these women do, and in this book we have seen how there are women who are quite happy to buy into the intimidatory power offered by gang affiliation. This might not always involve them committing violence, but many do, usually on other women. The female off-shoots of certain gangs, such as the Cherry Ladies in South London's Charlton, are a threatening and violent group that intimidate and harass the non-gang-involved females within their communities.

There is, however, a great deal more to be gleaned from *Goliath*. If, as stated earlier, we are to treat white working-class communities as beginning to acquire the traits of established interstitial zones during the Thatcher years, then Campbell's book teaches us a lot about the authorities' approach to them. More than anything, it shows us where we have come from. Campbell shows how a scheme like Neighbourhood Watch did little for communities dominated by crime, within which there is a communal complicity, framed by the idea that the working class could 'forgive fugitives from the class enemy': 'People knew what was going on, they were familiar with the power of the criminal fraternity. The lads ensured that the graffiti announced who was innocent and who was guilty. Some man up for murder in the week of the riot was, of course, deemed to be innocent; some man up on sex offences was a pervert; some girl was a slag; some person was a grass.'[15]

More than fifteen years on, official rhetoric is still centred on crime prevention and legitimate community policing, rather than the building of bridges between the interstitial community and the mainstream. The same graffiti abounds in the areas covered in this book, the same knowledge of who has done exactly what is shared by all. Likewise, one of the riots described in Campbell's book was initiated by the death of a pair of boys in a car accident after the police had chased them while they were in a stolen car. The father of one of the boys described his son as a professional car thief, rather than a joyrider, to the local press – a statement which was deemed reprehensible by its readers. Yet as Campbell argues: 'he had made a poignant effort to give his son the status of a skill . . . It was a quest to clothe a life in moral virtue when it had ended in disgrace: profession implied a social purpose.'[16]

As we have seen, this gap between the two worlds has, if anything, grown. In 2008 I am talking with a black gang member in east London when a middle-aged woman walks by. He says hello, and soon he begins to chat to her: 'You workin'? You going to the office? How late you working till? No fucking way . . . I thought they'd abolished slavery.' She laughs. She tells him – this drug dealer, this gun criminal, this kidnapper, this villain – about how he should get a girl. 'Fuck that, I'm still shooting. When I stop dodging bullets, then it's safe for the stork can come my way.' She laughs again. There is warmth, compassion. She knows him well. As Campbell argues, as rich and poor moved further apart geographically and economically, as crime among poor neighbourhoods rose, the politicians of the 1980s and early 1990s defended themselves by infusing respectable society with a very clear notion of 'Goodies' and 'Baddies'. It is a notion and a rhetoric which has taken hold. I speak to some of my friends about the book I am writing: 'Jesus, aren't you scared?' 'Why would they talk to you? How do you even find them?' 'Have they ever robbed you?'

Bad things happen in Gangland, and the amount of it that is never reported is stunning. It takes a little time to gain the trust of interviewees, and then they come in a great deluge: a boy is murdered, and the perpetrators phone his friends to tell them they will piss on his grave. A man refuses to act as a getaway driver, and so the gang heads to his house and slash his throat. Yet this happens among people who have known each other for years. It's the flip side of what happens to these communities when links to normality are damaged.

However, the most important lesson to be gleaned from *Goliath* is a positive one: it lies in the policing aspect. There is little room for community-based (let alone problem-oriented) policing in Campbell's book. The police here are brutal; a blunt instrument that serves only to estrange the communities they pretend to serve. She mentions the Scarman report into the Brixton riots of 1981, which cited the racism of the police as an issue.[17] The Chief Officers in the book are uncertain about their role in maintaining public safety, and have received little guidance from the Home Office. The overall impression is that the police force is a macho institution that serves only to heighten the savagery of the youths within the rioting areas. Today's police force, like all large organizations, is far from perfect. But if this book has highlighted the problems with trying to implement constructive police strategies in recent years, *Goliath* provides a telling reminder of how much worse the situation used to be.

Continuing with our wider definition of gangs as all violent youth groups, a lack of links upwards into more profitable criminality does not stop groups of youths being extremely violent. Indeed, the violence they commit is often directed at innocent members of the public – perhaps more so than the heavily involved gangsters with their limited perceptions of the world, whose violence is often constrained to the latest beefs, and for whom the general public are often less viable targets to assault or rob than members of their own community.

In August 2007, Gary Newlove, a 47-year-old father of three, was killed by three youths (Adam Swellings, 19, Stephen Sorton, 17, and

Jordan Cunliffe, 16) whom he confronted outside his house in Warrington. He believed they had been vandalizing a neighbour's digger, and remonstrated with them. They beat him to death, kicking his head like a football. It later emerged that Swellings had been released on bail on the day of the attack, under the condition that he was not to enter Warrington. Prior to the attack, he had drunk five litres of cider. Sorton had downed up to ten lagers and a litre of cider and Cunliffe three bottles of lager.

It was a heartbreaking case: it emerged that Newlove had previously set up a Neighbourhood Watch scheme and liaised with police to stop youths drinking and committing acts of vandalism around his home. His youngest daughter had written him a letter while he lay dying in hospital, in which she said: 'I love you with all my heart, so please don't give in. I know you can fight this, as you are a strong, loving man who I know loves me no matter what. I am asking you to be strong and don't give in as I love you too much to believe that you won't go without a fight. You mean the world to me and I wouldn't change you for the world.'[18]

Later his widow would give a furious speech. She said:

'Until the Government puts into place an effective deterrent, the youth of today know too well that they can get away with their actions . . . For all too long youngsters have been drinking and smoking into the early hours and then deciding to do acts of criminal damage and beat people up as a joke because of their influence by drink and drugs. They should not be allowed to congregate on street corners under the bridges putting fear into people who simply want to just pass them by without any foul-mouth back chat. Parents have to face up to their responsibilities. If the children do not face up to the action then we have to make the parents face the action. What these people need to understand is that it could be their partners or parents that it happens to.[19]

Her speech gave an indication of the misery and culture of fear that such youths create. While we are only talking about this kind of crime at a superficial level, there are a number of lessons which can be applied from earlier chapters. First, a crucial point on which media coverage tends not to dwell: such violence is still usually committed by young people who have been born into disadvantaged and disorganized communities. Again, poverty is not directly responsible for their crimes, but the background to them is the culture of frustration, low expectation and hyper-masculinity that has been allowed to build up where they live. Some of these children are particularly susceptible to the kind of risk factors that will be outlined in the Conclusion. And as in previous chapters, what this leads to is not a call for outright sympathy and tolerance for their actions: rather, it is a call for a balance within these areas between the punitive – focussed and strict policing – and preventative work – engaging with the youths that are most likely to commit these crimes. In the Conclusion I will show some ways in which this can be improved.

Moreover, it appears that the perpetrators of such crimes have plenty in common with the gangs we have investigated. There may be lessons to be learned from those who deal with more organized gangs of the inner cities. I spoke to a number of people who work with children in areas that have serious problems with anti-social behaviour, drinking and violence, but fewer of the gang problems found somewhere like London or Birmingham. The picture that emerged was similar to that which comes out of the larger cities. Here, for example, is one community worker: 'You can always tell when there's trouble coming. It's slow to come up to the boil, but you always know when it's about to burst. A young person was stabbed to death in the middle of town on a Friday night. By Monday morning, all the kids in our group were able to name exactly who the individuals were that had done it, and had seen it coming for weeks.

The reason is that there are often familial links between the kinds of people who commit this crime. The problem is that the men in this community move about the female partners so frequently. We identified eight young people in our area who we considered dangerous, and then found six of them had familial links – usually they were half-brothers. Given their connections I don't see how they're that different from gangs in London or wherever. I've been trying to get funding for a gangs project – but the police and councillors couldn't admit that we have a gang problem; it insinuates there are guns and organized crime here.'

Having looked at the background to crime prevention in the UK, it is possible to suggest solutions for the areas that suffer most from gangs.

TEN

Conclusion

'I can't tell you why I do this shit all the time. I'm just like Yogi
Bear . . . I can't leave those picnic hampers alone.'
   'Have you ever been on the London Eye?'
   'No.'
   'Why not? Wouldn't it be interesting?'
   'Yeah . . . I guess it would. I dunno. It's just . . . it's not on
my radar.'

Gang member and John Heale, 2008

Is the gang problem getting worse? I believe so. There have been
some genuinely shocking headlines in recent months. In March
2008 the *Daily Mail* obtained figures under the Freedom of
Information Act that revealed two children aged eight and three aged
nine were stopped on suspicion of breaking the Firearms Act.[1] The
picture that emerges from coverage in general is that the problem is
far worse than it has ever been across the country. The truth is more
complex.

   How, exactly, do we go about measuring the problem? There are
four main sources. The most obvious source for criminal statistics
lies in official figures presented by the police of arrests made, prosecutions, etc. However, it does not give a particularly accurate

portrayal of the situation, because so much crime is never reported. One way of measuring unreported youth crime is self-report surveys, such as the Offending, Crime and Justice Survey. However, the total sample of interviewees per year is relatively small. For what it is worth, this survey has shown little change in the last few years. Another way of knowing about crime is that recorded by other agencies, such as hospitals and refuges, a patchy way of painting a picture. For the fullest picture there is the public's response to victim surveys such as the British Crime Survey, which asks a large sample of people about their experiences of household and personal crimes on an annual basis. This is an important guide, but it does not interview children, only adults.

The fact that there is a paucity of data regarding the young is surprising given what we do know about children and unreported crime. On the one occasion that the British Crime Survey included questions about child and youth victimization, in 1992, the results showed that two thirds had been victimized in the preceding six to eight months, of whom one third had been assaulted. A 2002 Crime Stoppers survey of 1,064 boys and girls aged ten to fifteen indicated that 45 per cent did not tell their parents about their victimization and that 51 per cent did not tell the police. Children's disproportionate vulnerability to violence on the street is revealed in a recent Crime Concern survey in Camberwell and Gospel Oak, in London, which found that over 20 per cent of children and young people had been 'mugged' in the preceding year. This is 25 times the adult rate as recorded by the British Crime Survey.

If we are still to judge the gang problem in terms of number of recorded crimes, which? We could start with gun crime, as it has become synonymous with gangs. The relationship is complex, but there is evidence to suggest that at least half the gun crime committed in inner cities is perpetrated by gang members (though as we have seen, the definition of 'gang members' is far from simple itself).[2] And on the surface, the problem is clearly getting worse.

According to the Home Office, the number of all firearm crimes (including air weapons) has increased by over 50 per cent in seven years: from 13,874 in 1998/99 to 21,521 in 2005/06.[3] This is an ominous figure, yet in both 1998/9 and 2005/6 there were almost the same number of firearm homicides – 49 in 1998/9, and 50 in 2005/6, with wild fluctuations in between – it went up to 97 in 2001/2.[4] There were 58 in 2006/7 (widely reported in the papers as 'a rise of 16 per cent on last year'). This may not sound like a huge number of deaths, but there is a simple reason that many of the gang members to whom I spoke knew people who had been recently killed – the majority of gun crimes take place in Gangland.

It is a muddled picture, and this is just when trying to analyse a relatively uncommon crime: knife crime is four times more prevalent. All it really shows us is that crime figures are so arcane that they can be distorted for whichever aims are required. Even the British Crime Survey was called into question in 2007 after the think tank Civitas argued that caps on repeat victimization mean it ignores around three million crimes, and as mentioned earlier, it does not interview those under sixteen.[5]

This leads us to perhaps a more productive way of measuring the gang problem; by looking at youth crime. Can we say for sure that young people are becoming more violent? Again, the statistical picture is muddled. 2007 saw the record number of teenagers murdered in London, with 27. However, as with gun crime, homicide rates fluctuate by a huge amount: in 1995, 44 people between 5 and 16 were victims of homicide in the UK. In 2005/6 the number was 20, and it varied wildly in the years in between.[6] Usually around half of these victims are murdered by a parent. However, another concerning statistic was released in January 2008: the *Sunday Telegraph* cited Ministry of Justice reports that stated there had been a rise from 17,590 youths under the age of eighteen convicted of violent crimes in 2003, to 24,102 in 2006.[7] Is this a case of more arrests, as the Government claimed, or a decline in behavioural standards?

There are certain things we can say with certainty. First, if youth crime has risen sharply, it has certainly been accompanied by a continued demand for 24-hour news and headlines. There is a temptation to agree with the words of the American rock star Marilyn Manson in the wake of the Columbine tragedy: 'Times have not become more violent; they have just become more televised.' Second, there have been certain incidents involving teenagers in the last two years that have been more callous than usual youth violence. These incidents have been confined to a few inner-city areas, within which there are a number of obvious contributory issues: youths have easier access to guns (especially with the growing popularity of rebores), gang members are increasingly aware of the power a gang's name can hold and the youths are the first generation that has been born when gang involvement is at its peak. Contrary to various media reports, gangs are nothing new, and have operated in these areas for decades. But the growing role of the Youngers in some areas is a new phenomenon. For these youths, the ladder to serious criminality is becoming a lot more clearly defined.

It is, then, my opinion that violent youth crime – especially involving the use of guns – is on the increase within specific, small areas in the country, which are becoming more and more socially marginalized,[8] as opposed to a blanket increase. The apparently sudden appearance of violent youth gangs across the country is similar to the moral panic over muggings that took place in the 1970s. While it has some of its basis in fact, its seriousness in the public mind is first and foremost led by the media, primarily through the lumping together of all youth groups, whatever the seriousness of their crimes, as gangs.

There is also no doubt that there are more youths in gangs than ever before, for the reason outlined in Chapter 4: the changing importance of the very word 'gang'. This does not necessarily mean there are more youths carrying out crime, but the potential for this to happen is clear.[9] It could happen because of criminals exploiting the young-gang members' desire for respect, or through the escalation of conflicts that would be less serious were they not perceived by the youths as 'gang' battles, rather than old fashioned youth territorialism.

If we are to look for answers, we might start by looking at the areas where these gangs are found, and the problems they face. For the most part, it's a question of economics. To use a cliché, one does not find many gangs in Sweden. The changes that have happened to this country in the last few decades – the widening wealth gap, the decline of traditional working-class employment, the concentration of disadvantage, the cyclical nature of poverty and attendant low expectations – have been written about by others at great length. It might, however, be worth dwelling on three factors: these being inequality of education, housing and the lack of respect for, and availability of, working-class job opportunities.

Of the latter, the findings of the American sociologist John Hagedorn need only be repeated. For him, youth gangs are a natural phenomenon and had been present in the city he studied, Milwaukee, for a long time. However, these gangs had always dispersed once people grew older and began to have families and, more importantly, jobs to provide for them. Once a criminal lifestyle provided a viable alternative way of living, and working class jobs declined, the gangs became a more permanent fixture: 'The problem is not competition from whites, who don't compete with black youth for work at a ghetto McDonald's anyway, but the lack of skills needed to advance from a dead-end job to a "good job". In the absence of the "good job" the hustling outlook is entrenching itself among poor minority youth.'[10] We can dispense with the racial elements of this analysis and apply it to all the areas we have covered; as we heard in Manchester, replace 'black' with 'white working class' and many of the facts about their relationship with the general public and the authorities hold true.

This leads us to the issue of education. For an understanding, we have to head back into Gangland one last time. Eimer's secondary school lies right in the heart of a gang-dominated area in east London. She teaches English, mostly to thirteen- and fourteen-year-olds. A bright, well-spoken and articulate woman in her early thirties, she agreed to talk about her area's problems.

'Let's say I have a naughty child. Now, how might we define naughty? I suppose he's late to school most days, he plays truant, and he gets in fights in the playground. Those would be the obvious defining characteristics of a disruptive influence, wouldn't they? But think about each aspect in turn. Let's suppose he's late because he has to go round the houses – maybe he lives in one postcode and the bus to school takes him through a rival one. What about playing truant? What if someone on his estate is telling him he has to sell drugs, or do whatever they want him to do? He can't say no – he'd be risking his life to go to school. And the fights . . . what if he's getting into fights because most of the boys here are from that postcode he's just avoided, and they don't like him because of where he's from? You see, we see very little in here. That child might have avoided them all the way to school, and has to avoid them all the way back. I've had kids telling me, "Miss, I know it looks like we get on, but outside the gates it's different." But the thing is, by most definitions this *is* a naughty child. And so he needs to be expelled. Back to where he came from, where he ends up more involved than he ever was. And then his kids will do the same.

'There are other factors – what if he's not in trouble with gangs, but he's a carer, looking after younger siblings? A huge number of the pupils I teach are exactly that. But you don't realize this is the case – and if they get punished for looking after younger members of the family then of course they will become resentful of the system. I don't think we're in any way trained to deal with the risks that are behind people getting involved in the gang problem, and that in itself makes the problem worse – look at this . . .'

Eimer takes me into the playground, where for a class project the eleven- and twelve-year-old children were allowed to paint on the walls to one of the quads. You wouldn't notice it there, hiding among the pictures of houses, cats, stick-men playing football. In the top left corner there's a three-inch high postcode. It's a gang tag.

Another youth worker I spoke to worked for a Behaviour Improvement Programme within schools. He felt that part of the reason for high exclusion rates lay in schools' lack of willingness to deal with problematic pupils. He said: 'At the school where I was working, you had to read from the headteacher's hymn sheet. I was dealing with a thirteen-year-old girl who had family ties to one of the biggest crews in the borough. She'd get in trouble – partly she was a bit naughty, nothing out of the ordinary – and, moreover, people knew who she was and would pick fights. What she needed more than anything was a soft hand. I was getting a good understanding with her – anything wrong, she'd come and talk to me. Suddenly I'm told I'm spending too much time with her; but I don't spend any more time with her than with other pupils. I asked why that was, for professional development reasons, and was told in no uncertain terms that the decision was final and that was it. Pretty soon, she'd been expelled. Problem gone.

'There's a culture within schools of just passing the problem of difficult pupils on and getting rid of the problem – at another school I saw them practically duping the kids and their families into signing consent forms that would make them take alternative education in Year Ten. Schools should empower the parents to make choices –

instead too often they take advantage of the fact that parents don't understand the system.'

The most obvious cause for black youth offending that a 2007 Home Affairs Select Committee report could delineate was exclusion from school. In fact, it is one of the main factors that all youth offenders have in common: a recent MORI report showed that 60 per cent of them have been excluded from school.[11] Black children are consistently below the national average across all Key Stages, at GCSE and equivalent and post-16. The failure of black children within the education system puts them straight into the hands of the gangs. Once excluded, they are unlikely to be employed until the age of eighteen, so for several years they have time and a need to earn money. Again, this is a cyclical blight within the black community: it causes the disadvantage that will make it happen again and again.

When discussion of black people and gun crime takes place, the subject of black people's failure within the educational system is usually brought up. This axiomatic connection has prompted endless self-flagellation from the black community and adds fuel to any potential racist views: is it because of cultural factors – something within the black mindset that means education doesn't work? Or is the education system itself racist? A 2006 DfES report found 'a compelling case' for the existence of 'institutional racism' within schools. The report found that 'whilst overt racism (at least on the part of the staff) is now unusual . . . discrimination . . . persists in the form of culturally unrepresentative curricula and low expectations for the attainment and behaviour on the part of the staff'.[12] Strangely, these claims are often accompanied by a suitable caveat: it's not the teachers' fault. There is a wealth of research from different bodies which explains how the education system is 'unintentionally racist', all of which is backed up by anecdotal evidence concerning instances where teachers have accidentally discriminated against black people because of minor cultural differences.

No amount of anecdotal evidence can help the feeling that, behind it all, it is symptoms that are being addressed. A 2005 Joseph Rowntree Foundation report concluded: 'The strength of the relationship between educational attainment and family income, especially for access to higher education, is at the heart of Britain's low mobility culture and what sets us apart from other European and North American countries.'[13] The problem is not with race; it is with the quality of education available to the poor, and the fact that this education is not skilled in dealing with the rapidly changing lifestyles of the urban young. Again, unintentional racism perhaps compounds this problem; but it is not the dominant factor.

Both Tony Blair and David Blunkett denounced the aforementioned *Guardian* journalist Nick Davies's writings on the correlation between poverty and lack of educational attainment, but his arguments are persuasive.[14] Davies has shown how a school's position in league tables is determined by the social make-up of its intake. He cites research carried out by a former Chief Inspector of Schools in Sheffield. Matching census data on household poverty with individual pupil's addresses, he produced a table ranking all 27 secondary schools according to their social intake. He then compared this with academic outcomes: more than 90 per cent of the difference in exam results between schools correlated with the poverty of the children there. The influence of the schools on their results was negligible. Davies has also argued that education policy in the 1980s deliberately helped schools in better-off areas by encouraging them to opt out of local authority control. This decision increased the flow of pupils from more prosperous homes to certain schools, which also had the effect of raising their overall level of academic attainment. At the same time, the Conservatives pegged school budgets to the level of pupil intake. Since those schools that did not perform as well in the league tables attracted fewer pupils, they received fewer resources, promoting a cycle of decline.

The Audit Commission estimates that some 12,000 children are permanently excluded from school each year. This situation 'has far less to do with the discipline than it has to do with an epidemic of emotional damage, particularly among . . . British children who live in poverty', Davies states. This book has concentrated more on a willingness to exclude on the part of schools (mostly the result of a target-driven culture that determines whether or not a school continues to receive funding), but Davies is strong on just how unfair these exclusions can be. He argues that some 20 per cent of children growing up in homes where both parents are unemployed suffer mental ill-health. Children with mental-health issues are four times more likely to play truant than others and ten times more likely to be in trouble with the police. These problems are left almost entirely unchallenged by government strategy, he continues: less than half of the nation's health authorities have a policy for child mental health.

Housing is another very difficult issue. As Professor Pitts argued, most adult tenants on gang-dominated estates would move, but all the London boroughs have long housing waiting lists and, together with the transfer of housing responsibility to a plurality of housing associations, this makes it hard for them to move within, or out of, the borough.[15] Ironically, those who choose to battle the problems where they live can find themselves in a very different situation: Pitts cites a case in Waltham Forest when the leader of the Beaumont residents' association attempted to stand up to the gang – such was the threat to him and his family that the police and housing authority persuaded him to move elsewhere. There are varying qualities of youth provision and policing, which are determined by the power of tenants' associations and how the housing providers see their roles. For some, their job barely extends beyond simple maintenance, while others are willing to engage with the youths in the area.

*

In the absence of any quick fix, there is a need to look at alternatives, which returns us to our original question: what are we fighting? The media has tried to impose order on chaos in recent years: it has attempted to reduce gangs to individual bodies, and found itself confused as to how, despite being so fluid, they can exert such control and be responsible for such drastic deeds. The authorities, for their part, have usually accepted a tripartite definition of 'the gang': a pyramid of organized criminals, street gangs and peer groups. In searching for answers, it would be better to do away with both concepts, and instead look at how we can deal with individuals. As one criminologist put it to me while trying to contrast the allegedly more organized gangs in America with those here: 'We have gangsters in this country. We have gang territories. We have gang life. But we don't really have gangs.'[16]

What, then, of these individuals? Let us start with the youngest: how do we know which will become gang members? It is hard to find research, but some has, in fact, been carried out. It was done on behalf of the Metropolitan Police in 2004 by a charity called Communities That Care which paints a very accurate picture, but it has been kept closely guarded due to the fear that it might allow the media to paint a bad picture of specific communities.[17] The survey interviewed around 11,000 children aged between ten and fifteen who lived in Inner London. On the one hand, it was a typical self-reporting survey, in which the children anonymously described what crimes they had committed in the previous year. However, it also sought to identify the things that made the children more likely to offend and those which made them less likely: these are risk and protective factors. The charity threw questions into the survey that asked about seventeen potential risk factors – from poor parental supervision and discipline, availability of drugs, truancy and peer attitudes – and five potential protection factors, including school and family rewards for involvement. The findings of this survey cast a clear light on why it is that people become involved in gangs. The first thing to bear in mind is that its subjects are very young, and they are in school. They are not the most likely to be involved in gangs; so certain factors about the minority that are have been clearly highlighted.

Of the total number, 402 were found to be seriously involved in gangs with a name and their own territory; 482 had ten or more members in this group. Of this latter number, one of the biggest factors they had in common was the disorganization of their community: 84 per cent answered in the positive to questions about fighting, crime, drug selling, graffiti and adults with guns in their neighbourhood. This can be compared with 61 per cent of non-gang members. It is also interesting to note that the list of top seventeen wards with a large number of children involved in a gang of any type, without name, territory etc., is completely different to the list of wards with a high number of children involved in more serious gangs. That said, many of the areas covered in both lists became familiar to me in the process of writing this book.

Both gang and non-gang members are at risk due to community disorganization and neglect, availability of drugs and availability of weapons. Peers also pose risk for gang and non-gang members. Perhaps most interesting is the fact that the protection profiles of gang and non-gang members mirror each other. Similar proportions of students, whether in or out of a gang, experience family attachment and report more family opportunities for pro-social involvement and family rewards.

If it isn't the absence of these factors, what makes for a gang member? When you look at the risk profiles of members of large gangs, the elevated risk factors were community disorganization and neglect and those pertaining to the individual (their friends' behaviour, and their own feelings with regard to social commitment). The major difference between gang and non-gang members is found in relation to the latter: 92.6 per cent of gang members are at risk due to alienation in comparison to 53.7 per cent of non-gang members. The questions about social commitment included key statements to which students were able to give their degree of agreement, such as 'I do the opposite of what people tell me, just to make them mad', 'I like to see how much I can get away with', 'It is alright to beat people up if they start the fight'. It also asked whether the respondents thought it was wrong for people to drink, smoke, use drugs or pick a fight.

The reasons for the positive responses to these questions are manifold: family or peer influences undoubtedly play the biggest part – 73 per cent of gang members reported problematic family behaviour, compared to 36 per cent of non-gang members. When these children live in a disadvantaged community, the likelihood of them becoming gang members rises dramatically, and when excluded from school their chances of involvement skyrocket. The picture that emerges with regard to gang affiliation is of a complex series of social factors that play off each other.

As criminologist Steve Shropshire has put it: 'To reduce the problem to only a handful of causal factors such as poor parenting skills, low teaching standards, lack of male role models, security (safety in numbers and so forth) and the ease of profiteering from illicit drug markets is to fail to understand the dynamics at work. The street gang culture has multifarious causal factors arising out of a complex intertwining of social, educational and economic exclusion and marginalisation, familial patterns and inequalities both real and perceived.'[18]

What all this means is that any attempt to understand gangs sometimes feels like trying to catch the wind. There will always be questions that are near-impossible to answer. Why, for instance, might one sibling devote himself utterly to the gangs, while another leads an upright life? What is it that makes one community so ridden with gangs that it has the highest proportion of child members in London, while at the same time it is a great deal lower than many others in terms of its violent crime statistics?[19] Again, no single theory gives an answer to what makes a gangster: ultimately gangs are made up of individuals, and what we see in any place at any one time is a reflection of this. The best way to envisage the situation is to imagine a class in school: which children are naughty, which are bullies, and what are the reasons? In some, their home life is very obviously a factor; in others, less so. And for a teacher, these few individuals have a huge knock-on effect on the rest of the class. Some children will start to behave like them; others will have their studies affected by the behaviour of that group. So it is with gangs.

If this gives us an (admittedly limited) idea of the children we are dealing with, the next question is: who should take responsibility for them? As one youth worker said: 'There is a cycle of blame. Police blame parents. Parents say the kids' problems start in the schools. The schools say the police aren't protecting them from the risk pupils. In reality, it's the responsibility of all three.' As mentioned earlier, it is not a question of how 'high up' these individuals are, but one of 'how involved': a subtle but important difference. Let us start with those who are least involved – usually the youngest.

The Joseph Rowntree Foundation produced a Glasgow report in 2007 which showed that young people pooled their local knowledge to avoid hazards, including violence from more organized gangs and aggression from adults with drink and drug problems. They took responsibility for keeping themselves and friends safe by moving around in groups and looking out for each other, using mobile phones to stay in touch.[20] The danger comes when this territorialism becomes antagonistic or is subsumed into the image and deeds of criminal groups.

Youth workers must be at once detached and working with the police and Youth Offending Teams in order to retain credibility with their client base. Most gang members begin their lives in areas that suffer from social exclusion. By the time they are heavily involved, this exclusion runs so deep that they are unable to see beyond their estate or indeed other gang members and their relative allegiances and antagonisms. Bridges have to be built between this lifestyle and the mainstream economy, and the obvious sector to form these connections is the voluntary. The idea of peer mentoring, which these agencies carry out so well due to the client base they attract, is key: if gangsterism is a template that spreads as youths copy each other, then positive equivalents can also be placed within the community.

This book has shown differences between the areas that produce gangsters and those that do not, and problems that are common among youths in the former. Knowledge of these problems should not be simply factored into a response as elements into an equation. As another youth worker said: 'In the wake of a shooting I remember being at a house where there were some gang-involved youths, and two officers from the council's gangs programme turned up and tried to walk straight into the group and pick up information despite knowing no one there. It's indicative of a wider problem – you can't professionalize yourself to that extent when dealing with this issue. The people who set the strategies by which the workers operate see people in the abstract. You can't perceive these youths as little bundles of problems, all of which have theoretically defined and appropriate solutions. I don't like the concept of an underclass – it implies that these people are simply not a part of our society.' In short, gang members are human beings – to deal with them, they have to be treated as such.

And so there is one key reason that the voluntary sector should be seen as important: the fact that it often holds sufficient credibility within the community to engage with gang members. Put simply, many of its workers have lived in the community for years, know many of the individuals who might find themselves involved in gangs well, are used to working at a quick pace on a small budget, and are not viewed with the suspicion that many youths reserve for 'authority' figures. The sector has had an increasingly important part to play as gangs have taken hold in certain areas, a role that many in local or central government did not foresee.

Here is one worker speaking about his institution: 'All the statutory bodies are barred from working with gang members due to their policies. Look at their closing times: the only services available to gang members are at night. Most of these youths don't get up till six in the evening, which means they have access to hospitals or morgues for when they or their friends are shot, the police, prisons, and us.'

Charities traditionally do not receive the kind of funding that comes from central government to local authorities' agencies, yet even the simplest facets of their work cost a lot of money. A statutory agency can provide many of the same things that a voluntary agency can, but without the same infrastructure costs: certain venues can be provided for free, for example, while the voluntary sector has to account for every penny.

I spoke to a voluntary worker about a residential he was doing with some gang members from two opposing gangs. It was due to last a week. There were two trainers for the charity's workers, which would cost £900 a day plus travel. Then the residential would cost £3500, along with the trainers' input, while a youth worker would cost £800. And there is no doubt of the worth of such a scheme: it brings together the battling gangs, and it brings them to account for their actions. The worker described one incident: 'We sent one of the gang members home for smoking. He was escorted back to his parents and said, "Mum, I've messed up." It was the first time he'd ever been brought to account for his actions, the first time he'd begun to understand the relationship of give and take.'

There are issues with the money which the voluntary agencies do receive. A large amount of it comes in the form of grants for specific projects from various institutions. This may sound positive, but as one worker put it: 'It means everything has to be new and sexy in order to receive funding – either that or a transferable model; but there's no such thing with gangs. I don't believe the funders have social consciences. Their agenda is that they are seen to be doing good. They'd rather fund everybody, rather than fund quality. And how are these projects monitored, precisely? Usually through our filling out a proposal that looks like an encyclopaedia. Why can't they monitor us through networks, or even visit us? The funding is so short term too – a six-month project here and there. How can I employ people, especially former gang members, when there is no job security? How much can I hope to achieve in six months? It's taken decades for the situation to get this bad.'

The sight of a muscular, tattooed ex-gang member with a pained look on his face as he waded through a 60-page proposal while a group of Youngers began to convene in the hallway by his office and kick up hell was a memorable image to me; a visual illustration of the problems with trying to make these agencies accountable from afar.

There is a constant war of words between the voluntary sector and the statutory authorities in some areas; both claim they are the only ones with the capacity to engage with the most hard-to-reach individuals. During the course of writing this book I heard many dismissive statements about the statutory sector from voluntary workers and from various people within the communities regarding its ability to engage with gang-involved youths, among them: 'The kids can't stand the council workers', 'The trouble with the statutory sector is that you can't just do things', 'It doesn't listen to the kids', and 'By the time they get what they want it's not relevant or it just takes too long: there needs to be research, consultation, a committee stage. Young people find themselves frustrated by the whole process.'

These are the most basic allegations. Beyond them, many charities claim local authorities will use their work for means of publicity, taking it to Westminster as an example of good practice in order to receive funding which will top up existing services and which the voluntary sector will never see. Some also say the local authorities will latch on to their client base, allegedly in order to help them, but in reality as a means of gathering intelligence for the police. The message coming out of most of the agencies to whom I spoke was clear. As one put it: 'We are the ones doing the real work, filling in the huge gaps left by the statutory sector: and yet the local authorities neither trust nor support us. They're dismissive of the voluntary sector, commissioning a couple of bodies who are their friends.'

Who is right? Ultimately I feel the voluntary sector workers are justified in their criticisms, however much there may be an encroached 'Us and Them' attitude behind them. As one council worker said: 'The only reason the kids like me is because I don't walk in there with my suit and tie and council badge on and start promising them things like so many others do. They'd see me in the same way they'd see the police or probation.'

This leads to another problem within the statutory sector: the culture of cynicism and disregard for the communities with which it works. One local authority shows this problem at its absolute worse. Its approach has been almost a model of how short-term aims can override the long-term strategies which are required. This council has tried to negotiate with what it sees as the gang leaders, but unable to circumvent red tape in how it deals with these individuals, it has reneged on promises and succeeded in enraging them on occasion. It knows it must employ voluntary workers in order to engage with its communities, but it also knows it has to demonstrate that it is getting value for money from them. However, their work is of a nature that means success is particularly hard to quantify. The result is a constant row between the voluntary workers asking to be allowed to do their jobs, and the local authority demanding paperwork. This state of affairs is hardly uncommon, but the relationship within this authority was the worst I have seen.

The council also runs a number of schemes which are dedicated to working with gangs, one of which is compulsory to attend and has been deeply unsuccessful. The programme employs ex-criminals to talk to the children – this can be a good thing, but when they are untrained it leads to problems. These are men who have already lived the criminal lifestyle, so the youths can feel that their word is worth even less than any authority figure: why should they be telling them what to do – under an authority badge – when they have already earned their P's? There are few long-term strategies in place – just a series of programmes which suggest short-term success.

This is not being mentioned in order to inflame the disagreements between statutory and voluntary in this or any other area. It is a row that has been going on for too long, and all the while young people's lives have been lost. The key is the way that the relationship is managed. What has to be given serious consideration is the way that the two work in tandem. Common sense dictates that the statutory sector is necessarily limited, which means local authorities must be realistic in what they achieve. The alternative is to bend the rules: one former council worker cheerfully announced to me how he had embezzled money in order to employ young people to work with him, because he knew full well that they wouldn't pass their Criminal Records Bureau checks.

The balance which must be achieved is to make the voluntary sector accountable, while giving it support and freedom in how it operates. When it was launched, the Connexions service was seen as a way to bring statutory and voluntary youth work together, but in the eyes of many youth workers, it has failed miserably.[21] At its best it delivers exactly what its community needs, and the people in charge of it are credible and have the most important thing anyone working with gang-involved youths can wish for: respect. Yet every year well-respected and well-performing charities find themselves struggling for funding.

All this apart, youth work is one very small part of the landscape. The police have a vital role to play in terms of dealing with the most serious individuals. Like any other statutory body, the force's work is driven by short-term imperatives and rapidly changing performance indicators, when the aims in these areas must be long term. And when the police announces, as in November 2007, that it is to hold talks with the leaders of gangs to stem violence, it is scant reassurance for the people who live in the communities from which the gangs originate, who know all too well that they are too chaotic for any kind of 'top down' approach to have a genuine impact.[22]

One hopes that future Home Secretaries will see the benefits of giving the police the scope for more preventative, rather than reactive, work. In many of the areas covered in this book the relationship between the locals and the police, whether gang members or not, is one of outright antagonism. Interstitial zones traditionally have a negative relationship with the authorities, but that does not mean improvements can't be made to improve this situation. The drive towards stopping anti-social behaviour should be shifted away from the police. It will take time and a great deal of money, but the end product of not doing so will be a resentment towards the police among the youth, which will last into adulthood.

There is too much pressure between local need and centrally prescribed targets such as the National Policing Plan, the crime reduction targets from central Government and the HMIC inspection criteria.

A recent article in the *Community Safety Journal* argued: 'None of these include instructions on how to negotiate the policy minefield in respect of children and young people.'[23] As mentioned earlier, the use of stop and search powers must be reconsidered. The police have a duty to protect the community: but an emphasis must be put on the grounds for suspicion before a stop and search is carried out.

Indeed, more time in general must be given to enhancing community relations. There is a high level of scepticism about official intervention within any of these areas, and the restoration of trust will again take time. In the late twentieth century in Boston, police officers were instrumental in galvanizing public services, and this helped to generate support for the crackdowns on proscribed behaviours.[24] An enhanced relationship with the community will help the police to garner the type of intelligence required for preventative measures; and for this to happen, the residents must feel that the authorities can offer protection.

One of the major problems with huge bureaucracies such as Youth Offending Teams and the probation service is that the way they are set up, framed and managed means they can only provide a general service. To put it bluntly, simply making sure that people turn up to appointments has little impact in Gangland. You might argue that the more heavily involved a gang member, the more likely they are to complete their order. You need to sustain contact with them.

At the start of 2007, the Chairman of the Youth Justice Board, Rod Morgan, resigned. He told BBC *Newsnight* that Government targets for bringing offenders to justice are having 'perverse consequences' by swelling prisoner numbers unnecessarily: 'We're standing on the brink of a prisons crisis. We have tonight, lots of people in police cells because there is no space for them in custody, and that's true for children and young people also . . . I regard a twenty-six per cent increase in the number of children and young people that are being drawn into the system in the past three years as swamping.'[25] He added: 'Over eighty per cent of fifteen to seventeen-year-olds will be reconvicted within two years of release – and of those who've already got several convictions, the rate at which they'll be reconvicted is well over ninety per cent – almost certainly . . . I have to say to you that a custodial establishment, no matter how good we make them, is the worst conceivable environment within which to improve somebody's behaviour.' At the time of writing a new Chair has been appointed to the Youth Justice Board, which is now the joint responsibility of the Ministry of Justice and the Department for Children, Schools and Families. It remains to be seen how much weight will be put on the latter's input.

Morgan was not the only senior figure to question the government's track record on youths that year. In October 2007 the 'Children's Tsar', Professor Sir Al Aynsley-Green, attacked the government's youth justice policy. He said: '[The] demonization and lack of empathy for young people is a major issue for England. It causes anger and alienation. At the moment we have a youth justice system dominated by a punitive approach. It doesn't focus on children's needs. We have to ask questions about naming and shaming, particularly for people who have learning difficulties and can't understand why ASBO restrictions are being applied.'[26]

And sadly, this is indicative of Labour's years of fighting crime. A popularist and punitive approach has seen little drop in the amount committed. The Centre for Crime and Justice Studies reported in early 2007 that billions had been spent on reform, but it had brought no major improvement. The report's co-author Richard Garside told BBC Radio 4's *Today* programme: 'What we have seen is a massive expansion of non-conviction offences brought to justice.'[27] These included 'things like cautions, penalty notices and other administrative means of hitting targets', he said. And one of the government's 'most conspicuous failures' was on reoffending – with targets being modified, missed or dropped. 'On paper, nearly all the targets have been met,' the study said. 'In reality, Labour's record on its various overall crime reduction targets is at best mixed; at worst, its crime reduction claims are misleading.'[28]

Labour's Home Secretaries have been so punitive and so eager to create new laws that they require an independent commission to decide on sentences due to prison overcrowding, while three new super-prisons – housing 2500 people – have had to be built. And once released, the chances are that their inmates will commit more crime. As Erwin James has pointed out, the current rate of re-offending within two years for people who come out of prison is two-thirds. For the 18 to 21s it is as high as 78.4 per cent.[29] According to the Social Exclusion Unit reoffending by ex-prisoners costs society £11 billion a year; it costs an average of £37,305 to keep someone in prison. Yet this constant growth is not the result of more criminals being caught, as numbers being dealt with by the courts have remained comparatively static. Neither is it the case that more people are being found guilty of serious crimes. Most of the prison population increase is among non-violent women shoplifters, relatively petty offenders and those awaiting trial.[30] In addition, there have been 7000 ASBOs administered since 1999, of which over half are breached, according to the Youth Justice Board.

In September 2007 the Home Office announced the creation of the Tackling Gangs Action Programme (TGAP). A million pounds was to be spent across London, Birmingham, Liverpool and Manchester. The press release said: 'A new dedicated national unit will run the anti-gang programme, and its members will come from central government, local authorities and frontline agencies. With £1m in additional funding, it will be overseen by a central ministerial taskforce on guns and gangs and headed by the Home Secretary.'

The key activities stated in the press release were covert operations and surveillance targeting gangs, high-visibility police presence on the streets in troubled areas, especially around schools, use of civil orders to restrict the activities of known gang members, greater witness protection, including safe houses for victims and witnesses, mediation services for gang members, and a crackdown on illegal gun imports. There were two more activities mentioned at the end: enhanced local community forums to improve communication between police and residents, and extra activities at local schools to keep children off the streets. Despite the fact that the press release stated: 'All this will be led by efforts to prevent young people from being drawn into lives of crime in the first place', there appeared little chance that any of the £250,000 per city (a paltry sum, given the scope of the problem we are discussing) would go towards any kind of preventative work.

Two months later, Vernon Coaker, Under Secretary for Police and Security, gave an interview to the BBC website which allowed the public to ask the questions.[31] One question was: 'At the James Callaghan lecture in Cardiff earlier this year, former Prime Minister Tony Blair blamed violence on the culture within black and urban communities. Does the minister endorse Mr Blair's beliefs? If so, what does he propose to do to change that culture? If not, what does he think is responsible?' His response ('I agree that gun and gang crime are mainly urban problems which have a knock-on effect on all communities. It is the responsibility of us all to understand and tackle these issues') seemed to be a tacit 'yes'. At the same time, his interview mentioned the importance of 'the police and communities', without any mention of how the latter might play its part, nor interact with the former.

The bulk of criminologists have agreed that an integrated multi-agency strategy is required for each local area, which must be able to deal with every level of gang involvement. As Professor John Pitts has it, it must 'remain anchored in day-to-day reality, and [must] resist the siren call of central government targets'.[32] The strategy must 'have representation from, and ready access to, the young people and adults caught up in the problem'. Any strategy which, as Pitts advises, must include representation from young people, parents, the police, the Youth Offending Teams, community safety professionals, probation, children's services, education, employment, housing, Better Neighbourhoods Team, social cohesion teams and the voluntary agencies will need to be incredibly well organized.

All this will take time. We now live in a country where ten-year-olds and younger are involved in gangs and in gun crime. For the situation to become this bad in these areas has not happened overnight. It has taken years of neglect, years of hoping that inner-city areas would sort themselves out. It will take years to put right; and only if we stop labouring under the assumption that their problems are not our own.

Every moral panic brings with it new spokesmen who claim to be experts and who want to help – even charities for shooting and conservation have been taking an interest in gangs, in the belief that they can help by teaching children to respect guns. This book does not give the entire picture with regard to Britain's gangs, nor all of the answers. What I hope to do is widen the debate that is taking place within the public sphere, and to suggest measures which can run in tandem with those that, while not directly aimed at gangs, can improve social capital in the areas where they are found.[33]

If the situation itself and the ways in which it can be resolved are more mundane than the reader might have expected, that can only be a good thing. Ultimately this nation has a duty to understand and respond to the problems that are taking place within these areas. It has a duty to the parents of Billy Cox, of Nathan Foster, of Ben Hitchcock, of countless other victims of gang violence. It has a duty not to create folk devils out of the disadvantaged, and should feel not titillation but outrage when it hears about their problems. It has a duty not to believe politicians who imply that negative social change is part of the wider picture; that child-gunmen are an inevitable manifestation of today's society. It has a duty because while we may be two nations, we are one blood.

AFTERWORD

In the two years since I began to research this project, street gangs exploded from a sporadic blip on the nation's collective consciousness to a huge story that dominated every media outlet. When I started work on this issue (at the end of 2005), the public knew street gangs existed, but little about them. Terms like 'Elder' and 'Younger' meant nothing to most people. Street gangs were largely synonymous with terms like 'black on black gun crime'; and while youth crime was on the radar, it was rarely equated with gang violence. When Damilola Taylor was murdered in 2000 the fact that his killers were members of a gang was not considered a crucial part of the story.

Things changed in 2007. They changed because of a series of particularly brutal youth murders, in particular those of Billy Cox, Michael Donsunmu and James Andre Smartt-Ford in south London. Suddenly every incidence of violent crime gave credence to the theory that we were witnessing a shift in the behaviour of our nation's youth. This frenzy reached its zenith with the death of Rhys Jones in August that year. There were reams upon reams of features and news stories about youth gangs. The story didn't go away in 2008; it just changed its shape slightly. The word 'gang' took less precedence; now it was violent youth crime, in particular involving the use of knives, which dominated the headlines.

Commentators singled out the usual suspects: the right blamed media depictions of violence and the dependence of the poor on the welfare state. The left blamed poverty and underinvestment in deprived areas. Both blamed the parents, and both sometimes blamed schools. And both were often right, which is the problem with gangs. They inhabit a paradoxical world, one too complicated to be encapsulated by a headline or indeed by most forms of journalism. Sometimes gangs are organised, and sometimes they're not. They're territorial, but many gang members don't care about territory. They're a product of poverty, but poverty isn't always the reason why people get involved in them. The usual solutions were trotted out – more policing from the right, more investment from the left. No surprise to learn that both had a point, but that the policing needed to be carried out with more subtlety than those advocating it believed, or that money alone was not the answer – few people stressed the importance of how the funding should be allocated.

So it was with the extent of the problem. Until the tail end of 2008, when a recession and the US Election swept the story from the front pages, both right and left were united in their conviction that youth crime was rapidly rising. In 2008, every teenage death in London was grimly added to a total until the media could report that a record number of teenagers had been killed in the city. That much was true, but few outlets admitted that they only had figures going back to 2000, nor that homicide rates fluctuate wildly year on year. Whenever we talk about the 'extent' of the problem, all we have are crime statistics, which are flawed; what knowledge we take from them is partial.

My answer to the question of whether the problem of gangs is 'getting worse' or not is again predictable. It is and it isn't. Not the kind of answer that makes headlines. I stand by the points I made in the Conclusion, and in the light of that perhaps the most worrying cases of youthful gang violence in 2007 and 2008 were the ones that involved guns in places like Sheffield and Derby, where gangs are a newer problem.

Is there any hope for the future? I didn't see a Government that had a handle on this issue when youth crime was the dominant story back then, and I still don't today. Since finishing this book I've worked with a number of bodies that help gang-involved youths. I know there are a lot of good men and women in this country who do a lot of valuable work. More often than not they're kicking against the system in some way, a system that just isn't framed to provide long term support, whether to statutory or voluntary bodies. For now, the issue has gone away, in that it's left the front pages. But gangs did not appear out of the blue and are unlikely ever to disappear. With better funding and organisation we can drastically reduce the problem. The question is whether our leaders care about the perception or the reality.

John Heale, London, 2009.

NOTES

PREFACE

1 'The Life and Death of a Gangsta', *Daily Mail*, 26 June 2006.

1 FROM LEYTON TO CHINGFORD: WELCOME TO GANGLAND

1 John Pitts (2007) *Reluctant Gangsters: Youth Gangs in Waltham Forest*, University of Bedfordshire, p. 27.
2 *Ibid.*, p. 25.
3 *Ibid.*, p. 55.
4 Simon Hallsworth and Tara Young (2006) 'Getting Real About Gangs', *Criminal Justice Matters*, 55: 12–13.
5 Pitts, *Reluctant Gangsters*, p. 35.
6 Tim Hope (2003) 'The Crime Drop in Britain', *Community Safety Journal*, 2 (4): 32.
7 Jock Young (2001) *The Extent of Crime*, Middlesex University.
8 Pitts, *Reluctant Gangsters*, p. 44.
9 cf. *ibid.*, p. 43.

2 HACKNEY

1 cf. Frederic Thrasher (1963) *The Gang*, University of Chicago Press, p. 90 (first published 1927).
2 *Team Hackney Floor Target Action Plan on Guns and Gangs* (2006), p. 18.
3 *Income and Wealth: Report of the JRF Inquiry Group* (1995).

261

4 *Houses Below Average Income: A Statistical Analysis 1979–1994/5*, London: HMSO (1994).

5 *Income and Wealth*: http://www.jrf.org.uk/knowledge/findings/social policy/sprsum3.asp.

6 Nick Davies (1998) *Dark Heart*, Vintage, pp. 201–220.

7 *Poverty and Wealth Across Britain 1968–2000* (2007) Joseph Rowntree Foundation, p. 31.

8 Malcolm Dean (1997) 'Tipping the Balance', *Search*, 27, Spring, York, Joseph Rowntree Foundation.

9 *Income and Wealth*.

10 Sarah Payne (2000) *Poverty, Social Exclusion and Mental Health: Findings from the 1999 PSE Survey. Poverty and Social Exclusion Survey of Britain*, Townsend Centre for International Poverty Research, University of Bristol.

11 cf. Davies. *Dark Heart*, pp. 230–234.

12 House of Commons Home Affairs Committee Report (2007) *Young Black People and the Criminal Justice System*, 1 June, p. 30.

13 *Ibid.*, pp. 30–31.

14 *Ibid.*, p. 30.

15 *Ibid.*, pp. 12–15.

16 *Ibid.*, p. 38.

17 'Blair Blames Spate of Murders on Black Culture', *Guardian*, 12 April 2007.

18 *Statistics on Race and the Criminal Justice System* (2005) Home Office, pp. 18 and 21.

3 SOUTH LONDON

1 'They're Lethal, Unfeeling, and No One Can Touch Them', *Observer*, 28 April 2002.

2 Kevin Braddock (2007), 'London's Secret Teenage War', *GQ*, 25 September.

3 http://en.wikipedia.org/wiki/Milgram_experiment.

4 Steve Shropshire (2002) *Developing Multi Agency Gang Strategies to Address the Street Gang Culture and Reduce Gun Violence Among Young People*, Steve Shropshire and Michael McFarquar Consultancy Group (September).

5 Dick Hobbs (1997) *Criminal Collaboration: Youth Gangs, Sub Cultures,*

Professional Criminals and Organised Crime, Oxford Handbook of Criminology, Oxford University Press.

6 'Peckham Boys' "General" Faces Life Behind Bars' (2007) *South London Press*, 21 September.

7 Frederic Thrasher (1963) *The Gang*, University of Chicago Press, p. 90 (first published 1927), p. 20.

8 Dick Hobbs (2004) 'Violence and Organised Crime', in *Handbook of Violence*, ed. J. Hagen and W. Heitmeyer, Springer, pp. 679–700.

9 *Homicides, Firearms Offences and Intimate Violence 2005/6*, Home Office Statistical Bulletin (25 January 2007).

10 *Gun Crime: The Market In and Use of Illegal Firearms*, Home Office Research Study 298, p. 39 (December 2005).

11 *Gun Crime: The Market In and Use of Illegal Firearms, Case Studies*.

12 *Today*, BBC Radio 4, 21 August 2007.

13 House of Commons Home Affairs Committee Report (2007) *Young Black People and the Criminal Justice System*, 1 June, p. 37

14 Rebecca O'Neill, (2002) *Experiments In Living: The Fatherless Family*, Institute for the Study of Civil Society, September.

15 A number of witnesses to the aforementioned Home Office Select Committee Report, *Young Black People and the Criminal Justice System*, traced family break-up to the organization of family units within the plantation system which led to a lack of family stability, a fragility that survives to this day. Another school of thought is that these communities put more emphasis on their area than the family in terms of how children are raised – but due to the economic factors outlined in this book, this method of parenting is no longer viable: they may feel it takes a village to raise a child, but mutual mistrust within public housing estates means the village no longer exists. (*Young Black People and the Criminal Justice System*, p. 39.) Camila Batmanghelidjh of Kids' Company and Neil Solo of Barnardo's also expressed the opinion that part of this problem was down to the fact that many black women prefer to carry on without a male partner.

16 *Ibid.*, p. 36, whole section entitled 'Other Issues Within The Black Community Compound Disadvantage'.

17 'Welfare and Parental Responsibility', *Daily Mail*, 29 April 2002.

18 John Pitts (2007) *Reluctant Gangsters: Youth Gangs in Waltham Forest*, University of Bedfordshire, p. 62.

19 'Revealed: The Rise of the Muslim Boys', *Evening Standard*, 3 February 2005.

20 John Hagedorn (1988) *People and Folks*, Chicago: Lake View Press, p. 130.

21 'Al Qaeda Gang in Jail Pool Queue Riot', *Daily Mirror*, 5 May 2007, and 'Al Qaeda Plot to Kill Prison Warder Foiled', *Daily Mirror*, 8 January 2008. The link between the Muslim Boys and Al Qaeda, contrary to these reports, has never been proved, despite a number of its members claiming this to be the case.

4 GOING COUNTRY

1 Stuart Hall (1978) 'The Treatment of Football Hooliganism in the Press'. In R. Ingham (ed.), *Football Hooliganism: The Wider Context.* London: Interaction.

2 A 2007 Brunel University study analysed 2,130 news items involving youths across a single month and found that 82 per cent of them referred to crime, and 90 per cent of these to violent crime; cf. Mike Wayne, Julian Petley, Craig Murray and Lesley Henderson 'Television News and the Symbolic Criminalisation of Young People', *Journalism Studies*, 9(1).

3 'Tessa Jowell: Gangs Are Skilled Entrepreneurs', *Daily Telegraph*, 26 September 2007.

4 cf. Graeme McLagan,(2005) *Guns and Gangs*, Allison and Busby, p. 123: Ian Blair is quoted: 'If this was white young women being murdered at the rate black men are being murdered, it would be headlines everywhere. I think there's something really wrong. To me, it is pretty close to institutional racism within the media.' A tabloid crime reporter is also quoted: 'It's very frustrating because there are often very good stories behind these incidents, but my news desk is just not interested. To stand a chance of getting into the paper . . . these murders and court cases have to involve either two people being shot, a child, or an innocent passer-by, who's preferably white.'

5 'Gang "Bans" Rivals From Town Centre', *Croydon Advertiser*, 9 February 2007.

6 'Society Has Failed Us – But We Are a Success In a Gang', *Croydon Advertiser*, 25 March 2007.

7 Dick Hobbs (1997) 'Criminal Collaboration: Youth Gangs, Sub Cultures, Professional Criminals and Organised Crime', *Oxford Handbook of Criminology*, Oxford University Press, p. 50.

5 BIRMINGHAM

1 'How Gangs Terrorised a City for 20 Years', *Daily Telegraph*, 18 March 2005.
2 *Lozells Disturbances Summary Report*, Black Radley (May 2007).
3 'Gangs Build "Wall of Silence" after Birmingham Murders', *The Times*, 18 March 2005.
4 Dominic White (2004) 'Taba and the Rude Girls: Cultural Constructions of the Youth Street Gang', *Journals for Crime, Conflict and the Media*, 1(2); 41–50.
5 *Perry Barr District Plan: Community Safety*. Available at www.birmingham.gov.uk.

6 FROM BRICK LANE TO BRADFORD

1 Dick Hobbs (2006) 'East Ending: Dissociation, Deindustrialisation and David Downes', *The Politics of Crime Control*, Oxford University Press, p. 124.
2 *Ibid.*, p. 128.
3 'Surviving Brick Lane', *Evening Standard*, 10 February 2003.
4 Claire Alexander (2000) *The Asian Gang*, Berg.
5 *Ibid.*, pp. 150–160.
6 *Ibid.*, p. 111.
7 Hobbs, *East Ending*, p. 130.
8 Sandu Sukhdev (2003) 'Come Hungry, Leave Edgy', *London Review of Books*, 9 October.
9 'Deadly Asian Heroin Gangs Carve Up Lucrative New Trade', *Observer*, 14 July 2002.
10 'Revealed: Bollywood Craze That Is Fuelling London's Vice Rackets', *Observer*, 27 July 2003.

7 MANCHESTER

1 *Shootings, Gangs and Violent Incidents in Manchester: Developing A Crime Reduction Strategy*, Karen Bullock and Nick Tilley (2002) Crime Reduction Research Series, Paper 13, p. 18.
2 'Battle to Save Children From Gang Terror', *Observer*, 7 March 2004.

3 'Gang War on the Wards', *Manchester Evening News*, 7 May 2005.

4 'Justice At Last: Witnesses Emerge to Defeat Gang Who Thought They Were Above the Law', *The Times*, 20 January 2007.

5 'Gang "Armourer" Jailed', *Manchester Evening News*, 8 September 2007.

6 Greater Manchester Police Figures.

7 House of Commons Home Affairs Committee Report (2007) *Young Black People and the Criminal Justice System*, p. 46.

8 Both recommendation and response can be seen on *The Government's Response to Home Affairs Select Committee Report: Young Black People and the Criminal Justice System* (October 2007). The full text can be seen at: http://www.justice.gov.uk/docs/ybp-and-cjs.pdf.

9 Statement made on 29 November 2007, available at http://www.ipcc.gov.uk/news/pr291107_gmp.htm.

10 'Police Fears Over HQ', *Manchester Evening News*, 3 July 2003.

11 *In Bed With MeDinner*, LWT, Series 3 Episode 11.

12 Peter Walsh (2003), *Gang War*, Milo, pp. 58–59.

13 'Noonan Funeral "Should Not Have Shut Down Schools"', *Manchester Evening News*, 28 April 2005.

14 'How the Young Poor Measure Poverty in Britain: Drink, Drugs and their Time in Jail', *New York Times*, 10 March 2007.

8 LIVERPOOL

1 'Drug Turf Wars bring Gun Culture to the Streets', *Observer*, 2 September 2007.

2 'Gang Culture: On the Streets With No Name', *Independent on Sunday*, 30 September 2007.

3 'Rhys Jones Murder: Passer-by describes tending to shot schoolboy', *The Telegraph*, 14 October 2008.

4 'Rhys Jones Murder Trial: "A kid's gone down"', *The Mirror*, 11 October 2008.

5 'Boy X: the witness who betrayed his friends for a new identity', *The Independent*, 17 December 2008.

6 *Ibid.*

7 'Rhys Jones Trial: "I have shot a kid and he went down"', *Liverpool Echo*, 13 November 2008.

8 *Ibid.*

9 'Rhys Jones Trial: "I don't know why they call me a grass"', *Liverpool Echo*, 22 October 2008.

10 'Boy X: the witness who betrayed his friends for a new identity', *The Independent*, 17 December 2008.

11 'Rhys Jones Trial: phone call that ended a Florida holiday', *Liverpool Daily Post*, 28 October 2008.

12 'Boy X: the witness who betrayed his friends for a new identity', *The Independent*, 17 December 2008.

13 'The Fir Tree pub is a badly run pub strongly linked to gang culture', *Liverpool Echo*, February 6 2008.

14 Tony Aitman (2007) 'Massive Deprivation in Norris Green', *The Socialist*, 14 September 2007.

15 *Ibid.*

16 *Ibid.*

17 John Belman (ed.) (2006) *Liverpool 800: Culture, Character and History*, Liverpool University Press, p. 455.

18 Aitman, 'Massive Deprivation in Norris Green'.

19 Belman, *Liverpool 800*, p. 463.

9 THE END OF THE LINE

1 'The War On Crime: At The Frontline', *Guardian*, 10 July 2003.

2 Peter Homel, Sandra Nutley, Barry Webb and Nick Tilley (2005) *Investing to Deliver: Reviewing the Implementation of the UK Crime Reduction Programme*, Home Office Research Study 281 (January).

3 'How Politics Put Policing in the Dock', *Guardian*, 11 July 2003.

4 Geoff Small (1995) *Ruthless: The Global Rise of the Yardies*, Warner.

5 Home Office (1998) *The Crime Reduction Strategy*, London: Home Office.

6 Bernard Harcourt and Jens Ludwig (2006) 'Broken Windows: New Evidence from New York City and a Five City Social Experiment', *University of Chicago Law Review*, Vol. 73.

7 'The Giuliani Presidency?' *Slate*, 11 May 2006 (http://www.slate.com/id/2141424).

8 Steven D Levitt and Stephen J Dubner (2006) 'Where Have All the Criminals Gone?', Chapter 4 of *Freakonomics*, Penguin.

9 BBC website, September 1998: 'Detective Superintendent Ray Mallon, who is currently suspended as head of Middlesbrough CID,

has been the most colourful advocate of this strategy in Britain. In 1996 he famously promised to quit if he failed to cut crime on his patch by 20% in 18 months – gaining him the nickname "Robocop"' (http://news.bbc.co.uk/1/hi/uk/182553.stm).

10 Beatrix Campbell (1993) *Goliath*, Methuen, p. 189.

11 *Ibid.*, pp. 194–195.

12 *Ibid.*, p. 322.

13 *Ibid.*, p. 200.

14 *Ibid.*, p. 210.

15 *Ibid.*, p. 171.

16 *Ibid.*, p. 55.

17 *The Brixton Disorders*, HMSO, 10 April 1981.

18 'Daughter, 12, Pays Tribute to Father Killed in Street Row', *Guardian*, 14 August 2007.

19 'Newlove Widow Statement Text: "He was Light of Our Lives"', *The Times*, 17 January 2008.

10 CONCLUSION

1 'The Boy of Ten Caught by Police with a Machine Gun under his Bed', *Daily Mail*, 5 March 2008. The situation in which a child of this age was being asked to harbour loaded guns for older relatives is far from uncommon, according to various interviewees. Two of them expressed their fear at being shot by a small child – as one put it: 'When I was ten, if you'd upset me I'd have smoked you if I could. And now a kid really can.' Another claimed to have seen a child of six on his estate with a gun, though this was impossible to verify and may well have been exaggeration.

2 Bullock and Tilley's report estimates 60 per cent of gun crime in Manchester is thought to be gang related.

3 Home Office Statistical Bulletin: *Homicides, Firearm Offences and Intimate Violence 2005/6*, p. 19.

4 *Ibid.*

5 '3 Million Crimes a Year "Left Out of Official Figures"', *Guardian*, 26 June 2007.

6 *Homicides, Firearms and Intimate Violence*, p. 22.

7 'Violent Youth Crime Up a Third', *Sunday Telegraph*, 20 January 2008.

8 This opinion is primarily formed on the evidence of a number of off-

record interviews, which cannot be reproduced in more detail.

9 As mentioned later (see note 17) the 'Communities That Care' survey shows the relationship between number of gang members and amount of violence etc. is far from clear cut.

10 John Hagedorn (1988) *People and Folks,* Chicago: Lake View Press, p.123.

11 MORI *Youth Survey 2002,* Section 1.

12 DfES Review (September 2006) *Getting It. Getting It Right,* p. 3.

13 Joseph Rowntree Foundation (2005) *Migration and Social Mobility: the life chances of Britain's minority ethnic communities.* Summary available at http://www.jrf.org.uk/knowledge/findings/socialpolicy/0545.asp.

14 Nick Davies (2000) *The School Report,* Vintage, 2 November.

15 *Reluctant Gangsters,* p. 63.

16 Some academics have questioned the perceived degree of organization of American gangs. cf. Malcolm W. Klein and Cheryl Lee Maxson (2006) *Street Gang Patterns and Policies,* Oxford University Press.

17 *Safer London Youth Survey,* 'Communities That Care (2004)'.

18 Steve Shropshire (2002) *Developing Multi Agency Gang Strategies to Address the Street Gang Culture and Reduce Gun Violence Among Young People,* Steve Shropshire and Michael McFarquar Consultancy Group (September).

19 CTC Survey 2004. It would not do the ward any favours to name it.

20 Peter Seaman and Malcolm Hill (2006) *Parenting and Children's Resistance in Disadvantaged Communities,* Joseph Rowntree Foundation.

21 cf. a lengthy article about this issue at http://www.infed.org/person-aladvisers/connexions.htm.

22 'Met Summit With Gunmen', *Evening Standard,* 16 November 2007. As Steve Shropshire puts it: 'Bold statements that the problem has been solved because shootings are markedly down one month over the previous month only serve to demoralize communities when the violence returns with a vengeance' (*Developing Multi Agency Gang Strategies*).

23 J Mortimore (2007) 'Narrowing the Welfare Gap', *Community Safety Journal,* 6(2).

24 John Pitts (2007) *Reluctant Gangsters: Youth Gangs in Waltham Forest,* University of Bedfordshire, p. 81.

25 BBC *Newsnight,* 26 January 2007.

26 'Children's Tsar Attacks Youth Justice Policy', Society *Guardian,* 15 October 2007.

27 *Today,* BBC Radio 4, 15 January 2007.

28 *Ten Years of Criminal Justice Under Labour: An Independent Audit*, CCJS, January 2007, p. 24.
29 'Our Prisons are Failing', *Guardian*, 6 April 2006.
30 *Ibid.*
31 BBC website, 17 October 2007 (http://news.bbc.co.uk/1/hi/talking_point/7049337.stm).
32 Pitts, *Reluctant Gangsters*, p. 93.
33 Among those proposed by the JRF in 1995: 'Business leaders ensuring that such communities are not excluded from mainstream economic activity; more links between training schemes and nearby employers; local management, decentralized budgets, and resident involvement in decision-making in areas like schools, the police, social services and health care, as well as housing; training of residents in appropriate skills; radical improvement in the performance of local schools; a positive role for young people in local initiatives; physical improvements; improved transport so as to integrate outer estates with the wider city; in particular parts of the country an economic regeneration policy which goes beyond initiatives on particular estates.'

BIBLIOGRAPHY

Alexander, Claire, *The Asian Gang* (Oxford, Berg, 2000).

Bourgois, Philippe, *In Search of Respect* (Cambridge, Cambridge University Press, 2002).

Campbell, Beatrix, *Goliath* (London, Methuen, 1993).

Davies, Nick, *Dark Heart* (London, Vintage, 1998).

Hagedorn, John, *People and Folks* (Chicago, Lake View Press, 1988).

Hall, Stuart; Critcher, Charles; Jefferson, Tony; Clarke, Tony and Robert, Brian, *Policing the Crisis: Mugging, The State and Law and Order* (London, Palgrave Macmillan, 1978).

McLagan, Graeme, *Guns and Gangs* (London, Allison and Busby, 2006).

Pritchard, Tim, *Street Boys* (London, Harper Element, 2008).

Thrasher, Frederic, *The Gang* (Chicago, University of Chicago Press, 1963 ed.).

Venkatesh, Sudhir, *Gang Leader for a Day* (London, Allen Lane, 2008).

Walsh, Peter, *Gang War* (Preston, Milo, 2003).

INDEX